GLOBAL ORGANIZED CRIME AND INTERNATIONAL SECURITY

Dedicated to the memory of the countless victims of transnational organized crime worldwide in the hope that this volume will contribute to encouraging vigorous and well-coordinated efforts to combat and defeat this serious threat to the world's economy, stability and democracies.

Global Organized Crime and International Security

Edited by
EMILIO C. VIANO
American University, Washington, D.C.

Ashgate

Aldershot • Burlington USA • Singapore • Sydney

Ashgate Publishing Limited
Gower House
Croft Road
Aldershot
Hants GU11 3HR
England

Ashgate Publishing Company
131 Main Street
Burlington,
Vermont 05401-5600
USA

Ashgate website:http://www.ashgate.com

Reprinted 2000

British Library Cataloguing in Publication Data
Global organized crime and international security
  1. Organized crime 2. Transnational crime 3. Organized crime -
  Case studies 4. Transnational crime - Case studies
  5. Security, International
  I. Viano, Emilio C.
  364.1´06

Library of Congress Catalog Card Number: 98-74930

ISBN 1 84014 959 0

Printed and bound in Great Britain by Biddles Limited,
Guildford and King's Lynn.

Contents

List of Contributors   *ix*
Introduction   *xi*
Acknowledgments   *xxiii*

**PART I: TRANSNATIONAL ORGANIZED CRIME: THE
GLOBALIZATION OF CRIME**

1   The Evolution of Espionage Networks and the
     Crisis of International Terrorism and Global
     Organized Crime
     Joseph L. Albini, R.E. Rogers, Julie Anderson   3

2   The European Union and Organized Crime:
     Fighting a New Enemy with Many Tentacles
     Monica Den Boer   13

3   Confronting Transnational Crime
     Peter B. Martin   25

PART II: THE CASE STUDIES

4   The Infiltration of Organized Crime in the Emilia-
     Romagna Region: Possible Interpretations for
     a New Social Defence
     *Augusto Balloni, Roberta Bisi, Andrea Forlivesi,
     Flavio Mazzucato, Raffaella Sette*   33

5   Transnational Organized Crime in Spain:
     Structural Factors Explaining its Penetration
     Carlos Resa-Nestares   47

6   Global Organized Crime in Latvia and the Baltics
     Andrejs Vilks, Dainis Bergmanis   63

7   Opening and Closing the 49th Parallel:
Responses to Free Trade and to Trans-
Border Crime in Canada since 1989
Ian Taylor   71

8   "Contested Jurisdiction Border Communities"
and Cross-Border Crime: The Case of the Akwesasne
Ruth Jamieson   85

9   The Use of the "Shining Path" Myth in the
Context of the All-Out War Against the
"Narco-Guerilla"
*Rodolfo Mendoza Nakamura**
*pen name   99

10   Organized Crime in Russia:
Domestic and International Problems
Yakov Gilinskiy   117

11   Regionalization and Expansion:
The Growth of Organized Crime in East Siberia
Anna L. Repetskaya   123

12   Alienation and Female Criminality:
The Case of Puerto Rico
Zuleika Vidal Rodriguez   129

PART III: PUBLIC POLICY AND INTERVENTIONS

13   Criminal Financial Investigations:
A Strategic and Tactical Approach in the
European Dimension
Petrus C. Van Duyne, Mike Levi   139

14   Mafia-Type Organizations:
The Restoration of Rights as a
Preventive Policy
Maria Luisa Cesoni   157

15   Repeal Drug Prohibition and End the
      Financing of International Crime
      Arthur Berney   173

16   The Criminal Justice System Facing the
      Challenges of Organized Crime
      Emilio C. Viano   185

List of Contributors

Joseph L. Albini, University of Nevada Las Vegas, USA

Julie Anderson, John Jay College of Criminal Justice, New York City, USA

Augusto Balloni, Criminology, University of Bologna, Italy

Dainis Bergmanis, Criminological Research Center, Riga, Latvia

Arthur Berney, Boston College Law School, USA

Roberta Bisi, Criminology, University of Bologna, Italy

Maria Luisa Cesoni, University of Geneva Law School, Switzerland

Monica Den Boer, Justice and Home Affairs, European Institute of Public Administration, Maastricht, The Netherlands

Andrea Forlivesi, Criminology, University of Bologna, Italy

Yakov Gilinskiy, Russian Academy of Sciences, St. Petersburg, Russia

Ruth Jamieson, Department of Criminology, Keele University, United Kingdom

Mike Levi, University of Wales, Cardiff, United Kingdom

Peter B. Martin, strategic analyst, residing in France

Flavio Mazzucato, Criminology, University of Bologna, Italy

Rodolfo Mendoza Nakamura*, University of Lausanne, Switzerland
*pen name

Anna L. Repetskaya, Law School, Irkutsk State University, Russia

Carlos Resa-Nestares, Universidad Nacional de Educación a Distancia, Madrid, Spain

R.E. Rogers, St. Clair Community College

Raffaella Sette, Criminology, University of Bologna, Italy

Ian Taylor, Institute for Social Research, University of Salford, United Kingdom

Petrus C. Van Duyne, Tilburg University, The Netherlands

Emilio C. Viano, School of Public Affairs, American University, Washington, DC, USA

Zuleika Vidal Rodriguez, Social Sciences Faculty, University of Puerto Rico

Andrejs Vilks, Criminological Research Center, Riga, Latvia

Introduction

EMILIO C. VIANO

Global developments since the Second World War have combined to produce societal, economic and political environments which have increased both the profitability and destructive impact of systematic illegal activity. Ironically, the end of the Cold War which reduced or eliminated many traditional security challenges seems to have accelerated and magnified this trend. At the same time, technological and scientific innovations, the speed and ease of communications, instant financial transactions in electronic form, and databanks with massive amounts of information are tightening global interdependence and shortening the time-span of international operations. These developments greatly facilitate destabilizing and criminal activities, boost their effectiveness, and make it easier for them to proceed undetected. As a result, criminal groups can easily branch out into new forms of criminal, economic, and political activities at the regional, national, and global levels. They also affect critical national security interests.

Transnational crime is presently one of the most serious security threats to democratic institutions, the rule of law, community welfare, and basic values and norms. A corrupt society ravaged by greed, violence, lawlessness and drugs does not allow, let alone support, the flourishing of a democratic, stable civilization and of a peaceful world. Counteracting it requires fresh thinking, a redefinition of what "security" means at the regional and international levels and a re-examination of our legal systems and of the rule and function of law enforcement. The menace represented by emerging forms of transnational crime goes well beyond national police and domestic concerns. It goes to the heart of what is security, democracy, and development. Alliances and coalitions are essential because no country can effectively defend itself. Along with military power, law and its enforcement are indispensable integers in a transnational equation of peace.

This volume will focus on current research and information on global organized crime and on the development and implementation of appropriate counter-measures. It will stress the need for a cooperative and transnational approach; outline the parameters of solutions that must respect democracy and human rights; and begin a dialogue leading to redefining what international security is. It will also address emerging transnational policing and related legal reforms as an expression of the international cooperation needed to respond to the globalization of organized crime.

This book has the following objectives:

1. Sharing of research and information on current trends, developments, and research/intelligence findings on the globalization of organized crime

2. Analyze the consequences and repercussions of the globalization of crime and of the corresponding measures for social control introduced by States and by international organizations (e.g. the United Nations, the European Union, and others)

3. Discuss and illustrate contemporary approaches and strategies to fight organized crime

4. Facilitate understanding the complexity, methodologies, and specificities of organized crime in the contemporary "global village".

A New Perspective

Most books on organized crime reflect a vision and approach that is not up-to-date with current realities. They focus on organized crime from a classic criminology perspective. Thus, they view it as one of many types of crime and deviance and as mostly a "local" phenomenon occurring at the national level. They do not underline the *"transnational"* and "threat to security" aspects of current organized crime as the newest developments and permutations of this complex phenomenon.

This book focuses on organized crime:

- as a worldwide phenomenon that has taken great advantage of enabling technology in banking, communications, and transportation to build what is probably the first true "virtual" corporation in the world

- as a threat to national and international security stemming, in part, from the collapse of the Soviet empire. The demise of the Soviet Union provided a thriving, ruthless, and well-organized system of graft, corruption and crime already in existence, with a new lease on life and also unleashed it onto the world scene

- as a system of transnational alliances with the potential to destabilize democratic values and institutions; distort regional, if not worldwide, economies; and subvert the international order by allying itself with terrorist organizations, rogue states, and developing countries in search of rapid industrialization and market dominance.

There is heightened and considerable awareness of this problem at the international level promoted and supported, for example, by the United Nations Office for Drug Control & Crime Prevention in Vienna, Austria. The United Nations Under-Secretary General in charge of crime policy, Pino Arlacchi, has decided to make "international organized crime" the lead issue to be addressed by that office in the near future, leading to a United Nations international meeting on the subject in the year 2000. In a speech delivered at the Carnegie Endowment in Washington DC at the end of 1997, Mr. Arlacchi said: "Since I assumed office on September 1st of this year, we are reorganizing the division (Vienna office) to focus on the problem of transnational crime, a major threat to the world's political, economic and social order... The U.N. is both strategically and intellectually prepared to take the lead in developing a strategy to confront the diverse manifestations of international organized crime...."

Outline of the Chapters

The contents of the book are described below in some detail to provide a general overview of the book and to highlight the specific contributions of the many distinguished authors to our understanding of this complex and growing phenomenon.

PART I: TRANSNATIONAL ORGANIZED CRIME: THE GLOBALIZATION OF CRIME

1   **The Evolution of Espionage Networks and the Crisis of International Terrorism and Global Organized Crime**
     Joseph L. Albini, R. E. Rogers, and Julie Anderson

This chapter focuses on the breakdown and changes that have taken place in national security systems both in Russia and the United States and also, in particular, on the lack of recognition of the considerable changes in the world of espionage following the fall of the Soviet Union. This breakdown in turn is seriously affecting governmental effectiveness against terrorist groups. Joined with the development of international patron-client networks among terrorist groups, it has created the new extreme threat currently posed by such groups. Terrorist groups constitute forms of organized crime when there is an opportunity for mutual exchange of services with drug traffickers, money-launderers, hijackers, and other criminal groups. The chapter concludes by addressing the changes that are necessary to meet and contain this developing crisis.

2   **The European Union and Organized Crime: Fighting a New Enemy with Many Tentacles**
     Monica Den Boer

The fear of organized crime has propelled a wave of transformations through the national and international criminal justice systems, both at the organizational and normative levels. This chapter analyzes the way in which the concept of organized crime has become a nodal point in European law enforcement cooperation and how it is influencing the restructuring of law enforcement organizations in a number of European Union member states. It also contains some comparative observations on the employment of special investigative methods and accountability procedures. While organized crime functions as a marker in the redefinition of internal and external security concepts, it also underlines a number of weaknesses in security arrangements, notably the permeability of national borders, the strength of free trade, and the evolution of the global village. This paradox makes the fragile balance between economic and law enforcement interests a difficult one to tackle for politicians.

3   **Confronting Transnational Crime**
     Peter B. Martin

Democracy around the globe is facing formidable challenges today, not from martial enemies outside, but from subversive forces from within. Organized crime is progressively gaining control, enlarging its power structure and strengthening itself. This chapter examines the forces and trends that weaken the sovereign state and provide organized crime with a favorable growth climate: globalization, decentralization of state authority, and the search for regional identity. Finally, the chapter addresses how democratic states can be effective in combating the criminal syndicates.

PART II: THE CASE STUDIES

4   **The Infiltration of Organized Crime in the Emilia-Romagna Region: Possible Interpretations for a New Social Defence**
Augusto Balloni, Roberta Bisi, Andrea Forlivesi, Flavio Mazzucato, and Raffaella Sette

Emilia-Romagna is considered one of Italy's most productive, affluent and desirable regions. These positive characteristics have attracted the attention of external criminal organizations from within Italy and also from abroad (Russia, China, former Yugoslavia, Albania and Maghreb). The extensive immigration to the region by people from outside the European Union ("extra-comunitari") has been closely linked with the growth of criminal organizations. The chapter examines the problem of immigration-linked crime which is particularly complex and challenging. Statistics are presented and analyzed. Practical suggestions on how to address this problem are offered.

5   **Transnational Organized Crime in Spain: Structural Factors Explaining its Penetration**
Carlos Resa-Nestares

In this chapter, the author reviews the various organized crime groups that operate within and from Spain in the areas of money-laundering, international arms trafficking, drugs, extortion, particularly in the tourist areas, and others. All the major organized crime groups are present and active in Spain: the Chinese triads, the Japanese yakuza, the Italian mafia, the Colombian cartels, and the Moroccan mafias connected to Islamic fundamentalist movements. Different groups have different styles of operation. Basic differences are identified and described. The chapter also addresses structural factors that facilitate the introduction of transnational organized crime in Spain. Policies and measures that can be taken to stem the influx of organized crime in Spain are discussed.

6   **Global Organized Crime in Latvia and the Baltics**
Andrejs Vilks and Dainis Bergmanis

The authors state that, in post-socialist countries, the situation is very favorable for organized criminal groups to emerge. They present and analyze related statistics and other data and then discuss the reasons why such a development might easily take place in the region. The negative impact of transnational organized crime on the economies of the Baltics is also addressed as are corrective and preventive measures.

7   **Opening and Closing the 49th Parallel: Responses to Free Trade and to Trans-Border Crime in Canada since 1989**
     Ian Taylor

This chapter examines the relationship between "economic liberalization" taking place in North America as a consequence of the North American Free Trade Agreement (NAFTA) and the question of cross-border crime, specifically between the U.S.A. and Canada. A formal model describing the practices developing in Canada with respect to regulation of the border in relation to specific commodities, is presented. The elements of a more grounded theory of border regulation are offered at this point. Finally, the general tendencies taking place in respect to the attempted regulation of cross-border crime are addressed, set against the reality of a global movement toward the enhancement of the free market in goods and the easier movement of citizens.

8   **"Contested Jurisdiction Border Communities" and Cross-Border Crime: The Case of the Akwesasne**
     Ruth Jamieson

This chapter sketches out a specifically criminological approach to understanding the relationship between transnational crime, national sovereignty and the problem of jurisdiction through an analysis of the penetration of transborder and organized crime into the Mohawk (Indian) Territory of Akwesasne on the Canada-U.S. border. The impact of the rise of new forms of market activity, linked to new criminal enterprises, on the traditional forms of social organization of Mohawk governance is also considered.

9   **The Use of the "Shining Path" Myth in the Context of the All-Out War Against the "Narco-Guerrilla"**
Rodolfo Mendoza Nakamura*
*pen name

This chapter intends to show that the "Shining Path" movement in the Upper Huallaga Valley and Aguaytia, Peru is fundamentally a movement of armed resistance organized by local drug traffickers in 1983 against the anti-narcotics law enforcement policies of the Peruvian government, and not an armed revolutionary movement directly tied to the "Shining Path" party (which had itself previously begun an armed insurrection in the Ayacucho region of the Andes). According to the author's analysis, a deal was struck between the local drug-trafficking mafia and the army. A sufficient degree of violence was maintained in these regions for organized crime to continue forcing local farmers into cooperating with it in the production of coca, and for the Army, supposedly engaged in a fight against a "Shining Path" revival, to share in the profits. Particularly useful is the chapter's discussion of "myth construction" when an image not corresponding to reality is created for internal (Peruvian) and international consumption.

10   **Organized Crime in Russia: Domestic and International Problems**
Yakov Gilinskiy

The author states that criminal organizations are basically like social ones such as labor collectives. Highly adaptable and functional, they strive for expansion and monopolization of their markets. The chapter briefly covers the history of the Russian mafia, paying particular attention to the factors and variables that have spurred the development of transnational organized crime in that country after the disintegration of the Soviet Union. The element of "entrepreneurship" is examined and the commercial areas exploited and monopolized are analyzed. Basically, the author states that we are confronted with the criminalization of business and the economization and politicization of crime.

11   **Regionalization and Expansion: The Growth of Organized Crime in East Siberia**
Anna L. Repetskaya

Changes in the economical, political, legal and moral spheres in Russia are clearly connected with the visibility and growth of organized crime in the country. The increasing importance and autonomy of regions within the Russian Federation are forcing criminal organizations to expand their activities and pay attention not only to the bigger cities but to the far out regions as well. East Siberia, situated in the center of Russia and rich in natural resources, has attracted high interest on the part of organized crime. Ironically, the remoteness of the region justified locating a large number of prisons in it; thus providing a "criminal base" on which to build criminal organizations. The author presents and discusses her hypothesis that "the higher the industrial development, the higher the amount of organized crime moving in". Possible remedies are then presented and evaluated.

12   Alienation and Female Criminality: The Case of Puerto Rico
Zuleika Vidal Rodriguez

The complex aspects of female criminality have received little attention in traditional criminology works. This lacuna is particularly visible when it comes to illegal drug trafficking whose dimensions, dynamics, and impact have not been sufficiently studied in the context of gender. In this chapter the author intends to present an analysis of these phenomena utilizing multi-dimensional perspectives. She also discusses the principal findings focused on the female gender, the manifestations of female criminality and the selling and trafficking of illegal drugs on a transnational basis. Data are particularly related to Puerto Rico.

PART III: PUBLIC POLICY AND INTERVENTIONS

13   Criminal Financial Investigations: A Strategic and Tactical Approach in the European Dimension
Petrus C. Van Duyne and Mike Levi

The past decade has witnessed a broadening of the attention on income from crime and what is done with it. This is particularly true with the increased activities and earnings of transnational organized crime. This development can be observed first in the legislation on the confiscation and forfeiture of the proceeds of crime and anti-money-laundering legislation in most industrialized countries and, second, in the growth of policing (including customs and excise) involvement in financial investigations. The objectives of these investigations are no longer confined to arresting and bringing the ring-leaders to trial and to confiscating the proceeds of crime but to cripple such "crime enterprises" financially. One could argue that the classical fact-and-suspect investigation has been broadened to focus on the financial management of the crime enterprises involved. This eventually leads to a "pro-active" investigation, more accepted in the U.K. than in continental Europe where scandals arising from covert operations have made people more cautious. This chapter addresses the various forms, approaches, dynamics, and problematics of "financial investigations" in the various areas that can be infiltrated by organized crime like the catering business, the gaming machine market, the real estate market, the real estate development and construction markets, the transport business and others. Tactical financial investigations are carefully examined, like fraud, forfeiture, money-laundering investigations and in-depth analyses of crime enterprises. The "European dimension" of financial investigations is addressed in detail.

14   Mafia-Type Organizations: The Restoration of Rights as a Preventive Policy
Maria Luisa Cesoni

This chapter examines the various responses of justice systems to transnational organized crime. It points out the tendency of justifying the curtailment and/or violation of human rights as a necessary means to effectively combat organized crime and control its spreading. The author argues that, on the contrary, a full respect of human rights and of all the principles of legality will, on the long term, constitute the most effective crime fighting and crime prevention policy.

15   Repeal Drug Prohibition and End the Financing of International Crime
Arthur Berney

The author focuses on the insidious and pervasive violations of constitutional and democratic rights often connected with and justified by the fight against drug trafficking and organized crime. Ultimately this entails a form of statism that strikes at the values associated with individual autonomy. The author then examines corrective steps that are attainable and which may prepare the ground for turning away from the current repressive policies.

16   The Justice System Facing the Challenges of Organized Crime
Emilio C. Viano

This chapter offers an overview of the major federal laws recently enacted in the United States to combat organized crime. Surprising as it might seem, there are still countries that do not have any meaningful legislation that defines or addresses the problem of organized crime. While the transnational nature of today's syndicate makes it imperative that international conventions and treaties be developed, ratified and applied, the first step is still each country's development of the appropriate legal tools for the fight against organized crime. The United States has been at the forefront in developing related legal approaches, models and techniques that have greatly influenced other countries and provided appropriate models. This chapter intends to offer an overview and analysis of the U.S. legislation as an example of concerted and aggressive approach to combating organized crime.

Conclusion

There is no question that the fight against the covert phenomenon of organized crime demands that we drastically revolutionize criminal law and the criminal justice system. Both are based on the model of reacting to the criminal behavior of individuals who are found guilty of reprehensible actions. Organized crime, however, is radically different from such paradigms because it represents crimes perpetrated in a business-like manner by amorphous anti-social groups and organizations that can be local, national and transnational in nature and span of operations. One could even argue that classic criminal law may have become obsolete and even dysfunctional and be in need of being drastically overhauled utilizing a new set of principles, objectives and purposes.

New principles may emphasize collective rather than individual responsibility, accountability and punishment. New objectives may stress prevention and prophylaxis more than the current "after-the-fact" punishment and rehabilitation. New purposes may concentrate resources on the elimination of a criminal organization's economic base and on the identification and confiscation of its assets more than on the traditional individual deterrence, incapacitation or reform.

Criminal law and justice may very well be at a historic crossroads. The challenge of articulating and adopting new definitions, approaches and policies departing from centuries of tradition in legal thinking and law enforcement practices is before us. The major obstacle in reaching these decisions is the limited knowledge that we possess about the nature and strength of the threat that transnational organized crime presents to society, the worldwide economy, and national and international politics. There is still much about organized crime that we do not know. There is also lots of knowledge that we have that is not correct and on target because it is based on obsolete and classic models of the "mafia" that do not reflect today's highly flexible, mobile, and adaptable organized crime.

The goal and objective of this book is to contribute to this more current understanding and assessment of transnational organized crime so that appropriate measures and interventions can be introduced, adopted and implemented at the international level. It is hoped that this volume will effectively contribute to this much-needed international effort which will, in the end, revolutionize how we conceive the role, nature and impact of criminal law and of the criminal justice system.

Acknowledgments

I join the distinguished contributors to this volume in gratefully acknowledging the support of the International Institute for the Sociology of Law in Oñate, Guipuzcoa, Basque country, Spain that made possible the international meeting on transnational organized crime where papers were presented that, after revisions, became the chapters of this book. In particular, I want to thank Malen Gordoa of the International Relations office of the Institute for her hard work in attending to the many details that ensure a meeting's success.

My thanks also to my assistants at American University, Joshua Moon, Sarah Schlosser, Chuck Rainville and Matthew E. O'Dell for their excellent help and painstaking attention to details in preparing this manuscript in camera-ready form for publication. Their patience, commitment and dedication greatly helped make this book possible.

I also want to acknowledge with gratitude the sabbatical support that I received through a grant of the United States Institute of Peace (USIP) which greatly facilitated my editorial work on this volume. However, the opinions, findings, and conclusions and recommendations I expressed in this book are mine and do not necessarily reflect the views of the United States Institute of Peace.

Finally, my deepest thanks go to the authors and contributors to this volume who generously agreed to share their knowledge, insights and understanding of this complex and growing phenomenon with the international community of scholars, students and readers so that we can make substantial progress in our fight against this insidious form of transnational crime.

PART I:
TRANSNATIONAL ORGANIZED CRIME: THE GLOBALIZATION OF CRIME

1 The Evolution of Espionage Networks and the Crisis of International Terrorism and Global Organized Crime

JOSEPH L. ALBINI, R.E. ROGERS, JULIE ANDERSON

Terrorism is a menace to the modern world. It has always been present in various forms throughout history; however, until recently, terrorism groups and their acts have been confined, for the most part, to within the boundaries of the specific countries whose governments were the primary targets of their attacks. But terrorism has now followed the development of other forms of organized crime. It has extended the limits of its boundaries. It has become international in its purpose, structure and tactics. As such, it is following the development of other forms of organized crime because terrorism is a form of organized crime; specifically, it is classified as political-social organized crime (Albini, 1971, pp. 38-45).

Unlike armies that attack one another in war, where the soldiers officially represent their governments and can be recognized and held accountable for their actions, terrorist are hidden by the unknown. They define their power within the realm of the unknown. Because they do not openly announce or declare their war, because their victims often do not come from the ranks of the designated enemy but instead can simply be innocent bystanders; terrorists, in reality, enjoy the freedom of striking whomever and whenever they please.

The expansion and use of this freedom has progressively been increasing in the past four decades. In the 1970s, terrorist acts became a cause for concern but were confined primarily to Europe, Latin America, and the Middle East. Today terrorism has reached out over the globe, and indeed, now constitutes a menace to the entire world.

It is this change in terrorist activity but more pointedly it is the change in group organizational structure and function that lies at the center of the discussion of this work.

3

Generic to the discussion of the concept of "risk" here we mean the "risk" of an American or other citizen becoming the victim of a terrorist attack. As John Ross (1995, p.47) notes, "risk", even when the probabilities are communicated clearly, can be and is interpreted differently by experts as compared to the average citizen.

As such then, risk is perceived differently at different levels of society. This fact is generic to our discussion in that we must and will contrast the difference between how government agency experts and leaders in various countries rate or view such risks as compared to the mass public or average citizen's reaction in such countries.

Let us now turn to the basic content or themes of this work. Firstly, we discuss and describe the development of and increase in a changing structure of relations between various terrorist groups as they interact within current international systems of global networks; this system, as we will illustrate, consists of a continuously changing "patron-client" network of a multitude of different types of relationships.

The second theme follows from this discussion to show how the future of terrorism will involve the use of these relationships and, with the availability of new weapons and technology, will seek to create new forms and targets of victimization, thus changing and expanding the power of per-suasion and influence of terrorist groups. Finally, the third theme we will deal with is the challenges which these new developments present for the intelligence agencies and security forces of the United States.

Let us now discuss the issue which we feel is focal to our discussion: the breakdown and changes that have taken place in national security systems both in Russia and the United States. This breakdown is noticeable among the security systems of various major countries. It appears that the structure and operating tactics of intelligence systems in themselves seem to have become dysfunctional and obsolete. There were, as early as the 1970s, issues signaling that the system, irrespective of country or agency, indeed suffered from generic problems. The Aldrich Ames case among others have currently confirmed this to be true.

But more central to the issue is the fact that we have not recognized the severe changes that took place in the world of espionage with the fall of the Soviet Union. Not only did its demise spawn changes in East-West relations, the very structure of the Soviet-Russian and US espionage systems was affected by the fall. Firstly, it severely altered a system of spy networking that had taken both sides decades to create. Contrary to the James Bond movies which entertained the public with the superspy description of how political support and by providing the patron with information that is vital to his personal and social welfare.

We should emphasize that patron-client relationships are not governed by legal norms but instead are based upon social norms in which there is an accepted faith between the two participants that each will carry out his or her end of the bargain. More importantly, we should note that the power relations between patrons and clients are constantly in a state of change so that a "patron" at one time or in one situation may later become the "client" of his or her original "client". So, too, a "patron" while serving as such to a "client" may himself or herself simultaneously be serving as a "client" to another patron. Thus, the patron-client relationship must be understood as a system of interaction taking place at and between various levels of social strata and one that involves constantly changing positions of power.

The nature of patron-client relationships varies from society to society, but the system generally operates to form networks of relationships in which the more clients a patron has, the more power the patron gains from favors he or she can request. This power is enhanced further by the vital information the patron obtains; in turn, the more patrons a client has, the more power he or she obtains from the protection and service the client can receive. As such, it is a mutually-reinforcing system in which, in terms of cost-benefit analysis, it serves both parties to cooperate and help one another. As such, both parties can gain and retain power.

As terrorist groups constitute forms of organized crime where there is an opportunity for mutual exchange of services, this makes for a natural, symbiotic blending for their cooperation with other organized crime groups such as drug traffickers, money-launderers, hijackers, and other types of criminal groups. But they cooperate with non-criminal groups as well. Thus, Phil Williams (1995) alerts us to the fact that in the geopolitics of international organized crime, not only do criminals interact but the underworld links up with the upper world of legitimate business people, law enforcement officials and government officials, the latter two often providing counterintelligence services for the criminals (p. 7).

From the shores of China, Nigeria, Japan, Russia, Cuba, India, Sri Lanka, the US, and other countries of the world each government is faced with its dissidents and terrorists, some whose object of attack is their own government, others who carry their terror beyond their own territorial boundaries into the territory of foreign governments.

The possibilities, then, are endless for the number and types of "patron-client" networks that can be created on an international scale.

In concluding this work, we now turn to the synthesis of the themes presented thus far in an effort to highlight the major issue of our discussion.

We believe that the recent incidents of terrorist acts including the World Trade Center and the Oklahoma City bombing are the beginning signs of a new approach and style of terrorism, the target which is, specifically, the United States government.

We cannot make accusations as to which particular terrorist groups or groups are its major perpetrators, which is one of the major points we wish to highlight - the fact that terrorist groups have proliferated so rapidly that it is now extremely difficult to discern with any reasonable accuracy which group has executed the act. This proliferation and the increase in terrorism in the US is accompanied by a significant change in the modus operandi of such groups. Whereas in the past and in acts committed outside the US, terrorist groups were instantaneously ready to claim responsibility for the act and in many cases made demands with a promise that if these were met, the terrorism would cease, today, they are silent - a silent message that seems to further the real effectiveness and terror of terrorism; mainly, the added fear of not knowing who perpetuated the act. We realize that the claiming of responsibility, in past terrorist acts, in itself did not lighten the impact of destruction and death that often accompanied these acts; however, to have the perpetrator claim responsibility at least gave the victimized country a vehicle for potential communication with the group and the possibility of arbitrating their demands.

To say that the threat of terrorism comes from within America is to accept as true some current misunderstanding about so-called American terrorist groups; mainly, the citizens' militia groups, otherwise known as "the patriot movement", that has gained much attention within recent years.

The patriot movement, we feel, has been misunderstood. These are Americans who fear their government and want to remain in a state of armed readiness in case they have to defend themselves against the federal government agencies. The incidents of Waco and Ruby Ridge have caused these groups to become concerned about the government's excessive use of force. Their fear of this potential use of force, not the hatred of the American people, lies at the root of their efforts to develop and maintain a state of military readiness. As many of them put it - "I love my country; it is my government I don't trust". These militia groups do not, it seems, view other Americans as the threat; hence, terrorism against Americans simply does not fit their profile.

We profess then, that the current wave of terrorism in America has its major perpetration and perpetrators coming from outside its boundaries.

We feel that the crisis takes on significant seriousness because of two factors, both of which have clearly been described in detail: first, the breakdown in the US espionage network following the end of the cold war and, second, the development of the current "patron-client" networking system of terrorist groups and its proliferation of new groups.

In short, then, terrorist groups have become very prolific in number, have acquired sophisticated tactical knowledge and weapons, and receive advanced forms of training. Since many of these groups consist of new splinter groups, their names and composition are elusive. Yet, because of the destruction and terror they can create, they have become in many cases autonomous agents of power; in some respects they have become small, elusive armies responsible to no government but, instead, self-governing entities with self-serving goals and ideologies.

And, so, America has become the target of world-wide terrorism and the central target is the US government and its intelligence agencies.

As difficult as it is to come to terms with reality, we believe that if America is to face the current crisis of the threat of terrorism, the government must take action in dealing with the current reality.

The Unites States is the most powerful military force in the world, that is, if it were fighting a war against other recognized and identifiable military forces. But the war with terrorists is not and can not be fought in that manner. Instead of raising Theodore "Teddy" Roosevelt's big stick, we are now forced to, and must, reconsider new strategies for facing this crisis.

Let us end, then, by suggesting what we feel are basic, general changes and approaches which we believe are necessary to meet this crisis. We hope these will open a forum for discussion.

Firstly, the government must rethink its past and current approaches to government-sponsored covert actions within a realistic, cost-benefit oriented framework that can co-exist functionally and effectively with its foreign policy. We agree with Roy Godson (1993) when he states that, "covert action is not a substitute for foreign policy"(p. 21).

Espionage structures and operations in the future must and will change. They already are changing, and the spy satellites that are about to go into space will herald that new era.

In the future, covert operations must have some form of monitoring and must be carried out with an evaluation of the consequences they present for future domestic and foreign policy. We need a better developed and clear strategy. And further, we must focus on improving our tactical intelligence system.

We can no longer afford, as was the case of our covert actions with guerilla forces in the past 40 years, to fight what Robert Asprey (1975) so aptly call a "War in the Shadows". Asprey, quoting Prime Minister Lord Palmerston, reminds us that, ". . . we have no perpetual allies and we have no perpetual enemies"(p. 1525).

From outside the shadows, the United States must rapidly begin changing the stereotype which America has so successfully created about terrorist and their followers. We can no longer afford to use ethnocentric and unscientific stereotypes to describe them for such stereotypes are based upon emotion, not reason. As *The National Times* (August, 1996, p. 13) notes in its thought-provoking article reprinted from *The Economist*, entitled "Inside the Mind of the Terrorist", "the terrorist. . . is not different from other men" and sometimes, "they can advance both a general cause and themselves". So, too, "Terrorists like governments, may be rational: they are pursuing a policy they hope will succeed. And the more it works, the more vigorously they will pursue it"(p. 12).

We do not support or condone terrorism, but as it exists, we must confront it on the basis of what it is - the production of terror in order to achieve its goal.

The federal law enforcement agencies must make adjustments to meet the current crisis. Both the FBI and the ATF have experienced a great deal of strain trying to meet the demands placed upon their agents by the new terrorist threat. We realize that both agencies have been overworked. But that is another tactic of terrorist groups; mainly, to keep instigating incidents, large and small, which will necessitate more time and use of both human and financial resources in order to investigate them.

In this fight against terrorism American citizens must become more aware of what their leaders are doing, particularly in the realm of foreign policy. The American public has well been characterized and criticized for its political apathy. It is a reactive public, reacting to specific issues which threaten segments of voters at certain times, such as the issues of the loss of social security and health benefits within the past two years. But, if democracy is to survive, we must heed the words of sociologists Karl Mannheim (1950) who, in the 1950s, predicted a crisis in our western democracies. In order to avert this crisis, he noted that citizens of democratic governments must develop democratic responsibility, which includes becoming and continuously remaining aware of issues so that they can vote in a knowledgeable manner. Only by knowing the issues can the voting public exert influence on the creation, maintaining and/or changing of its government's foreign and domestic policy.

In ending this work, we do so by repeating again what we said before - that terrorists are not much different from the rest of us. They feel pain, anxiety, love, hate, and the whole gamut of other emotions. Perhaps if we can start at this level of understanding, if we can comprehend the basic elements that mitigate their need to use terror, then perhaps that will be the first step toward producing a world free of terrorism.

References

Albini, J. (1971), *The American Mafia*. New York: Appleton Century Crofts.

Asprey, R.B. (1975), *War in the Shadows*. Vol. 1 and 2. New York: Doubleday.

Boissevain, J. (1966), "Patronage in Sicily". *Man* I, March, pp. 16-18.

Cooper, H.H.A. and Redlinger, L.J. (1986), *Making Spies*. Colorado: Paladin Press.

Godson, R. (1993), *Covert Action in the 1990s*. Washington, D.C.: Consortium for the Study of Intelligence.

Las Vegas Review Journal. (1996), July 11, pp. A1, A4.

Mannheim, K. (1950), *Freedom, Power and Democratic Planning*. New York: Oxford University Press.

Newsweek. (1996), July 15, p. 36.

Ross, J.F. (1995), "Risk: Where Do Real Dangers Lie?" *Smithsonian*, November 1995, pp. 43-53.

Steel, R. (1996), *The New Republic*. July 29, p. 23.

The Atlantic Monthly. (1996), July , pp. 24-28.

The National Times. (1996), August, pp. 10-13.

Williams, P. (1995), "The Geopolitics of Transnational Organized Crime". Paper presented at the Meetings of the American Society of Criminology. Boston, November 14-18.

Wolf, E.R. (1966), "Kinship, Friendship and patron-client relations in complex societies," in M. Blanton (ed.), *The Social Anthropology of Simple Societies*. New York: Praeger.

2 The European Union and Organized Crime: Fighting a New Enemy with Many Tentacles

MONICA DEN BOER

Introduction

The old Trevi-regime subsided just when the threat of the old communist enemy was beginning to fade and when the fight against organized crime was experiencing a "boom". In their first efforts against organized crime, the Member States of the European Community made numerous attempts to draw up a comprehensive inventory of the organized crime groups that were active in their territory. However, these attempts disappeared to the background when it turned out that considerable differences existed between the Member States in the kind of criteria they used and in their perception of the threat of organized crime (Anderson, 1993, 1; Anderson c.s., 1995, chapter 1).

Despite this initial failure at EC level, the fear of organized crime has propelled a wave of transformations through the national and international criminal justice systems, both at an organizational and normative level. This chapter analyzes the way in which the concept of organized crime has become a nodal point in European laws enforcement cooperation. Within nation states, it has reinforced the call for the enlargement of scale and centralization. The chapter includes notes about the (re-)structuring of law enforcement organizations in a number of EU Member States. Furthermore, it contains some comparative observations on the discussion with regard to the employment of special investigative (undercover) methods and accountability procedures that apply to these methods. Between nation states, the emphasis on the fight against organized crime has helped to legitimize the creation of a joint police organization and the drafting of joint legal instruments (in the context of "Justice and Home Affairs co-operation"). Finally, within the

13

European region more widely, organized crime symbolizes a new iron curtain between the poorer "source" countries, where illegitimate goods are mostly produced, and the richer "destination" countries, where illegitimate goods are traded and consumed (Williams, 1996).

While organized crime functions as a marker in the redefinition of internal and external security concepts, it simultaneously symbolizes a number of weaknesses in the security arrangements, notably the permeability of national borders, the vigour of free trade and the evolution of the global village. A paradox, perhaps which makes the fragile balance between economic and law enforcement interests a very difficult one to tackle for politicians.

The Challenge to Define Organized Crime

Since the creation of the Trevi Working Group on Serious and Organized Crime the Member States have been at pains to establish a common definition of organized crime. Even nowadays, when serious work is being undertaken to consolidate intelligence sharing and to establish a network of magistrates,[1] there is still a noticeable struggle to come to an agreement about the exact target of recent strategies and new police investigative methods.

It is obvious that the phenomenon of organized crime is a rather differentiated one across Member States. Research has demonstrated that the phenomenon of (transnational) organized crime is fluid and heterogeneous in nature (Williams 1995), especially when it concerns the structure of the criminal organization. In some Member States, there is still a rather strong emphasis on the hierarchical nature of organized crime, especially in those countries where law enforcement agencies focus on Mafia-type criminal organizations. In other Member States, there is more attention for a "flatter", coalition-type of organized crime (Van de Bunt c.s. 1996, 114). The Parliamentary Inquiry Committee on Special Investigation Methods[2] in the Netherlands for instance, which submitted its final report in February 1996, perceived organized crime as being facilitated by networks, immigrant economies and profitable coalitions between (individual) entrepreneurs.[3] In some Member States there is also a growing tendency to highlight the corruptive aspects of organized crime, alias the penetration of the "underworld" in the "upperworld". This awareness has promoted the undertaking of more research on the identification of vulnerable aspects of markets and public administrative bodies.[4]

In practice, internal cooperation structures use various references to serious crime (like in the definition of Europol's subject of investigation[5]), but not always by stating the requirements of double criminality or extraditability. The emphasis on "serious crime" rather than "organized crime" leaves scope for a wider interpretation, and thus application, of international law enforcement action. Moreover, the inclusion of the serious crime definition in the action-radius of Europol allows for a focus on the constitutive elements of organized crime, and for the investigation (and prosecution) of criminal activities committed by individuals.

It is interesting to observe that working with a legal definition of organized crime is still relatively rare within the EU. Definitions of organized crime are often absent in the national criminal laws of the Member States (Germany works with a definition by means of constitutive criteria, whereas for instance Italy and the Netherlands work with the concept of "association with or membership of a criminal organization"). Despite the availability of legal definitions and concepts in a few Member States, it has not yet been possible for the Ministers of Justice and Home Affairs to achieve a single, unambivalent definition with the EU-context. However, in a recent report the High Level Group pinpointed at this problem, and following its recommendations, the Justice and Home Affairs Council decided at its meeting on 26 and 27 May 1997 that a multi-disciplinary working party on organized crime ought to be instituted to develop a joint definition and policy on organized crime.[6]

In operational terms, law enforcement organizations operate with a *Fingerspitzengefühl*, whether or not an investigation of a crime provides links to further criminal activities. Article 2 of the Europol Convention lists a number of criminal activities. Before the Europol Convention will be ratified, these criminal activities comprise unlawful drug trafficking, trafficking in nuclear and radioactive substances, clandestine immigration networks, traffic in human beings and motor vehicle crime. Within two years at the latest following the entry into force of the Europol Convention, Europol will have a mandate in the investigation of "crimes committed or likely to be committed in the course of terrorist activities. . ." The competencies of the Europol Drugs Unit (EDU) - as Europol is officially called in its pre-convention stage - currently also covers associated money laundering activities and related criminal offences. The list provides a focal point for law enforcement organizations throughout Europe: if a criminal activity can be interpreted as any of the listed criminal activities, it is (will be) possible to initiate international co-operation. The subsidiarity requirement provides additional criterion for international co-operation.[7] Therefore, even if a criminal activity may not directly be legally construed as a form of (transnational) organized crime, a certain operational level of co-operation is facilitated by the crime categories that the Europol Drugs Unit works on.

Another development that could be highlighted in this context is the decision to create a joint mechanism for the collection and systematic analysis of information about international organized crime.[8] This decision dates from November 1993 and was later laid down in a Joint Action.[9] In the meantime, the Council has decided that an annual situation report will be made up under the responsibility of the EU Presidency,[10] which will be supported by a contact network of persons in the Member States. The annual situation report will be fed by national situation reports originating from the national criminal intelligence services. The methodology for these reports has been standardized, to the extent that the reports will have to take into account a certain number of listed issues, such as the nationality and geographical data of a person(s) who is suspected of involvement in organized crime, his/her form of co-operation with other suspects and the location where the criminal activities take place. The following list of characteristics will be used for reporting purposes:

1. *Co-operative structure of more than two persons*
2. Each with his/her own specific task
3. *For a longer or indefinite period time (this criterion applies to the stable and (possibly durable character of the group)*
4. With a form of discipline and control
5. *Suspect of serious crimes*
6. Internationally active
7. With the use of violence or other means of intimidation
8. With the use of commercial or business structures
9. Involvement in money laundering
10. With an influence on politics, the media, public administration, justice or the economy
11. *With the purpose of gaining profit and/or power*

A crime or criminal group is defined as a form of organized crime if at least six of these characteristics apply: four of those have to be 1, 3, 5 and 11. It is too early to judge whether this standardization of definition criteria will have a noticeable effect on the reporting performance of the Member States.

Organized Crime: A New External Threat?

Meanwhile, it is clear that the concept of organized crime has attracted an almost disproportionate attention from law enforcement agencies, politicians, policy makers and academics. A shift has been noticeable since the beginning of the nineties, when Trevi established a Working Group on serious and organized crime. As organized crime was important in the eyes of law enforcement, it became a popular target that, if adequately encountered, could add a significant score to the performance record of individual law enforcement agencies. The fear of (transnational) organized crime has facilitated international networking and the obtaining of resources. Moreover, organized crime has become an appealing working terrain for law enforcement agencies. The disappearance of the bipolar system made it also necessary for Secret Services to explore new areas of crime: the ending of the Cold War "removed the rationale for much internal security planning" (Bunyan, 1993, 33). As Europe has pulled down its defenses against communism, it has begun to confront the enemy within (Den Boer, 1994, 182). The exterior menace has been transformed from communist regime to immigration and organized crime, which has reinforced the emphasis on security threats coming from outside "the" community. International security agreements increasingly often include the factor of migration. Organized crime, particularly associated with mobility and transnationality (Den Boer, 1997a), has rapidly become a suitable substitute for the old external security threat. In the law enforcement discourse, references to the "external" aspect of organized crime are not unfamiliar, particularly when it concerns illegal immigration and trade in human beings, Russian organized crime, and the smuggling of radioactive and nuclear substances. In short, "internal" and "external" security have to a certain extent become merged (Bigo and Leveau, 1992; Den Boer 1997b).

Furthermore, organized crime, illegal immigration networks and imported terrorism are all high-profile crimes which have somehow overshadowed ordinary, small-scale crime. The fight against high-profile crimes may have been instrumental in the enlargement of scale of police organizations and in securing new resources and facilities (Den Boer,forthc.). However, many police officers would argue that, first, local crime is still a lot more visible in local communities and also undermines feelings of safety and stability in communities; and second, that crime is closely related to context and opportunities in the vicinity of would-be offenders.

The effect of preoccupation with the external security aspects of organized crime is that it can be construed as a common threat to the European Union, particularly also when destabilizing effects can be ascribed to it. Some of these associations fall in line with the revelations about the strong intertwining between terrorist related crimes and organized crime. The construction of a common threat may have become an instrument in the formation of a common identity (which is still noticeably absent in a united Europe).

However, this focus on the new threat, i.e. organized crime that pervades the West European economies, has a number of side-effects which may exactly run counter to the establishment of a common identity. First the "victimless" nature of organized crime makes law enforcement efforts against it less tangible for the (European) citizen: counter-measures remain largely beyond the scope of day-to-day community policing as they are conducted mainly at a central and international level. Second, the methods used for the investigation of organized crime are innovative and often not legally regulated, which means that they are accompanied by minimal levels of legal and political accountability. It is unclear whether the (European) citizen appreciates the gradual extension of special police competencies: which benefit does s/he get in return? Is organized crime indeed tackled more effectively with the help of undercover investigation methods?

Organizational Consequences

A more skeptical question ought to be raised therefore: has the heavy emphasis on the threats from outside the community been used as a rhetorical tool to justify the call for more co-ordination within national criminal justice systems and the creation of centralized police bodies? The need for more coordination between the EU Member States in their measures against organized crime has certainly had a number of organizational spin-offs. Indeed, one could argue that the internationalization of policing activities has propelled a range of internal measures within the Member States (Den Boer, forthc.).

The creation of international co-operation structures, such as Schengen and Europol, has imposed a demand upon the criminal justice systems in the Member States to enhance the co-ordination of information flows and to make accountability procedures more transparent at higher law enforcement levels. One motivation for this demand is the diplomatic importance that is rendered to well co-ordinated covert operations against transnational criminal networks. Another reason is that international co-operation has made the internal organization of the criminal justice system a more obvious subject for inspection from the outside world. The increase of law enforcement co-operation has also led to more competition between the national criminal justice systems in Europe (Den Boer, forthc.).[11] Organized crime, with its typical characteristics "international" and "serious," has functioned as an important catalyst in the call for a more centralized co-ordination of intelligence-exchange within and between the Member States, and this argument strongly reverberates in the High Level Group *Action Plan to Combat Organized Crime*.[12]

Although there are good arguments for coordination and centralization (more efficient, more transparent, more accountable), local and regional criminal intelligence agencies are not always enthusiastic about the sharing of criminal intelligence at the national and international level. It should be regarded as a cultural challenge to unravel the "cocooning" culture in which many police intelligence officers still operate (Zanders 1997, 127); very often they keep intelligence to themselves in the expectations that it will lead them to the solution of the case(s) under investigation. However, in practice this isolationist "breeding" of intelligence has too often culminated in an undesirable ignorance about the use of certain informers between two or more police regions, thereby allowing the criminal informer to play off the one intelligence department against the other (as demonstrated also by the Dutch Parliamentary Inquiry Committee).[13]

Future Developments in EU Anti-Organized Crime Efforts

The future of co-ordinated efforts against organized crime within the EU does not only depend on the introduction of legal and organizational changes, but also (and perhaps mainly) on transformations in the police culture. The thwarting of the secrecy culture in the criminal intelligence branches will be the largest challenge, but it will be impossible to impose it "from above". If the intelligence cocoons in the Member States can be tackled successfully, the future Europol will gain more credibility, which will also be supported by its post-convention mandate in the international exchange of intelligence. It is expected that Europol will also play a growing role in the facilitation and support of the international co-ordination of cross-border undercover operations. In his annual report on EDU activities in 1996, the EDU coordinator says that the national Europol-satellites have more frequently appealed to the EDU to support and facilitate the coordination of international controlled deliveries and international supervisory operations. Even though the exchange of information between the EDU liaison officers has remained the principal activity, 6% of all assistance requests concerned the support given by the EDU liaison officers to the coordination of running multilateral law enforcement activities (e.g. controlled deliveries of which 33 were facilitated by EDU in 1996).[14] Europol /EDU has been active in holding seminars and in drawing up documents. Recent documents include the *Policy regarding Special Techniques* and a Study regarding *Controlled Deliveries*, in which the legal, judicial, factual, structural and financial problems in such operations are dealt with.

It is regrettable that Europol's "operative" mandate - now anchored in Article 30 of the EU Treaty of Amsterdam which was signed on 2 October 1997 - has not yet been complemented by a sounder system of active judicial supervision and control. A proposal by the Dutch Minister of Justice to have a European Prosecutor attached to Europol was torpedoed by a majority of the Member States. The creation of a European Prosecution Service has been put forward as a suggestion, but is highly contested (Bruggeman 1997). Instead, and following Recommendation No. 21 of the High Level Group on organized crime, we will see the introduction of a network of liaison magistrates.[15] Preferably, liaison magistrates should be seconded to Europol in the form of a network, with a mandate to perform judicial pre-screening of international undercover operations, and to assess the criteria upon which action is to be undertaken (Vermeulen 1997). A recommendation to this extent was submitted by the expert conference on intelligence-sharing (INTELLEX '97) which was held in Noordwijik in May 1997.[16]

A promising strand is the preventative (administrative) approach to organized crime, which has been advocated by the Dutch Presidency, and which also forms part of the political guidelines that were put forward by the High Level Group on Organized Crime (No. 5f). Research has demonstrated that organized crime thrives on several opportunities in the public and private sphere, which present themselves as legal loopholes, lack of organizational supervision, lax internal auditing, or a decentralized public expenditure. The preventative approach to organized crime focuses on ways in which opportunities in the public sphere can be removed or substantially undermined, such as: the improvement of integrity in public administration (e.g. by codes of conduct); an intensified (multi-agency) co-operation with private enterprises (e.g. insurance companies); the exchange of information between Member States about physical persons involved in the creation, direction and funding of legal persons; the development of criteria for the issuing of licenses; the exclusion of organized crime from participation in tendering procedures and (EU-)subsidies; and ultimately also harnessing of socio-economic environments which are prone to exploitation by criminal networks (in its public guidelines no. 14 the High Level Group has proposed to use the EU structural funds, namely the European Structural Fund and the Urban Fund).

It is clear that if organized crime is to be combated effectively, a complex range of measures is required. In this regard, covert investigation practices ought to be compensated by a preventative approach that targets the very *raison-d-être* of organized crime, namely economic profit. The EU Money laundering directive and the administrative investigation competencies of UCLAF[17] are instruments at hand; recently expanded by the anti-corruption convention that introduces sanctions against corrupted civil servants who work at national and EU level.[18] Hence, operation *mani pulite* may soon take on a European dimension.

Notes

1   Recommendation 21 of the *Action Plan to combat Organized* OJ 97/C 251/01; 15 August 1997).

2   Enquêtecommissie Opsporingsmethoden 1996; Professor Fijnaut and his team, who undertook the analysis of organized crime in the Netherlands, used the following definition: One can speak of organized crime if groups of persons primarily aim at illegal profit; if they systematically commit crimes with serious consequences for society, and if they are able to protect these crimes effectively, in particular through the use of physical violence or corruption (*Ibid.*, on p. 25).

3   Especially this latter point was brought forward by P. Van Duyne during his interrogation by the Dutch Parliamentary Inquiry Committee (*supra*, no. 1 on p. 27).

4   E.g. T.M.C. Asser Instituut 1997.

5   Article 2 of the Europol Convention (Council Act of 26 July 1995 drawing up the Convention based on Article K. 3 of the Treaty on European Union, on the establishment of a European Police Office; 95/C 316/01) states that the European Police Office should combat "terrorism, unlawful drug trafficking and other *serious* forms of *international* crime where there are factual indications that an *organized criminal structure* is involved and two or more Member States are affected by the forms of crime in question. . ." (emphasis mdb).

6   Recommendation No. 20, *Action Plan to Combat Organized Crime*, OJ 97/C
         251/01, 15 August 1997.
7   Article 2-1 of the Europol Convention (*supra*, no. 5) rules that for Europol
         to stage an investigation, it is required that two or more Member States must
         be affected, and the crime in question must "require a common approach by
         the Member States owing to the scale, significance and consequences of the
         offences concerned".
8   Doc. 9908/2/93 (CRIMORG 1 REV2).
9   Joint Action of 29 November 1996 adopted by the Council on the basis of
         Article K.3 of the Treaty on European Union, concerning the creation and
         maintenance of a directory specialized competencies, skills and expertise in
         the fight against international organized crime, in order to facilitate law
         enforcement cooperation between the Member States of the European Union,
         96/747/JHA. OJ L 342/2.
10   Note from the Working Party Drugs and Organized Crime to the K.4
         Committee (6204/1/97 - ENFOPOL 35), Brussels, 6 March 1997.
11   The point about competition was also brought forward by the assistant
         coordinator of Europol, Dr. Qilly Bruggeman, during a conference of
         Committees for European Affairs of the national parliaments of the EU
         Member States and of a Committee of the European Parliament(Staten-
         Generaal, vergaderjaar 1996-1997, 22 660, Nrs. 77 and 9, p. 4).
12   See e.g. Recommendation No. 1 OJ 97/C 251/01, 15 August 1997.
13   *Supra*, no.2, on p. 305.
14   Report from EU-coordinator over 1996, from the Europol Working Party to
         the K.4 Committee, Brussels, 19 March 1997 (6711/97, EUROPOL 14).
15   See also Joint Action (96/277/JHA) on framework for the exchange of liaison
         magistrates for the improvement of judicial cooperation between the EU
         Member States; OJ L 105, 27 April 1996.
16   *Intellex '97. Conferentie inzake tactische en strategische informatie-
         uitwisseling over georganiseerde criminaliteit.* Den Haag: Ministerie van
         Justitie, on pp. 261-262.
17   Anti-Fraud Coordination Unit of the European Commission. See also the
         Annual Report on 1996 by the European Commission on the Protection of
         the Financial Interests of the Community (Fight against Fraud). Brussels,
         European Communities, 1997.
18   Council Act of 26 May 1997 drawing up, on the basis of Article k.3 (2) c) of
         the Treaty on European Union, the Convention on the fight against
         corruption involving officials of the European Communities or officials of
         Member States of the European Union. OJ 97/C 195/01.

References

Anderson, Malcolm. (1993). "Control of Organised Crime in the European Community". Working Paper IX, *A System of European Police Co-Operation in 1992.* Edinburgh: Department of Politics, The University of Edinburgh.

Anderson, M.; Den Boer, M.; Cullen, P.; Gilmore, W.; Raab, C.; and Walker, N. (1995). *Policing the European Union: Theory, Law and Practice.* Oxford: Clarendon Press.

Asser Institut, T.M.C. (1997). "Prevention of and Administrative Action against Organised Crime", A Comparative Law Study of the Registration of Legal Persons and Criminal Audits in Eight EU Member States, carried out for the purpose of the EU Conference on Crime Prevention in Noorddwijk, May 1997 (draft report).

Bigo, Didier and Leveau, Rémy. (1992). "L'Europe de la Sécurité Intérieure", Rapport de fin d'étude pour l'Institut des Hautes Études de Sécurité Intérieure. Paris.

Boer, Monica den. (1994). "The Quest for International Policing: Rhetoric and Justification in a Disorderly Debate". In *Police Co-operation across National Boundaries,* edited by Malcolm Anderson and Monica den Boer. London: Pinter.

Boer, Monica den. (1997a). "Criminalisering van immigranten en asielzoekers in Europa: de interactie tussen criminologie en rechtshandhaving". *Recht en Kritiek* (forthcoming).

Boer, Monica den. (1997b). "Wearing the Inside Out: European Police Cooperation between Internal and External Security". *European Foreign Affairs Review.* Volume 2, Issue 4 (Winter).

Boer, Monica den, ed. (1997c). *Undercover Policing and Accountability from an Inernational Perspective.* Maastricht: European Institute for Public Administration.

Boer, Monica den. (forthcoming). "Internationalism: A Challenge to Police Organisations in Europe". In *Policing Across the World: Issues for the Twenty First Century.* Edited by Rob Mawby. UCL Press.

Bruggemann, Willy. (1997). "Creating a European Public Prosecution Service". In *Schengen, Judicial Cooperation and Policy Coordination.* Edited by Monica den Boer. Maastricht: European Institute of Public Administration.

Bunt, Henk van d; Fijnaut, Cyrille; Bovenkerk, Frank and Bruinsma, Gerben J. (1996). "De georganiseerde criminaliteit in Nederland". *Tijschrift voor criminologie.*Volume 2. 102-119.

Bunyan, Tony. (1993). "Beyond state-watching". In *Statewatching the new Europe. A Handbook on the European State,* edited by Tony Bunyan. London: Statewatch.

Enquêtecommissie Opsporingmethoden. (1996). *Inzake Opsporing*. Den Haag: SDU Uitgevers.

Vermuelen, Gert. (1997). "A European Judicial Network Linked to Europol". *Maastricht Journal of European and Comparative Law*. Volume 4, Number 4.

Walker, Neil. (1997). "Deficient Weaponry, Reluctant Marksman and Obscure Targets: Flaws in the Accountability of Undercover Policing in the EU." *In Undercover Policing and Accountability from an International Perspective*, edited by Monica den Boer. Maastricht: European Institute of Public Administration.

Williams, Phill. (1995). " Transnational Crime Organizations: Strategic Alliances," *The Washington Quarterly*, Winter, Volume 18, Number 1: 57-72.

Williams, Phill. (1996). *Grave New World: Transnational Organized Crime on the Eve of the Twenty First Century*, Mimeo.

Zanders, Patrick. (1997). "Europese regionale politiesamenwerking. De Europese politiediensten als informatieintensieve bedrijven." *Intellex '97. Conferentie inzake tactische en strategische infomatie-uitwisseling over georganiseerde criminaliteit*. Den Haag: Ministerie van Justitie, 199-142.

3 Confronting Transnational Crime

PETER B. MARTIN

Democracy around the globe is facing formidable challenges today, not from martial enemies from outside, as we saw heretofore, but from subversive militants from within. Democracy is infected by a pernicious affliction initiated and propagated by organized crime that gains control progressively, maybe first as only a communal criminal gang, to later transform itself into a market driven force, eventually infiltrating the legitimate government at all levels, and finally rendering the government powerless. Throughout the metamorphosis organized crime enlarges its power structure and fortifies itself as democracy atrophies or is lost altogether. Organized international crime is a multi-billion dollar business, experts estimate it can gross $190-250 billion a year.

Jean Monnet thought the key to peace, security and prosperity would be economic interdependence; obviously, he did not factor in the impact of organized crime. Besides globalization, another new trend is the decentralization of state authority, which might be a good thing in its own right if it did not have a weakening effect on the state. Associated with this decentralization of authority is the search for regional identity, so we have the resultant corollary whereby nationalism expands while the sovereign state shrinks.

Family Connections

Nationalism, and its subsequent sense of collective identity, assists in the development, mobilization and coordination of organized crime. Keeping it "all in the family" makes for better security. Entry into these various crime syndicates is exclusive, deliberate and methodical with very little left to chance, which makes them difficult to infiltrate for intelligence gathering. They are often very adept at counter-surveillance, using state-of-the-art penetration methods against authorities. For example, a while ago the Cali cartel purchased sophisticated telecommunications and surveillance

25

instruments from Israel. With that hi-tech equipment they were able to tap into the Colombian Intelligence Agency and the United States Embassy. In addition, crime syndicates employ private detectives and corrupt lawyers to protect themselves from law enforcement agencies.

With such a single ethnic character or signature, whether it be Colombian, Russian, Albanian, or Italian, they can enter into other countries, bond with the local ethnic group, set up networks or affiliation and thereby further increase their global network. Occasionally, there are "marriages of convenience" whereupon certain organized crime families will make an alliance with another for security or business reasons, therein internationalizing the crime syndicate. This has been observed among Colombians, Italians, and Russians uniting to facilitate markets in the drug trade - increasing the global reach of both organizations. However, for the most part, cultural differences, language incompatibility, and security considerations, keeps organized crime more transnational than international.

Money Matters

The power and potential threat of transnational crime is predicated on corruptior of government officials and law enforcement personnel. Considering the vast amounts of money organized crime has amassed from the drug trade, the total liquidity available for bribes is colossal and epitomizes the growing economic power of organized crime and its affiliated threat to the stability of nations. According to David Bickford, former legal advisor to the British Security and Intelligence Services, more than $1 trillion generated by organized crime, is laundered through offshore banks benefitting from secrecy laws. "International Business Companies" (IBC) serve as fronts for transnational criminal activity where the funds can not be traced; plainly substantial revenues are netted by the host countries. Money launderers have now started buying equity in international banks gaining recent control of legitimate banks. Unequivocally, the electoral process can be corrupted when organized crime promotes and finances the elections of their chosen candidates. Once these bought-off members of government are in place they are often protected by parliamentary or diplomatic immunity. Corruption in politics corrodes public trust and the legitimacy of the regime, wearing away the very foundations of civil society, eventually even threatening the stability of the democratic states and engendering transnational economic problems.

A good example of this is Albania's pyramid crisis. With the dissolution of communism and the break-up of Yugoslavia the criminal factions in the region have vied for control of various forms of illicit activity. Nowhere has this criminal activity been so coordinated and transnational than in Albania. The Albanians, especially the Kosovars, have consolidated their once disorganized criminal gangs, using émigré support, into a powerful, highly secretive and ruthless syndicate that has spread out its network across even the Atlantic. All this was made easier with the recruitment of a legion of corrupt politicians, policemen and other government officials throughout the region and into Italy.

Once the communist state was no longer around to structure and organize crime, as it did in the past, Russia fell under the shadow of disorganized crime. Since the demise of communism in Russia every criminal is out for himself, albeit there has been some signs of consolidations among criminal elements. Ironically, organized crime was probably the detonator that blew up the economy and ruined the USSR, much as inchoate disorganized crime today is disastrous to Russia's economic development. Even Russia's privatization efforts have bred criminal activity. According to the chairman of the Security Committee of the Duma, the mafia controls 81% of the voting shares in privatized companies. And according to Moscow's police inspectors, one third of Russia's new private entrepreneurs are involved in the drug trade. Pretty much the same can be said for ex-Soviet States. And due to huge international debts in many of these countries, in addition to the rising interest rates of commercial loans, many legitimate enterprises are turning to organized crime for loans and credit. The FBI reports that criminal computer hackers, or "crackers" as they are now called, operating out of Eastern Europe, lifted approximately $5 billion out of the Internet. And it has recently been reported that Bulgaria has a school to form future hackers. As barriers fall, and as control over the world economy decreases, the void in regulatory control risks being filled by organized crime, as they infiltrate the economy, state, criminal justice system and the media.

Mind Control

Like some international sects, organized crime can intimidate by gaining control via the media, With many newspapers around the world in desperate need of funds, it is all too easy for organized crime to subvert the media by funding them and thereby controlling them. Organized crime can also intimidate the press by swamping them with law suits (as we have seen done by quasi-religious sects) thus stifling any further revelations they might have on organized crime and jeopardizing freedom of the press.

The law is often unable to protect the very citizens who try and challenge organized crime. To maintain their power, authoritarian societies rely on their corrupt legal system and their instruments for social control. Violence, or mind control is used as an instrument of control to produce a submissive population. Individuals often can not start up a legitimate business in many countries because the criminal clans in place will not stand for any competition. If you do not play by the rules you simply do not play. Such an authoritarian scourge reduces an individual's civil liberties and relegates him or her to an exploited individual, dependent on the mafia or other authoritarian society to survive.

Checking Transnational Crime

How can democratic states, who are traditionally bureaucratically bound and tied to laws, be effective in combating the agility of these criminal syndicates? Possible solutions include

1. A transnational approach to the problem is needed. Unless we want to live the social order of termites, dangers to our individual freedoms are going to continue until we improve our intelligence gathering and have better counterintelligence. The other side already has sophisticated intelligence and counterintelligence; our job is to stay ahead of them.
2. You have to know your enemy, his methods, and use them against him. We have to drop our armor of civility and fight them on equal terms if we are going to persevere and preserve our democracy.
3. Transnational crime has to be monitored much more closely exploiting bilateral and multilateral forms of cooperation. Intelligence has to be apportioned to other intelligence services around the globe. Intelligence ought to move laterally, not just up and down.
4. The stream of intelligence has to flow faster so as to break up the bureaucratic log jams so often encountered.
5. Police jurisdiction has to be made more flexible; after all, criminals have never honored borders.

6. Strategies to combat money-laundering have to be reinforced; assets have to be seized before they can be reinvested - tantamount to a disruption to the criminals organization's safe havens.

But the foundation of a successful strategy against transnational crime is political will. A democratic state can have any number of laws, enforcement units, intelligence agencies, and hi-tech hardware, but unless its government is willing to campaign against transnational crime the opposition will prevail; for when they see political weakness they make the most of it.

PART II:
THE CASE STUDIES

4 The Infiltration of Organized Crime in the Emilia-Romagna Region: Possible Interpretations for a New Social Defence

AUGUSTO BALLONI, ROBERTA BISI, ANDREA FORLIVESI,
FLAVIO MAZZUCATO, RAFFAELLA SETTE

Emilia-Romagna, between wealth and social conflict

Emilia-Romagna is considered one of Italy's most productive regions: with its enviable geographic location, its thriving businesses and industries, an industrious populace, efficient local administration, life style and level of employment which are noticeably above the national average.

The Emilia-Romagna region, with its central geographic position characterized by a social-economic environment in which social development processes typical of the entire nation have been particularly accentuated and evenly distributed, changed profoundly after the 1950s when, although considered a typically agricultural zone, it rapidly moved towards economic structures and life styles typical of an industrial society.

Global demographic movements were limited during this transformation, but if exchanges with other regions were scarce until the 1970s, internal migration proved intense, characterized by transfers from rural zones to the cities, with the consequent passage from agricultural jobs to industry and services. These population movements may be explained by the natural tendency towards urbanization, but were also significantly motivated by the disparity of economic development from one zone to the next in the Emilia-Romagna region.

In fact, the industrialization process tends to develop in an accentuated fashion at the heart of the region, moving along the axis of the via Emilia, site of the maximum concentration of population, with few exceptions, which always gravitate towards the "megalopolis" extending from Piacenza to the Adriatic, along the via Emilia. Another strong area from the economic and demographic viewpoint is the Adriatic coast, with the Ravenna industrial pole and the Romagna area tourist industry, which in the past was based on small operators, expelled or transferred from other sectors, but has taken on a more complex and industrialized form.

All of these positive characteristics of the Region combine to attract the attention and aggression of external criminal organizations. Interviews with magistrates from the Bologna district antimafia office, the heads of social monitoring agencies and the documentation acquired, reveal the presence - in varying degrees - within this area of Italian criminal organizations whose origins lie outside the region (since the 1980s), and which have direct links with the mafia, camorra, 'ndrangheta, sacra corona unita and the Brenta mafia. There are also significant indications as to the presence (since the 1990s) - again in varying degrees - of organizations or criminal bands from abroad (Russia, China, Yugoslavia, Morocco).

These organizations, of foreign extraction, have not encountered problems in their cohabitation with local organized crime of varied origin, nor with indigenous common criminals, who occasionally support their activities as well as their own endemic operations.

In this context, the extensive immigration phenomenon of recent years must not be overlooked, having provided Emilia-Romagna with demographic resources essential to its production activities. This phenomenon, progressively increasing, inevitably draws criminal activities and interests, especially to the Romagna area, which are increasingly closely linked with the objectives of consolidated criminal organizations (Savona and Di Nicola, 1997).

In light of this, we must attempt to understand in what way the migratory flows towards Emilia-Romagna from European and other nations affect the characteristics of crime in the region. For this reason, it is useful to briefly illustrate the elements with the greatest influence on the relationship between immigration and crime, bearing in mind how the quantitative data about the involvement of citizens from nations outside the EU in crimes in the Emilia-Romagna region indicates an alarming situation, both in terms of absolute values, i.e.: with reference to the number of foreigners reported to the police, and as regards their percentage of the total reports made.

However, the problem of immigration-linked crime is particularly complex, for three main reasons. Firstly, it is difficult to make valid comparisons between crime rates and the size of the migratory flows, due to the presence, on one hand, of the so-called "unknown number" and on the other, of a significant number of illegal immigrants. Secondly, the problem of the relationship between migration and crime is open to conflicting interpretations, dictated by political motives, since the subject in question is inevitably linked to the questions of intercultural tolerance and the willingness and ability of the institutions to take in immigrants. Finally, recent studies on the phenomenon show that the prevalent approaches are statistical and legal, to the detriment of a social-ethnic viewpoint which is still practically inexistent but which could offer valid contributions in terms of knowledge (Palidda, 1996, p. 161).

Before examining the quantity and quality of the crimes committed by foreigners in Emilia-Romagna, it may be useful to provide some information about the presence of immigrants in the region (Favaro, 1996, pp. 193-194). Emilia-Romagna is one of the regions with the highest number of foreigners, a number destined to increase in coming years. The presence of foreigners in the region increased noticeably between 1989 and 1996, tripling the number of resident foreigners, which went from 23,000 to around 67,000. The reasons for this rapid increase should be sought, to a minimum degree, in the new entries in Italy and, to a greater degree in the movement of immigrants from southern to northern regions. Their distribution in the various regional provinces is more even than in other regions, the main concentrations being respectively in Modena, Bologna, Forlì and Reggio Emilia.

However, it should be emphasized that the above information refers to foreigners who are holders of an official stay permit, whilst it is difficult to estimate the number of illegal immigrants, that is to say, those without a stay permit, and irregular immigrants, i.e.: those to whom a stay permit was issued but who failed to renew it. According to data supplied by the Caritas organization for 1995, estimating a total national presence of around 300,000 irregular and illegal immigrants, and breaking this number down in the various regions so that it corresponds with the percentages of stay permits, the number of foreigners without official permits in Emilia-Romagna would be around 22,000. However, this is probably an overestimate, since the number of irregular and illegal immigrants in this region is significantly less than in regions such as those of the south (Pinto 1995, p. 17). The problem of illegal immigration becomes very important to the problem in question, since, as explained below, it may be considered one of the causes of the tendency, on the part of a certain number of immigrants, to adopt deviant behaviour.

Regarding the specific link between immigration and crime in Emilia-Romagna, several important statistical elements arise. Firstly, during the period from 1991 to 1995 there was a large increase in the percentage of foreigners reported to the police in the region relative to the total number of foreigners reported at national level, a percentage which passed from 1.7% in 1991 to 8% in 1995 ; there was also a significant increase in the percentage between 1991 and 1992 (from 1.7% to 6%) and a slight reduction the following year (from 6% to 5.5%).

No less important is the data about the percentage of foreigners among the total of persons condemned for some particular crimes in Emilia- Romagna during the four-year period 1991-94. For example, for theft, the percentage went from 2.6% in 1991 to 25.2% in 1994 ; the same applies for robbery with violence, a crime for which the percentage of foreigners among the total number of persons condemned in Emilia-Romagna went from 7.2% to 20.2%, again during the four-year period 1991-94. Equally worrying is the percentage increase in the number of foreigners among the total persons condemned in our region for pushing, possession and production of drugs, which jumped from 4% in 1991 to 35.1% in 1994. The percentage of foreigners among the total condemned in Emilia-Romagna for wilful murder and rape is a case apart. Again, there was a percentage increase during the four-year period 1991-94 (from 4.8% to 15% for murder and from 8.3% to 21.6% for rape), although the peak was in 1993 (respectively 22.6% and 22%) with a reduction the following year (Barbagli and Colombo 1996, pp. 48-53). It should be noticed that the victims of the murders in question were often other immigrants (Palidda, p.171).

The main countries of origin involved in the immigrant crime phenomenon in Emilia-Romagna are Morocco, Tunisia, former Yugoslavia, Albania and Algeria, although precise information must be provided about the temporal trend of this aspect. If we consider the number of foreigners reported to the police in Emilia-Romagna during the period from 1991 to 1995, it becomes evident that during the first year examined, the majority of foreigners reported were from the former Yugoslavia (41.8% of the total 175 cases), yet over the entire period considered, although the number of cases increased, reaching 446 in 1995, their percentage of the total fell to 13.1%. At the same time, the number of reports increased noticeably relative to Moroccans (from 69 in 1991 to 1145 in 1995), Tunisians (from 71 to 623 cases) and Algerians (2 reports in 1991 compared with 241 in 1995), whilst with relation to Albanians, there was a gradual increase until 1994 (from 5 to 84 cases) and a large sudden increase in 1995, with 312 reports, equaling 9.2% of the total cases.

The most common crimes are drug pushing, mainly by Albanians and Maghrebians, and theft, mainly involving citizens of the former Yugoslavia. The brawling phenomenon is also worthy of attention, especially brawls between North Africans, chiefly attributable to alcohol abuse: to this end, some operators in the Bologna Municipality, when asked about initial hospitality centres, claimed that they were important in facilitating the immigrant's integration into the local society and culture, but also said that they are dangerous when they become hot-beds of tension which periodically leads to more or less violent clashes between the guests of the structures.

If we return to the problem of drug pushing, it is possible to identify some characteristics of the methods used by foreigners to commit this crime. As already indicated, the Maghrebians and Albanians are chiefly involved in drug pushing, above all in the region's most important cities and on the Adriatic coast, where most money circulates. Whilst in the past similar criminal behaviour was limited to a brief period (two or three months), after which the foreigner returned to his/her country of origin to invest the money obtained in legal activities, this crime has recently become an increasingly stable means of making money for the pusher. Data obtained from interviews with experts from Bologna's social monitoring agencies reveals that foreigners involved in drug pushing form the group of "labourers" which substituted that represented by Italian drug addicts, although it is suspected that in Bologna, as has already occurred in other northern cities, part of this group is passing to the middle level in drug trafficking (*La Societa Multietnica* 1995, p. 117). Moreover, recent episodes on the Romagna coast lead observers to believe that some Albanian pushers have improved their standing, no longer dedicating their time to the traffic of marijuana, but rather to the direct control of a share of the distribution of heroin and cocaine.

The reasons why foreigners become involved in criminal activities in Emilia-Romagna can be attributed to two main factors, that is to say, widespread wealth and the problem of illegal immigration. The Emilia-Romagna area provides a plurality of opportunities for legal and illegal gain, thus attracting those populations which are similar, above all due to their close geographic situation, to Western culture, based on personal success and the obtainment of wealth, confirming the idea according to which the deviance attributed to immigrants is one of the perverse results of the relationship between "dominant" and "dominated" societies (Palidda, p. 170).

Regarding the second reason indicated, it should be understood that illegal activities such as theft and drug pushing are an obligatory path for that group of illegal immigrants who, unable to enter the regular work force, have to turn to crime in order to survive.

A further consideration should be made about the above data relative to foreigners reported and condemned in recent years in Emilia-Romagna. Various sources (Barbagli and Colombo, p. 48; Palidda, p. 170) have expressed the opinion that, besides an effective increase in the involvement of foreigners in crimes in our region, there seems to have been a change in the selective criteria of the criminal justice system, oriented against these minorities. For example, for the foreigners arrested it is often impossible to adopt alternatives to incarceration, due to the lack of family, social and work reference points normally required in order to enjoy these benefits. It is for this reason that the need to acquire precise information about the problem will stimulate future studies and research.

Apart from these considerations, the part played by immigrants in crime affecting the Emilia-Romagna region cannot be denied, nor can the affirmation that the presence of criminals of foreign origin in the region is linked to events related to organized crime, both when immigrants become the manual labourers of Italian criminal organizations and when they form independent bands.

Therefore, immigration may be seen not only as a new case of exclusion of citizenship rights, but also as a transformation factor. It is difficult to create standards and services which do not discriminate, yet at the same time do not ignore differences, particular needs and specific details. On the one hand, a person is entitled to be treated like others, irrespective of sex or ethnic origin, and on the other hand the community has the right to be respected and provided with help to maintain its traditions and culture.

In light of this, the new questions of tolerance and pluralism must be posed above all by new immigrants, but not exclusively. The subject of citizenship and of class and ethnic ties also allows us to consider the growing influence of the "culture of interests" as compared with traditional cultures, aspects which lead us to believe that ethnic protests may be class protests, that is to say, unrest in groups which are not favored within a capitalist structure, or to believe that they are cultural battles intended to allow the prevalence of traditional values over the pervasive influence of capitalist values (Zincone, 1997, pp. 11-19).

Having said this, it should be emphasized that the crime sectors in which a complex organizational structure is most evident are those of drug pushing, robbery of security trucks and banks, control and management of illegal gambling houses and money laundering. Extortion deserves a separate mention, although it does not yet comply with the traditional "racket" model in the area. In fact, there is no evidence of a levy systematically imposed by criminals on shopkeepers and entrepreneurs, even though the social monitoring agencies have recorded an increase in this particular type of crime.

A typical product of the arrival of Calabrians and Sardinians was the recrudescence of kidnapping for the purpose of extortion, which stopped at the start of the 1990s, mainly thanks to successful police work, but which is still a phenomenon that must not be underestimated, due to the huge concentration of possible profitable targets worthy of attention in the zone.

In regards to money laundering, the zone most at risk is the Adriatic coast, where it is assumed that mafia organizations have made insistent attempts at infiltration by the purchase of tourist-hotel structures. However, the true dimensions of this problem are still not known.

Statistics and some practical suggestions

If this is the phenomenon which appears in the documentation, it is a good idea to examine the statistics.

The research is based on the study of the development of organized crime through the official criminal justice statistics made available by the ISTAT (Central Statistics Office) which we then processed.

In the Italian criminal code, associative crimes appear in Book II ("Particular crimes") Heading V "Crimes against public order", art. 416 ("Criminal association") and art. 416bis ("Mafia-style association").

According to a ruling of the Court of Cassation dated 11/10/1991, "in criminal association the criminal agreement is directed towards the implementation of a vast criminal plan, to commit an unspecified number of crimes, with the permanence of an associative tie between the participants; each of which has the constant knowledge that he/she is associated with the implementation of the criminal plan, even independent of and outside the effective committing of the individual crimes planned, with the result that, it is the permanence of the associative tie between two or more persons linked by the same criminal end, which represents a danger to public order and is the reason behind the configuration - as an autonomous crime heading - of the crime of criminal association".

Moreover, according to a ruling of the Court of Cassation dated 15/04/1994, "the criminal figure envisaged in art. 416 bis of the Criminal Code is distinguished from that at art. 416 of the Criminal Code, not only for the disparity of the aims which the association attempts to achieve, and therefore the object of the criminal plan, but also for the use of intimidation by the association in order to fulfil its aims; the intimidation enacted by the associative tie is an instrumental element, not a means of associative behaviour, and must not necessarily be used by the individual associated parties expressed from time to time in acts of physical and moral violence to achieve ends alternatively envisaged by the incriminating provision, since the mafia-style and similar associations are characterized by subjugation and omertà which is the effect of the said intimidation on the individual both within and outside the association".

This research will be based on the crime statistics which illustrate events constituting a violation of criminal laws, and the persons responsible for such violations. The data refers to crimes for which legal authorities have begun criminal proceedings. For statistical purposes, the ISTAT considers criminal proceedings begun in the following cases:

in the case of crimes where the person responsible is known, when the person subjected to preliminary inquires is formally charged, as per art. 405 of the Criminal Code;

In the case of crimes where the person responsible is unknown, when the crime is recorded in the "Unknown Register".

In criminal legal statistics, the crimes as at art. 416 and art 416 bis were classed together as crimes against public order until 1993, from when they were also classed analytically.

To analyze the trend of crimes against public order in Italy, we constructed the historic series, shown in Table 4.1, with absolute values and percentages of persons reported for these crimes from 1980 to 1995. An analysis of this table and the relative graph allow us to divide the series trend into different periods:

- an initial period, from 1980 to 1984, characterized by relative stability in the number of persons reported for these crimes and a similar relative stability in the percentage of persons reported for crimes against public   order among the total persons reported, this percentage fluctuating between 0.3% and 0.38% ;
- a subsequent period, until 1989, characterized by an increase in the absolute number and relative percentage of persons reported for crimes against public order among the total;
- 1990 saw a fall in the absolute number of persons reported for these crimes, although the percentage of the total remained at 0.36%;

- a period of growth, culminating in 1994, of both the absolute and percentage values, which reached 1.15% of persons reported for crimes against public order among the total persons reported;
- in 1995 the number of persons reported fell, although it stabilized at values which were still higher than those for the period previous to 1994.

We compared the statistics for Italy with those for the Emilia-Romagna region, both for crimes against public order in the aggregated category and for analytical crimes relative to articles 416 and 416 bis of the Criminal Code, for the three-year period 1993-1995 (in April 1996, the date of drafting of the present research, the ISTAT had still not supplied the data relative to 1996).

Table 4.2 shows that, although the number is much lower, the percentage of persons reported for crimes against public order among the total persons reported in Emilia-Romagna continued to rise from 1993, until in 1995 it equalled that relative to the data for the whole of Italy (0.7 %). The trend in overall crime rates is similar (Table 4.3.).

We shall now analyze the two types of crimes disaggregated from the "crimes against public order" category. Regarding criminal association, we emphasize that the number of persons reported "peaks" at the same point as the aggregated class, in 1994 both for Italy and for Emilia-Romagna (Tables 4.4 and 4.5). Emilia-Romagna is differentiated from the rest of Italy not only by the absolute numeric values, but also by the percentage of female criminals, which during 1993 was greater than that for Italy as a whole (16.8%). The perpetrators of this type of crime under the age of 18 appeared in Emilia-Romagna only in 1994 and represented 5% of the persons reported. Moreover, again regarding persons under the age of 18 in 1994 the females recorded in Emilia-Romagna represented 7.69% of the total minors reported. In contrast, for Italy as a whole, persons under the age of 18 reported were present over the entire three-year period examined and represented a percentage from 1.7% in 1993 to 0.9% of the total persons.

In Italy, the persons reported for mafia-style criminal association were less than those reported for simple criminal association (Table 4.6), whilst in Emilia-Romagna during the three-year period 1993-1995, there were no persons reported for this crime against which the Legal Authorities have begun criminal proceedings. Finally, in Italy, this number was practically constant in 1993 and 1995, whilst it "peaked" in 1994. Minors were present only in 1993 and represented 11.67% of the overall number of persons reported.

The crime rates used for this research are not sufficient to provide a qualitative evaluation showing effective variations in crime, since the calculation of the rates does not take into account the seriousness of the crimes. Therefore, we feel that it is advisable to use the weighted crime rates, constructed by applying a weight to the individual crimes so as to express their degree of seriousness (Table 4.6). The weights consist in the average sentences decreed, expressing the average number of months of imprisonment inflicted for the crime committed, deduced from the criminal regulations in force during the years referred to (values supplied by the ISTAT).

In order to further develop the analysis of the development of organized crime in Emilia-Romagna, we felt that it was a good idea to examine the reports compiled by the Attorney General of the Bologna Court of Appeal at the start of each legal year, since these represent a further source of information (Meeting of the Court of Appeal of Bologna, inauguration of the Legal Years 1994, 1995 and 1996).

During the period from 1 July 1992 - 30 June 1993 the region was not "immune from infiltration by mafia or mafia-style criminal associations, previously formed around mafia exponents who were distanced from their places of residence and subjected to special surveillance and obligatory stays in municipalities within our region. During the period considered, these nuclei developed the tendency to join forces or integrate with local criminals, whether individuals or groups, as well as drawing fellow-villagers, friends and relatives, thus forming a network of operators in various criminal directions" (e.g.: drug trafficking, sale of arms and explosives, receiving of stolen goods, money laundering).

In the report for the subsequent year, relative to the period from 1 July 1993 - 30 June 1994, the Attorney General stresses that drug trafficking in the Emilia-Romagna region is facilitated by the coastal line towards the Adriatic sea and by the branching of the road network. The marketing of drugs in the territory uses criminal groups "which are autonomous or connected in varying degrees, yet to which the characteristics of mafia-style associations are not easily attributable. Associations with marked characteristics of this type even in areas of crime other than drug trafficking, e.g.: arms sales, extortion, prostitution, gambling and usury, are not endemic in the district territory".

Therefore, it may be said that, in terms of obvious crime, Emilia-Romagna remains below the national average and at an intermediate level relative to other northern Italian regions. However, considering the Region's economic and productive potential, particular attention must be paid to those sectors most vulnerable to the aggression of mafia interests. The most urgent preventative action appears to be required for :

- immigration from countries of the former Soviet block, which is quite consistent, with increasingly scarce practical control possibilities, which project phenomena into the Romagna area that the Russian mafia will count amongst its primary management activities, e.g.: money laundering and prostitution;
- public competitions, which represent one of the preferred vehicles for the penetration of mafia interests into the entrepreneurial sector of a territory.

These factors, which promote the development of crime in a regional context, reveal the great complexity of the environment in which the social monitoring agencies must operate : it is a context which sees the creation of new relationships between people, new forms -legal and illegal- of confrontation and so of conflict. It is this that necessitates culturally and professionally skilled operators, who demonstrate competence and correct behaviour.

The need to encourage skills linked to professional training models at European level is evident, where the presence of the University is required, so that other organizations, not always suitably qualified, do not take on inadequate substitute didactic roles in these particular, delicate sectors.

In conclusion, study programmes must be set up and used to advantage, as a contribution to be provided by the criminologist in order to help reduce crime and make life safer, even as regards the protection of the assets of companies and private and public institutions.

In fact, as well as dedicating time to the study of the causes of crime and research on crime as a social phenomenon, the criminologist can train operators who contribute towards crime prevention and suppression and provide programmes and instruments for social and personal safety.

Table 4.1 Persons Being Investigated for Criminal Activity

Italy

Year	against public order	Total	%
1980	1946	508116	0.38
1981	1699	567050	0.30
1982	1911	540151	0.35
1983	1698	553540	0.31
1984	1877	549860	0.34
1985	2221	657586	0.34
1986	2704	698808	0.39
1987	2867	765253	0.37
1988	2769	764610	0.36
1989	2818	744421	0.38
1990	1251	347998	0.36
1991	2231	506170	0.44
1992	2518	561230	0.45
1993	3205	550267	0.58
1994	6898	601369	1.15
1995	3932	565366	0.70

Source: ISTAT

Table 4.2 Persons Being Investigated for Criminal Activity (Years 1993-1995)

Crimes in Emilia-Romagna

Year	against public order	Total	%
1993	125	25727	0.49
1994	250	30406	0.82
1995	220	31508	0.7

Source: ISTAT

Table 4.3 Crime Rates per 100,000

Crime Rates

Year	Italy	Emilia-Romagna
1993	5.61	3.19
1994	12.04	6.37
1995	6.86	5.61

Source: Our processing of ISTAT data

Table 4.4 Persons being investigated for criminal association in Italy

Year	Total M	F	Total	%F	Minors (under 18) M	F	Total	%F
1993	2570	361	2931	12.32	46	2	48	4.17
1994	4597	1024	5621	18.22	47	14	61	22.95
1995	3093	498	3591	13.87	25	9	34	26.47

Source: ISTAT

Table 4.5 Persons investigated for criminal association in Emilia-Romanga

Year	Total M	F	Total	% F	Minors (under 18) M	F	Total	%F
1993	104	21	125	16.8	0	0	0	0
1994	209	41	250	16.4	12	1	13	7.69
1995	181	29	210	13.81	0	0	0	0

Source: ISTAT

Table 4.6 Crime Rates (Basis 1993=100)

	Average Sentence decreed (Months)	Italy	ER	Italy	ER	Italy	ER
Year		1993	1993	1994	1994	1995	1995
Criminal Association	72	100	100	191.3	200.1	122.1	168
Mafia-style criminal association	84	100		550.3		118.9	
Total		100		220.6		121.8	

Source: Our processing of ISTAT data

References

Baragli, M. and Colombo, A. (1996), "La criminalità in Emilia-Romanga. Un Profilo Statistico". In *Quaderni di Città Sicure (Journal on Safe Cities)*, 5th edition.

Favaro, G. (1996), "Immigrati adulti e bambini: dritto alla comunicazione e allo scrambio tra culture", in *Immigrati e comunità locali (Immigrants and local communities)* edited L. Pepa, Angeli, Milan.

Palidda, S. (1996), "Irregularity and Crime by Immigrants in Italy", in *Secondo rapporto sulle migrazioni 1996 (Second report on migration in Italy)* edited by the Cariplo Foundation for Multi-Ethnic Initiatives and Studies, Angeli, Milan.

Pinto, P. "Changes in presences and residence", *La società multietnica*, edition 1, December 1995.

Savona, E.U. and Di Nicola, A. (1997), "Migration and Crime. Thrity Years On", report presented at the XI National Conference of Italian Criminology Society, Gargano del Garda.

La Società Multietnica, edition 1, December 1995.

Zincone, G. "Citizenship - instructions for use", *Animazione sociale*, editions 8/9, August-September 1997.

5 Transnational Organized Crime in Spain: Structural Factors Explaining its Penetration

CARLOS RESA-NESTARES

Organized Crime in Spain: An Overview

In the social sciences, an extensive bibliography exists on the phenomena of organized crime. However, there is little material treating this issue with a specific focus on Spain. The increased presence of international criminal organizations in Spain has come about as a direct result of a number of specific circumstances, historical and cultural as well as economic and territorial.

The presence of organized crime in Spain, as well in many other European countries, is not limited to recent decades. Gangs of swindlers, bandits and organized smugglers, among others, have operated, to one degree or another, throughout history. After the Spanish Civil War and the subsequent Second World War, the worsening of the socio-economic situation in Spain, the country's international isolation and the scarcity of many consumer goods in the Spanish market contributed to the strengthening of an already existent modality of organized crime: the "estraperlo"- or black market. This concept includes a wide range of activities related to black markets for primary goods, illicit service payments, extortion, threats and racketeering. Its context is one of widespread corruption and of the exceeding arrogance of the victors of the Civil War (1936-39), together with industrialists and shopkeepers.

It was not until the early 1970s that the large international crime groups began to establish themselves in a major way in Spain, and then mainly in the tourist region of Costa del Sol, in Southern Spain. The main activity of these groups consisted of laundering money generated through drug and arms trafficking, extortion and kidnaping. Organized crime groups have set up operation bases and have expanded their presence while remaining virtually unnoticed by the majority of the general public of Spain. The only violent incidents in Spain have been mainly a consequence of internal power conflicts in the organization's headquarters. International criminal organizations in Spain have always tried to avoid ostentatious violence in order to maintain the country as a secure base for money-laundering, an activity for which they consider it especially suitable, and as a refuge. According to official figures, about four billions US dollars are laundered in Spain annually (*El País* 1996a).

International arms trafficking groups are the oldest global crime groups in Spain. They are principally Arabs, who have a long history in the Costa del Sol region, where they manage their arms trafficking operations throughout the world. Many other crime organization have arrived, mainly looking for secure territories for money-laundering. Colombian narcotic cartels, essentially involved in cocaine trafficking, have used Galicia (in Northwest Spain) as a bridgepoint to Europe since the mid 1980s. Besides these cartels well-known relations with Galician smugglers, they have also established contacts in other coastal regions in northern Spain. As police pressure on the Galician coast has increased since the early 1990s, drug traffickers have resorted to the centuries-old networks of fishermen in the Atlantic ocean. Thus, even with the most important Galician druglords in prisons and second-line elements managing the business, Colombian cartels have started to introduce cocaine into the ports of Asturias, Cantabria and the Basque Country.

In terms of heroin trade, the Turkish mafia traditionally has channeled this illicit trade, in collaboration with the Calabrian N'Drangheta and the Neapolitan Camorra. The retail traffic in heroin is partly controlled by the gypsies. The gypsies are accustomed to dealing with violence and their dense social networks have proved almost impenetrable by the police- factors which make them optimum candidates for trade with violent heroine addicts. As one gypsy commented on television: "They [the non-gypsy population] are the ones who make the money. All we want is to feed our children" (Telemadrid, 1996). In recent years, the Sicilian mafia has bypassed the Turkish connection, using their own routes to introduce heroin. In December of 1995, the police arrested a clan from the Neapolitan Camorra. This group had been operating in Spain since the end of the 1980s in the same style as the Sicilian mafia in New York (although on a much more modest level). This drug ring was uncovered and the case became known as the "Pizza Connection". They operated under the front of a chain of pizzerias in the southern city of Granada. Among the twenty-one people arrested was a sergeant from the

Central Unit of Fiscal and Anti-drug Information, who had been passing along information to the clan.

The Chinese Triads, established in Spain in the early 1990s, have imported their traditional model of extorting their compatriots who live in Spain. The relatively scarce number of Chinese in Spain in comparison to the number of those in other developed countries, a factor which has impeded the formation of a self-contained Chinese-Spanish community, is in all probability the reason for the Chinese not having established themselves in the drug market in Spain. A Triad group which operated out of Barcelona was a arrested in 1995 and accused of the death of a fellow Chinese in a restaurant. Apparently this man had refused to pay the protection tax of $16,000 per year. Explosions had previously been detected in Chinese restaurants. The infrastructure of the Chinese Mafias, directed from outside the country, was left intact in this sting operation, which leads to the suspicion that this group could be reorganized at any time. In addition, through the falsification of documents and their strong connections in other areas, these mafias are operating in the illegal entry of Chinese immigrants in Spain, primarily from the underdeveloped agricultural province of Zhejiang. The trip costs the immigrants $16,000, of which a half is paid in China while the other half is liquidated by working in Spain. The work conditions are of semi-slavery in restaurants, houses of prostitution, and garment factories. The Japanese Yakuzas, with their traditional methods, have come in the wake of Japanese investment in Spain, but their networks are still poorly developed. The latest arrivals in the club of organized crime have been the Russian mafias, who have dedicated themselves primarily to the extortion of their countrymen and to money-laundering.

It would seem that Spanish groups have served primarily as second-level subsidiaries in drug trafficking. In addition they control groups dedicated to white slavery, which trade primarily in women from Brazil and the Caribbean.

In the drug business, different drugs have different routes in their passage through Spain, a fact which is central in determining the structure and size of each organization dealing with them. In the case of heroin, Spanish inte.:ests are of small importance within the Balkan Route and the drug road from South-eastern Asia. The same could be said about chemical drugs, which play a secondary but increasing role in the international drug market, coming primarily from Holland, the United Kingdom and the reconverted industries of Eastern Europe. Nevertheless, estimated consumption of ecstasy and heroin in Spain is one of the highest in the European Union. On the contrary, for hashish and cocaine, Spain is a country of fundamental importance in international drug trafficking, for it serves as an entry point to the wider European market. In 1995, 197,024 kilos of hashish (26,3 per cent of the amount intercepted in the European Union), 6,897 kilos of cocaine (33,1 per cent), and 546 kilos of heroin (10,6 per cent) were seized. These data make a total for the 1990-1995 period of 869,337 kilos of hashish, 32,409 of cocaine, and 5,012 of heroin seized (Plan Nacional sobre Drogas 1996).

It is well known that cocaine, controlled by the Colombian drug cartels who have established their operating bases in Spain, originates in Colombia and other South American countries, (Argentina, Paraguay, Venezuela, Brazil, Ecuador and Peru). Concerning cannabis derivatives, the only thing that is clear is that their production is controlled by Moroccans, with the support (either explicit or implicit) of that country's political leaders and police force. The lack of cooperation that the Moroccan authorities provide toward the eradication of cannabis plantations in their country is remarkable. The Moroccan government continues to ask for greater economic cooperation by European Union, purportedly to assist its domestic campaign against drugs. The introduction of hashish from Morocco into the European Union as well its distribution within Europe itself is diversified among various small-sized European organizations, including Moroccan communities in different European countries and among the large mafias, for whom it is basically a second-class product. The techniques for the introduction of hashish into Spain are diverse, ranging from individuals crossing the Straits of Gibraltar as passengers in commercial ferries with little amounts of hashish stowed in their bodies (so-called "mules", for which 142 Spanish citizens are in jail in Morocco) to coaches in regular travel to European countries and fishing boats from the nearby towns in Southern Spain or high-speed motor boats crossing the Strait by night.

Operating from their own national territory, the Moroccan mafias also dedicate themselves to the task of introducing illegal immigrants of all nationalities into the European Union. These immigrants traverse the Straits of Gibraltar in fishing boats from the south of Spain or in small wooden boats which, when they are not lost in stormy weather, have the advantage that they cannot be detected by police radar. According to official calculations, only thirty percent of these "wet backs" who risk their lives to cross the Straits of Gibraltar in small boats are caught. And in the last five years, six thousand have been captured. The price per immigrant is between $8,000 and $40,000. On the payment of this sum, the immigrants receive not only clandestine passage into the European Union but also a number of very practical tips on how to take advantage of the legal system of the European countries, in particular, Spain, their port of entry.

Other activities, such as tobacco smuggling are of a smaller scale and are conducted through multinational mafias who operate in complicity with the world's principal tobacco companies. Each year, 700 million smuggled packs of tobacco are sold in Spain. This merchandise comes primarily from the East through different land and sea routes, from the United States and from Andorra. It makes up ten per cent of the tobacco consumed annually in Spain, which implies a loss of 120 millions US dollars for the Spanish tobacco industry. Contraband tobacco can be found throughout Spain and is smuggled in primarily through Andalusia, Galicia and Catalonia. This tobacco traffic is controlled by large mafias dedicated to contraband goods.

Two Different Groups, Two Different Styles of Operation

The types of crime and the nature of criminal operations are largely dependent on the country of origin of crime groups operating in Spain. This can be seen by a comparison of the Colombian drug cartels and the Russian mafia.

The newcomers: the Russian Mafias

In their generic denomination "Russian Mafia", the police include all individuals from the former Soviet Union, who are ethnically very diverse, but operationally, very similar. These groups proliferated out of the ruins of the former Soviet superpower, and have arrived in Spain during the 1990s. They include Ukrainians, Belarussians, Georgians, and Chechenians as well as others from former satellites of the Soviet Union, such as Poles, Serbs and Bulgarians. Since 1994, these groups have been establishing themselves primarily in three areas: the Costa del Sol in Malaga province, the area of Valencia and the Catalonian coast.

Given the instability of the economic institutions of their mother country, Russian crime groups have decided that Spain is an ideal base for money-laundering. The major form of laundering money is in "clean" investments. It is thought that these mafias have invested thousand of millions pesetas in the acquisition of tourist apartments and bungalows in posh urban developments as well as in the installation of restaurants and other services related to tourism. Investments are principally dedicated to foreign trade, real estate sales, food and tourism, businesses which are always conducted with cash. Between 1994 and 1995, the presumably "clean" operations operating out the of former Eastern block were worth 16 million US dollars.

In the last two or three years, organizations dedicated to the thefts of luxury cars have also sprung up in the Costa del Sol and in Madrid. Once stolen, these cars are transported by Russian or Polish mafia groups to the former Eastern countries to be resold. The proliferation of Russian controlled prostitution rings, so frequent in other countries of the European Union, and especially in Turkey, is still scarce in Spain. The same can be said of the falsification of passports, visas and residency permits, as well as of the importation of Belarussians children for adoption purposes, made possible by the falsification of official documents. Although it may be too early to say, it seems that certain Eastern groups are also becoming involved in drug trafficking, mainly of heroin, due to their advantageous position on the heroin routes from Southeastern Asia.

The cruelty of these groups has been amply demonstrated by the half-dozen tortured corpses they have left in their tracks in Andalusia. These murders may have been due to a settling of accounts. At any rate, this cruelty clearly differentiates the Russian groups from other international criminal organizations established in Spain, which observe the unwritten law of avoiding shoot-outs and murders. Although the Russians' principal activity in Spain is money laundering, extortion occurs, to the tune of 10 to 15 percent of the vast amounts of money that these groups invest in tourist lodging. The methods used are similar to the "protection tax" that the Chinese mafia demands from restaurants, and which is advisable to pay if they do not want to see their businesses burned or destroyed.

In many cases, the Russian mafias take advantage of the lack of co-operation of the Russian police with Spanish investigations. The collapse of governmental structures that has decimated the police force, is one reason for this lack of co-operation. Others are the pervasive corruption which plagues the Russian police.

The Veterans: the Colombian Cartels

The Latin American drug dealers have had their eye on Spain since the late 1970s, in large part because they were fleeing the pressure exerted on them by the United States within their respective countries. In the mid 1980s, the Colombian drug lords had to flee their country due to the pressure being put on them for the first time in their history. Two of these druglords, Jorge Luis Ochoa and Gilberto Rodríguez-Orejuela, ended up in Spain, where they had already established some friendships and had strong economic interests, mainly as a result of the open relationship between Spain and her ex-colonies. They felt that Spain was a safe haven in which to set up camp away from the American DEA. An additional plus was the fact that the recently elected socialist government in Spain was reluctant to collaborate with the North Americans. Since they thought that their stay would be a long one, the two druglords began to organize new markets for cocaine in Spain. However, they were both arrested and extradited to Colombia in 1986. In the meantime, they set about making Spanish contacts in the prison where they were being held. In Colombia they were shortly set free and renewed their contacts in order to set into motion the introduction of cocaine in Europe. In 1989 DEA already had proof that the Iberian peninsula was the main point of entry of cocaine in Europe. It was also the principal receptor of moneys for laundering.

In Galicia, an agricultural and less developed province in the Northwest of Spain, smuggling has a long tradition (Conde, 1991). Since the Civil War, smugglers have acquired the reputation of public benefactors, supplying essential goods such as food and medicine. They do not only arouse admiration for their daring and adventurous image, but also undertook certain functions of public protection such as providing penicillin to those who could not afford it and a mutual tolerance of clandestine fishing. They were highly regarded as recently as 1987, in which a mayor from the conservative party on a Galician coast village stated that "the smugglers are the most honest people in the world", Well into the 1960s, they continued trafficking in foodstuffs, alcohol, clothing and minerals. During this time they discovered the benefits of trafficking in American tobacco, which they smuggled in mainly through the forbidding estuaries of the Galician coast. The Portuguese introduced them to this business, but were soon displaced by the Galicians, who began to deal with the different organizations dedicated to tobacco smuggling, among which were the Italian Mafia and well-organized Greek groups. At that time they expanded their distribution networks into the rest of Spain and began to employ money-laundering techniques. It was also at this time that low-level violence made its appearance. Large amounts of money began to flow into the backwoods area of Galicia. The social and political context was extremely benevolent with this state of affairs, with the important complicity of the police forces and financial institutions. The smugglers enjoyed flaunting their money, and Galician children wanted to be smugglers when they grew up. Sito Miñanco, one of the principal Galician drug dealers was known as "the benefactor" or "Robin Hood", was the president of a youth group from his village and paid for the church altar out of his own pocket. Other drug traffickers made their own contributions to public welfare, which ranged from village celebrations to road repairs.

In the mid 1980s, the Galician smugglers were the key to the practically unexploited European cocaine market that the Colombian cartels were dying to get their hands on. The Colombians were able to offer a product which would exponentially increase the profits of the Galician groups, although with a similarly steep increase in risks. From that time on, Galicia was to become the principal point of entry of cocaine into Europe.

The operations of smuggling cocaine into Galicia seems to have followed unchanging patterns throughout the past decade. The Colombians put the shipments on motor boats flying flags of third countries, paid for by the Galicians, which bring the shipment across the Atlantic Ocean. This shipment is smuggled into European territories in various ways. One possibility is that the ship docks in Galician ports in order to unload the drug shipment together with other merchandise for businesses which, provided by the Galicians, serve as fronts. The other is that the drug shipments are picked up on high seas from the mother boat by fishing boats or high-speed motor boats, which then bring the merchandise to land by way of the craggy coasts of Galicia in collaboration with reinforcements on the shore. At a later time, Colombian and Galician drug smugglers each take their fifty percent of the merchandise. Since the distribution networks are different, the two sides do not enter into conflict: while the Galicians dedicate themselves to the Spanish market, the Colombian cartels send their merchandise by highway towards other European countries.

Nevertheless, the Colombian cartels have always had a two-pronged operational strategy in Spain. On one hand, they introduce the drug into the country through the Atlantic coast of Galicia, and on the other had, either alone or in collaboration with French or Italian organizations, they enter Spain through the Mediterranean coast, funneling the shipments through their own businesses, which receive the merchandise in which the drug is hidden. In October 1994, the head of the declining Medellín Cartel was arrested in Barcelona and accused of introducing large quantities of Colombian cocaine into the country through the port of Barcelona by means of a complex web of companies. Recently the cartels have diversified their points of entrance to include the Spanish airports, which now receives part of the drug shipments in a direct connection from Latin American countries.

At the end of the 1980s, the Galician smugglers, now integrated into the international drug smuggling network, entered into a relationship with Turkish heroin groups and began to deal in this drug. They have also been connected for some time now with the Moroccan hashish traffic. The normal route of entry for this drug is in Galician fishing boats which go to fish off the Moroccan coast. It was a strategic error on the part of these bands, for the drug began to leave a trail of death on the Galician coast as addiction among young people soared. The prestig.: of the smugglers, which had, if possible, risen with the entrance of large amounts of money into Galicia, took a steep decline. As judge Carlos Bueren declared recently, the smugglers and drug traffickers are regarded favorably within the general population, "they give out favors right and left" and "have the nerve and the arrogance not to hide the origin of their money". They began to come up against hostility on the part of a great number of their fellow Galicians, particularly among the mothers of heroin addicts. At first the protest was a silent one, but it is now beginning to take the shape of a head-on confrontation, in the shape of the associations of mothers against drugs which are springing up on the Galician coast. These mobilizations were crucial to the increasing involvement of political and judicial authorities in the fight against drug trafficking as they become increasingly aware of the dimensions of the problem, which until recently they had tolerated. The children of Galicia no longer want to be smugglers when they grow up (*El País* 1996b).

Differences, Similarities

It can be said that there are five basic differences between the operating styles of these groups in Spain. The first has to do with location. While the Colombian clans have chosen Madrid and Barcelona, the two principal cities in Spain, as their center of operations and as the main destination for money to be laundered, the Russian mafias have installed themselves on the coasts from Galicia to Catalonia.

The second difference is the level of contact with native Spaniards. Although in both cases the majority of the contacts are limited to those established with such professionals as lawyers, economists and so on, the Colombians' contact with the society is much more diversified. Because of the very nature of their operations, they are obliged to make contact with Spanish entrepreneurs who can receive shipments of drugs without arousing suspicion. These contacts are not necessary in the case of the Russians, whose money-laundering operations can be carried out within their own communities. The Colombian druglords also need Spaniards, usually from lower classes, for intermediary jobs in the structure of their organization: low-level traffickers, mules, warehousemen and so on.

The third difference can be established in terms of violence. Russian mafia groups are especially virulent and cruel in the former Soviet Union, just as they are in Spain. The Colombian drug dealers, on the other hand, have always acted with more restraint, trying to avoid the use of violence although, of course, they do make ample use of threats. Nevertheless, in recent months the violence employed by these Colombian groups has escalated, a development which may be a reflection of the convulsive national scene in Colombia or again, may be owing to a settling of accounts. In 1995 a Galician "pentiti" and a Spanish lawyer who was also giving indications of wanting to repent were murdered by Colombian hired assassins. The corpses of four murdered Colombians have turned up in Madrid during the last year in strange circumstances.

A fourth difference is the relationship of these groups with national banks. The Colombian drug traffickers have been able to function perfectly within the Spanish financial system, which has turned a blind eye to their suspicious deposits and transfers of money. In addition, the cartels have been able to count on the collaboration of key people within the Spanish system. In the case of the Russian mafia, however, one of their first steps upon arriving in Spain was an attempt to buy a Spanish bank. The organization of their respective headquarters has a great bearing on these groups' different relationships with the Spanish banks. In Russia, the mafia controls a large part of the financial system. Were they to enjoy a similar situation in Spain, they would be able to move much more rapidly than they are presently able to do.

Last of all, the Russian mafia has a range of activities which is more varied than that of the Colombian drug traffickers, who have dedicated themselves almost exclusively to the distribution of cocaine in Europe and the subsequent laundering of part of the profits. On one hand, this situation limits their future evolution, but it also affords them an almost complete monopoly of a product which continues to be highly profitable.

However, these differences between the two criminal organizations are volatile, depending on several variables, which are directly dependent on the internal situations of their respective countries of origin. It is perfectly possible that the present situation leading Russian groups to become more directly involved in heroin trafficking. Colombians, continue to demonstrate an increased use of violence in order to establish control over their drug-trafficking ranks.

Structural Factors Facilitating the Introduction of International Organized Crime in Spain

The reasons that international organized crime has expanded into Spain are various:

- The geographical situation of the Iberian peninsula. The close proximity to the logistical bases of powerful criminal organizations, such as the Marseilles clans or the Sicilian Cosa Nostra, definitely makes Spain a hotbed of criminal presence. In some cases, it is simply inevitable for certain drug traffic to pass through Spain; this is the case of the Moroccan hashish destined for Central Europe.

- Spain's legal situation. The absence of specific and concrete legislation on organized crime coupled with the existence of a legal framework excessively protective of the rights of the criminally accused make the prosecution of criminal groups nearly impossible. Legislation on money-laundering is practically non-existent and what does exist contains extremely important gaps. At the present time various legal modifications giving better protection to anti-drug operations which use undercover agents are in the works. However, according to Gonzalo Robles, general director of the National Plan against Drugs, they will not be similar to "the American model of provoking criminal actions in order to repress them"(*El País* 1996d). In addition, in order to combatting drug traffic, parliamentary approval will be requested for controlling the entry of capital (*El Mundo* 1996a).

- Spain's justice system. There are no judges who specialize in these affairs, which are taken up by the National Court (Audiencia Nacional). This court also deals with terrorism cases and has been bogged down for years. The structure of the National Court, with only five examining magistrates, has given rise to a situation in which only one of the magistrates, Baltazar Garzón, is investigating the extremely complicated GAL(state-terrorism) case. In addition, Garzón is the only magistrate investigating a pile of briefs which have to do with the terrorism of ETA, on top of a number of drug trafficking cases. This situation has brought about excessive personalism, in which judges are more interested in appearing in the press than in correctly investigating cases. All of these problems, in addition to the wide-spread corruption among judges and magistrates has led to some questionable decisions almost always favorable to the accused.

- Spain's economic policy. Over the last fifteen years, the governing socialist party allowed foreign investment with a "no questions asked" policy. During successive socialist governments between 1982 and 1996, there were three periods of fiscal amnesty for illicit funds. Liberalized practices of international capital transactions have made it easier to launder money in Spain. Although these transfers are neither illegal nor secretive, they are later "covered up" though complex financial operations.

- Spain's commerce. One major industry of Spain is that of the tourism sector, which generates ten percent of the Gross National Product. Tourist activities are difficult to regulate, the moneys generated are largely cash payments and the transient nature of such trade abets money-laundering. The construction industry in Spain also serves as a cover for money laundering.

- Spain's financial system. Spanish banking institutions, who also have an extensive network of offices in Latin America, have never been very inclined to collaborate with the justice system. Conversely, they have been more than willing to carry out large-scale operations of financial engineering with objectives such as capital flight or money-laundering. In August of this year the Home Secretary observed that the collaboration of financial institutions with his office to uncover and pursue money laundering is at the very most, "in need of improvement." In 1995, principally in order to get good press, the Banco Santander, one of the most important banks in Spain, created an original unit specialized in detecting where money was coming from. For purpose of this unit, the bank has signed on the services of an ex-police officer, expert in such matters. According to the bank's Board of Directors, the purpose is to avoid illicit funds being passed through the bank for purposes of legalization and to introduce them into legal circulation. The bank's personnel are also being given training in this area.

- A lack of coordination among police forces. The existence of a numerous police forces (both civil and military) accompanied by a confusing division of jurisdictions, which practically all converge on drug traffic and border patrol, makes unclear the ultimate responsibility for containing drug traffic. Until this year, there was no unified database on the activities of organized crime. In addition there is no special police force dedicated to money laundering.

• A lack of resources of the police force. In the area of organized crime the dearth of mechanical resources and the obsolescence of the ones in use is alarmingly obvious. For example, the boats used to chase down drug runners are adapted tourist yachts, small and slow, with any number of technical problems, mainly due to the intense workload to which they are subjected.

• Police corruption and incompetence. Members of the police forces are frequently being questioned in sting operations against different organized crime groups in Spain. Their functions are to pass on relevant police information in exchange for payment, and in some cases to muddle police investigations. Advance warnings to crime lords have made the success of police operations against drug trafficking impossible. The following two cases may be regarded as symptomatic. In the first, the General Director of the Police warned a well-known journalist friend a day in advance of a large- scale police sting operation about the problems that one of the journalist's friends, a known member of the jet-set, was going to have for drug trafficking. In the second, the head of the National Guard's Fiscal Service (Servicio Fiscal de la Guardia Civil) stated to the newspaper with the largest circulation in Spain the "in Galicia we have set up an important network of telephone taps and we have dossiers on almost three thousand people who could potentially have some connection to smuggling activities". This declaration was made while the Judicial Police force was carrying out an investigation into the intrigues of smuggling bands in Galicia.

• Spain's social characteristics. A factor which has been decisive in the establishment of Latin American drug traffickers in Spain is the common language and culture and large communities of immigrants shared between these countries. Other organizations have also considered Spain an ideal country to avoid political pressure and the settling of accounts for a completely different reason from the above; that is, the large number of tourists which come to the country. There are some examples of this. In 1986, some Colombian drug lords arrived in Spain fleeing from an escalation in violence and pressures put on them by the government of their country. Gaetano Badalamenti, a New York capo dedicated to heroin traffic, landed in Spain due to internal struggles between the Grado and Greco families. In August of 1996, a runaway member of the Calabrian N'Draguetta, Giuseppe Carnovale, turned up in Barcelona after having escaped from an Italian prison. The Marseilles mafiosi often take refuge in Catalonia when they sense a toughening of political pressure in France and continue controlling their business from Barcelona until the storm passes. This fact has converted Spain into a headquarters for both chance and pre-arranged meetings in order to set up large-scale dealings between different criminal organizations. The Mediterranean coast, from Catalonia to Andalusia, provides the ideal place of refuge for organized crime groups, who can blend in with the large number of foreigners present all times of the year. In the short term, this situation is ripe for encounters between different criminal organizations who have the common goal of increasing the size of their operations.

- Spain's lax policy with respect to drugs. During 1980s, the socialist government implemented laws which allowed the possession of small quantities of drugs in addition to public and private drug consumption. This fact may have generated a more permissive atmosphere among the security forces with respect to large consignments of drugs and drug trafficking.

- The utilization of existing small-scale bands of criminals. The smugglers located throughout Spain, especially in the border regions, have put together well-organized networks, whose plans of entry and distribution could be used by large-scale organizations trafficking in hard drugs. In addition, the gypsies constituted a group traditionally associated with petty crime throughout Spain whose methods of operation were a bit archaic, but who had the advantage of being socially very cohesive and of having well-established internal group laws.

Conclusion

Although the presence of organized crime is not as intense in Spain as in other Western European countries or as in underdeveloped countries, it poses economic and international problems that could threaten national security. The fact that Spain is not the country of origin of any of the large-scale organizations of world-wide crime has contributed decisively to this situation. In purely economic terms, it can be said that financial crime played an important role in the strong economic growth that Spain experienced at the end of the eighties. This growth was made possible mainly by a revaluation of assets due to large investments in real estate for money-laundering purposes. As a result, the price of buildings skyrocketed in Spain. The co-operation between the police forces of different national security agencies (mainly Italian, Portuguese and French) has and will continue to contribute to partially limiting the massive entrenchment of large scale international criminal organizations. The harmonization of the legislation of the various European countries related to organized crime, as well as the recent unfreezing of the Europol should prove to be effective tools for combating organized crime. Interpol, the Schengen system, the extinct Trevi Group, and the new European Union structures, including K4 Committee and the European Drug Unit-Europol, have been the most important formal arrangements for promoting police co-operation in Europe in recent years. However, an impediment to effective structures for police cooperation is the current lack of knowledge and understanding about the types of cross-border crime (Benyon, 1994).

Given the ever-increasing internationalization of crime, the future does not look too bright for Spain's legitimate institutions. As these mafias come into contact with local groups, the latter begin to adopt the structures and methods of their foreign colleagues. This danger should be taken seriously in Spain, given the inadequacy of its legislature in this respect and its ideal geographic situation. Judge Carlos Bueren, one of the most committed in the fight against drug trafficking, was not very optimistic last autumn when commenting on the future in Spain he said: "we are going to be surprised by new and more violent drug-related murders" (Abc 1995).

References

Abc, 1995. "Bueren aboga por la creación de juzgados autonómicos contra la droga", 20 October, 30.

Albani, J.L. (1971) The American Mafia: Genesis of a Legend, New York: Appleton-Century Crofts, 1971.

Benyon, J., 1994. "Policing the European Union: the changing basis of cooperation on law enforcement", International Affairs, 70: 497-517.

Conde, P., 1991. La Conexión Gallega: Del Tabaco a la Cocaína. Barcelona: Ediciones B.

Dombrink, J., 1988. "Organized Crime: Gangsters and Godfathers". In J.E. Scott and T. Hirsch (eds.), *Controversial Issues in Crime and Justice.* New Burypark: Sage.

El Mundo, 1996a. "Mayor Oreja solicitará al gobierno que regule la figura del 'agente encubierto'", 1 August, 19.

El Mundo, 1996b. "La justicia belga investiga a Banesto por blanquear dinero", 8 August, 50.

El País, 1996a. "La lucha contra el blanqueo de dinero, objetivo central del Plan Nacional sobre Drogas", 10 July, 20

El País, 1996b. "Esto no es Sicilia", 28 July, Sunday Supplement, 8.

El País, 1996c. "Entrevista con Gonzalo Robles", 12 August, 21.

Imbert, P., 1994. "Crime without frontiers", *Police Review*, 97.

Levi, M., 1993. "The extent of cross-border crime in Europe", *European Journal on Criminal Policy and Research*, 1: 57-76.

Martin, J.M. and Romano A.T., 1992. *Multinational Crime: Terrorism, Espionage, Drug and Arms Trafficking*. Newbury Park: Sage.

Plan Nacional sobre Drogas, 1996. *Estado de Situación y Respuestas a los Problemas*. Madrid: Ministerio del Interior.

Telemadrid, 1996. Madrid Directo, 14 de september.

6 Global Organized Crime Latvia and the Baltics

ANDREJS VILKS, DAINIS BERGMANIS

The close of the 20th century has been marked by a rapid expansion of organized crime. It must be realized that organized crime is not only a problem at national or regional levels, but that it constitutes a global concern. We share the view of American criminologists (Mueller et al., 1995) who argue that in the last two decades international crime has increased almost the same amount as international import and export operations.

The evolution of organized crime and its distinct globalization are linked to social and technological progress world-wide: the achievements in technologies, advanced communications, interdependence of international finance and business operations, extension of electronic financial transactions and international tourism.

The Polish criminologist Mosciskier (1995) argues, "for the emergence of organized crime, a specific legal-economic situation is needed". It can be stated that, in the post-socialism countries, the situation is very favorable for organized crime groups to emerge. This is also true for the development of international crime: countries undergo transitional periods, marked by reorganization and reforms in political, economic and social spheres. Economic and social standards are deteriorating, anxiety and depression grows, so does the overall levels of confrontation, and all these aspects favor the development of organized crime.

The Crime Situation in Latvia

The rapid growth of crime can be seen between 1985-1992. The total amount of crimes increased 2-3 times, while the number of severe crimes were ever slightly higher. During the last three years the crime rate in Latvia has decreased by one-third. The crime situation is characterized by the amount of crimes committed per 10,000 residents, which is 154.7 in Latvia.

Irrespective of the decrease in the number of registered crimes, public institutions such as law enforcement bodies, are neither optimistic nor satisified that crime structures have changed considerably. Many crimes involve the use of firearms and explosives. In 1996, 508 crimes were committed, of which 51 were murders and 348 were criminal assaults involving the use of firearms. In 1995, 70 cases of explosions were registered as a result of which there were 4 casualties and 6 people injured. Material damages exceeded $1,000,000. The latency of certain types of crimes, associated with organized crime groups, remains high, among them bribery, extortion and economic crimes.

Legislatures are slow to react to organized crime. Late in the game, on August 28, 1992, Article (143) on the liability for extortion performed by an organized group, was incorportated in the Criminal Code of the Republic of Latvia.

According to the data of the Latvian police, 78 criminal groups have been detected. The majority of these groups are small consisting of 8-10 people who conduct relatively small operations. This type of criminal cannot be considered independent as they rely on the help of leaders from more influential groups. At present, there is no indisputable crime leader in Latvia as many underworld authorities have either perished or are residing abroad or are under arrest.

Concepts and Characteristics of Organized Crime

Organized crime - like any phenomenon - has its own functional criteria. Identification of these criteria allow's us to make conclusions on the potential growth and stage of development of a nation's organized crime.

The most essential criteria is the existence of personnel working concertedly on some form of criminal activity- organized crime groups. From the aspect of criminology, it is important that these groups may appear to be legitimate ones, having been established without the intention to commit criminal offenses. Within the structure of the organized crime group, sub-groups involved in less obviously illegal duties may function (structures engaged in money laundering, management groups, etc.). Ultimate power in organized crime groups is concentrated in the hands of one or a couple of leaders, although the number of members vary from five to several hundred or even thousands of people.

It is evident that groups are not homogeneous by their organizational level, structures and type of criminal activities. These features are linked to social, economical, ethnic and geographical factors. Therefore the levels of organized crime should be taken into account, enabling a more accurate estimation of organized crime in different regions.

Primitive level groups include stable independent groups having simple organizational structure: a leader and a few members. Everybody has his own role, and planning follows a certain established model. Group capacity varies from 3 to 5 members. Theft, robbery, swindle and hooliganism are the crimes mostly preferred.

The intermediate level of organized crime is a transitional stage to more elaborate and dangerous formations. This kind of association consists of several subordinate units: fighters, secret agents, executors, bodyguards, "financists" and others. The number of group members amounts to 50 or more people. Groups at this level usually engage in racketeering, drug business, smuggling, illegal bank operations. As a rule, these groups have connections with state officials.

The highest level appears as criminal organizations with a so-called network structure. In other words, these associations consist of 2 or several management levels and represent the concept of "Mafia".

Criminal organizations at this level have several principal features:

- existence of capital resources - such as a common financial fund, as well as bank accounts and real estate. This principal indication is linked to the importance of a funding system within any complex structure. Common "reserves" for the convicted in prison are created, illegal networks of money lenders and bankers are formed, and banks are created to house money of dubious origin.

- official cover-ups for their illegal activities in the form of different registered foundations, joint ventures, restaurants, casinos and other establishments. To obtain a legal "facade", limited liability companies, stock corporations etc., are established, thus creating possibilities for money -laundering. Sometimes these organizations engage law-enforcement functions (provide security for companies, recovery of debts etc.) They undertake extortion, control definite territories and enterprises etc.

- a governing body consisting of a board with members of equal standing. Successful operation is ensured by a unitary management structure which decides the group's functions, principles and strategies, and has responsibility for dispute resolution and maintaning appropriate ideology and philosophy.

- functional hierarchy system and international connections. Chiefly due to the anonymous nature of international crime, the organized criminal groups are able to r intain long-term unpunished functioning and even to essentially increase their efficiency. In addition, law enforcement institutions lack necessary international co-operation. There is also a lack of relevant legal norms and acts regulating the functioning of law -enforcement instututions, especially with regard to the fight against organized crime.

Standards of conduct are very clear in organized crime groups. In cases where these rules are violated, a range of different sanctions is possible. On the whole, this hierarchy system is established and directed toward gain, i.e. illegal profit. The main ways of obtaining these profits are:

- narcobusiness, illegal arms trade, prostitution, illegal financial operations, extortion and control of enterprises, etc.
- a specific language-system for communication, including slang and such peculiarities as nicknames, tattoos etc.
- to justifiy their criminal and antisocial way of life, organized crime groups possess their own ideology and philosophy (like "money does not smell" etc.). The new moral and ethical standards also fulfill the role of propaganda.
- an information base, built up through scouting and geared to neutralize the activities of social control and law-enforcement institutions.
- modern technical equipment is employed to secure this result.
- the presence of their intelligence people within the systems of authorities and legal institutions. Often young people are recruited and the costs of their education provided for, in order to later work in the institutions to be infiltrated. Another popular way is to coerce high-ranking officials to employ members of organized crime groups.
- a stable nature of the activity. Organized criminal groups are materially and financially secure enough to perfom long-term activities, regardless of any social, economical or political changes. The stability of their operation is not jeopardized by counter measures, which many governments try to undertake.
- organized crime groups and their representatives may act legally and even occupy rather high positions in some social or political structures.

- territorial integration - means that organized crime groups are based in a definite area - territory. There are some "favorite" areas for the commission of crimes, to obtain material resources, to launder money, to go on holidays etc. However, organized criminal groups divide their influence spheres not only geographically, but also in respect to concrete functions so that some kind of specialization occurs. Some groups control gambling businesses, prostitution, some provide all forms of criminal services etc. Regardless of mode, the motive of illegal profit remains the same.

- The next criteria is the actual engine of organized crime (Siegel, 1992). As already stated above, the main objective is to accumulate a fortune through illegal actions. Illegal profits are laundered through complicated bank operations, remaining in foreign bank accounts or invested in real estate.

- The last criterion is corruption, which is one of the most essesntial features of organized crime, if regarded as a socio-political phenomenon. Corruption depends on the venality of state officials. Corruption may be defined as a system of relations based on unlawful practices by officials undermining state and public interests. Organized criminal groups gain significant support by bribing officials into serving the Mafia's interests. When bribery fails, blackmail, extortion and gradual cooptation of an official into illegal affairs occurs (Europe 2000, 1997).

Risks for Society Posed by Organized Crime: Tendencies and Prognosis of Dynamics

The damages that organized crime cause are not always adequately estimated. First of all, organized crime damages the governing institutes through corruption. It inspires spiritual and the moral degradation of the nation, especially affecting the youth, creating the stereotype of a "beautiful" life that excludes responsiblity and promotes violence, anarchy, sex and drugs. Organized crime endangers the ecology, as it participates in the smuggling of nuclear and chemical waste. Organized crime also destroys the economy, as funds are taken out of national circulation illegally. Very evident are the threats organized crime pose to the banking system. "Commercial terror" initiated by the mafia is especially damaging in the period of transition from a collective economy to a free market. Moreover, the activity of organized crime groups in economics advances their involvement in politics. Organized crime either directly or indirectly harms constitutional order.

Organized (international) crime is a large-scale phenomenon in modern society, representing a huge potential threat for countries regardless of their political systems and ideological beliefs. This phenomenon is virtually unaffected by national frontiers or by law enforcement activities. We can concede even further. Organized crime not only has a direct and lasting effect on national justice systems, it also influences many national political, economic and democratic developments.

Organized crime, by its inherent practice of uniting, organizing, promoting and empowering criminal elements, hinders the legitimate development of nations. The further integration of organized associations is to be expected. To a large extent, it is linked to the expansion of racket, which functions as a catalyst for the formation of organized crime groups. Instability of political and economic situations accelerate criminal group involvement in a country's politics and economy.

A very dangerous trend is the strengthening of international criminal relations, encouraged by transparency of national borders, globalization of economy, insufficient legal regulation, etc. Another alarming trend is that organized crime increasingly appeals to and recruits the new generations. Apart from that, there's also a tendency for organized criminal groups to establish links with extremist elements. Concerning prospective criminal business areas, there certainly will remain illegal drug and arms trade, speculations with real estate, racket of banks and enterprises, professional racket, smuggling of nuclear substances, ordered homicides, child prostitution, money laundering service, protection from tax authorities, etc.

Organized crime is a regular and objective phenomenon. It conforms to certain preconditions necessary for it to emerge and function. It develops and takes new forms and undergoes evolution, under definite economical, social, political, moral and cultural conditions. By the end of the 20th century, the further development of organized crime will be determined by the following global factors:

- economic crisis in Eastern European countries (decline of industry, high prices and low quality);
- sharp deterioration of standards of living, increase in rates of unemployment, insufficient social security;
- in political spheres, the incapacity to realize power potential, insufficient governing mechanism, reorganization of administration structures;

- growth of social depression, negativism, increased t\ likelihood of confrontation;
- deformation of cultural values and concepts, formation ot orientations and social norms;
- destabilization of the legal system, with legislation being too distant from actual social realities, reorganization of law enforcement institutions with an overall decrease of justice awareness among the population.

Problems of Organized Crime Prevention

Under conditions of reform and transition, the prevention of organized crime can not be addressed. In this period of free market conditions (privatization, decentralization, increased relations with Western countries), organized criminal groups develop unhindered. Under transitional circumstances, unclear norm structures abet the development of criminal subcultures, which, in time become major, nearly mainstream institutions. Indeed, by their nature, content and potential sometimes they become as influential upon the cultural values as the legislatures, the executive power, courts and the media.

In many countries, the future of democratic develoments depends on successfully overcoming the criminal influence. We cannot hope for any completely favorable result in our intentions to counter organized crime. Organized crime will always enjoy influence and footing in the legitimate power institutions.

Moreover, organized and criminal formations sufficiently possess immense material and financial resources to satisfy their criminal interests indefinitely. The resources of a "hidden" economy, in some countries, reach 1/3 - 1/2 of a nation's gross domestic product, (Russia, Belorussia) and are controlled by the structures of organized and internatinal crime.

From the global view, organized crime as a transnational anti-social reality is phenomenon with a powerful intellectual and material potential. However, on the other hand, this phenomenon also inspires a few positive consequences:

- it is able to initiate consolidation of countries with different orientations and legal systems;
- it determines the development of new legal systems, organizational forms, technologies and methods intended to control the phenomenon itself, and from a dialectical aspect, it can encourage the progress of society.

I completely share the view of Professor Viano (1995) who stated, "What is needed for economic revitalization in Russia is quite basically a genuine social partnership that embraces all elements of the people in a common economic task. The trust on which such cooperation must be founded and the effectiveness of the democratic institutions that guide public action can only be ensured by overall fairness and a decent amount of equity in the distribution of property, income, and social services". I think this also counteracts organized crime and its consequences.

Contemporary organized crime has become impersonal and anonymous, operating in several countries, making profits from the proceeds of its activities throughout the world, always using the latest technology for its activities. It disregards borders and becomes a universal force. The new world with open borders and open national economies with a rapid pace of international trade represents progress for the international society, but it must be ensured that these world-wide activities are carried out within and supported by the framework of the legality.

In order to curb the problem of organized and international crime, governments fully committed to adopting national law and developing enforcement structures that are designed and constructed to effectively deal with organized crime and its practices, need to exist (free from corruption and cooption). Only then will it be possible to fight this dangerous phenomenon in a concerted international fashion and to address it in an international forum.

References

Mošciskier, Andrzej. (1996), "New Forms of Crime in the Time of Transformation from Socialist to the Market Economy", *Impact of Political, Economic and Social Change on Crime and its Image in Society* (51st International Course of Criminology), Warsaw, pp.157-162.

Mueller, G.; Friday, P.; McCormack, R.; Newman, G.; Ward, R.H. (1995), "American Crime Problems From a Global Perspective", *The Criminologist*, v. 20, no. 6, pp.11-12.

"Organized Crime Becomes a Threat to Economic Reforms and Democracy", *Europe 2000 (Quarterly Newsletter)*, 1997, no. 12, pp. 34-35.

Siegel, Larry. (1992), *Criminology*, pp. 379-389.

Viano, Emilio. (1995), "The Russia Mafia and its Impact on the Privatization of Markets", *Organized and Transnational Crime*, Riga, pp. 140-172.

7 Opening and Closing the 49th Parallel: Responses to Free Trade and to Trans-Border Crime in Canada since 1989[1]

IAN TAYLOR

Theorizing Border Regulation in Canada

We do not have the space here to recount the detailed work we have completed on the rapid changes taking place in the regulation and surveillance of the cross-border trades in guns, drugs, alcohol and cigarettes and people into Canada. These are matters discussed in some detail in our longer report (Jamieson, South and Taylor, 1997). Here we have two other purposes. We want, first, to offer out a descriptive model of what our research suggests are distinctive, ideal-typical features of the institutional and ideological responses of key governmental and police agencies in Canada to trans-border trading in guns, cigarettes and alcohol, drugs and people. By institutional responses, we mean the particular innovations that have been made in terms of actual practice of work, new "cooperative" arrangements (or "partnerships") established with other agencies, the introduction of new technology into the work task, etc. By ideological responses, we mean the different kinds of common sense interpretation which are brought to the practical understanding of particular cross-border threats, their origins and source, their relevance in terms of border-crossing, and the most likely ways in which such cross-border threats are to be encountered. Taken together, these different institutional reconfigurations (and the rethinking of the cross-border threat associated with these changes) may be thought of as a major ingredient in the response of the State itself to cross border problems, though we recognize that the intensity and commit ent brought to particular campaigns to underwrite the integrity of the border will also be a function (as, for example, in the case of cigarette smuggling in 1994) of specific political initiatives. We should clarify that the main focus of this model is on developments within one national society, within "a territory within demarcated boundaries. . . with one administrative monopoly (the State)" (Sheptycki, 1995, p. 615): that is, that we are presenting a model here on the impact of the new cross-border reality as it was described to us by some Canadian police officers, customs officials and other agents of border regulation in 1996. This is not a model of the kinds of partnerships and understandings that are currently being institutionalized above the level of any one nation state - in "transnational" social and political space itself - or a description, in itself, of what Leslie Sklair, in pioneering analysis of the great variety of organizational or systematic links emerging within what he calls "the global system", has referred to as "transnational social practices" (Sklair, 1991, c.2).

The descriptive model has certain formal qualities which might encourage its application in analyses of the responses of national police, customs and immigration agencies working within other transnational economic unions, like the European Community or the South East Asian Free Trade Area, and we offer it on that basis.

Our second concern in this concluding section of this chapter, however, is to try and capture not only the different developments in the regulatory responses to transnational economic liberalization that seem to be generic to most such transnational developments, but also to understand the specificity of those developments within one local or national society - in this instance Canada. That is we believe that the emergence of new forms of inter-state (transnational, cross-border) systems of regulation and policing have a set of common features, which must properly be understood, but also that the particular mix of strategic vision and institutional activity which emerges in any one national society derives in part from a pre-history, which continues to leave an imprint on the "common sense" which agents working with border agencies bring to their work.

We want to identify four discrete features of the organization of border-control and border-surveillance in Canada.

The Identification of Risk

Nearly every border agency with whom we spoke in the summer of 1996 commented on the emergence and continuing re-inflection within their workplace of some form of "Risk-Assessment". Revenue Canada Customs has been working for some time with an ongoing program which assesses the "risks" involved in the deployment of different staffing levels at airports or at established customs locations on land (for example, the Ambassador Bridge and tunnel between Detroit and Windsor, Ontario) at different times of the day or night. In British Columbia, customs officers, working with RCMP officers, have targeted previously "unguarded" parts of the border in that province, in order to identify the numbers of people crossing the border at these points, to what purpose and with what goods in their possession. Nationally, Revenue Canada Customs has institutionalized a set of practices articulated around a distinction between the "High Risk" and "Low Risk Traveler", with those people designated as low risk travelers having their passage over the border (at airports or at land crossings) eased very considerably. So business people who make frequent trips across the border and who have been identified as "low risk" can now fill out their own customs declaration before departure from home, whilst also entering Canada without showing of documents and without interdiction.

In June 1995, National Revenue Minister Jane Stewart also announced the creation of the CANPASS system for travelers entering by private plane or pleasure boat, operating on the basis of pre-approved permit and telephone reporting system. Revenue Canada and Immigration Canada will henceforth screen all applicant wanting to enter Canada on existing records to ensure that they are not customs or immigration risks.[2] The emergence of this broad based bifurcation of the traveling population into high and low risk individuals has many parallel in other areas of social regulation inside the country: in Canada's new system of firearms regulation, for example, firearms owners on whom there is no record in the Canadian Police Identification System can now apply for additional weapons, or renew their existing weapons, on their Firearms Acquisition System by electronic mail, fax or other modern communication technology without having to present themselves for interview, and they will have their new FAS processed much more rapidly than they would have before the Firearms Act of 1994 came into force.

The emergence of "Risk Assessment" in the practices of social control is a phenomenon of the 1980s and 1990s, closely associated, at least initially, with the increasing use by police managers, private consultancies and public authorities of economic and statistical modeling in auditing the effectiveness of policing in the regulation of crime in particular localities. In its most straightforward application, "risk assessment" may involve analysis of patterns of crime in a particular geographical location or space (a parking lot, a local park) as a guide to the short-term deployment of police officers. However, the development of risk assessment is also an expression of a more general transformation in the stance assumed by the Government or by the Authority towards the kinds of services they provide and/or promises they make with respect to citizens' needs and demands, across a wide range of areas. Whether in the field of social welfare or health, or in the control of everyday forms of crime, the contemporary, post-industrial, or post-modern nation-state is withdrawing from the universalistic set of promises and commitments that characterized the earlier post-war period (the modernist period of welfarist mixed economics, driven by the commanding but benevolent state) (Simon, 1987; Ewald, 1991; O'Malley, 1992). This transformation is seen, in some quarters as a function simply of the exhaustion or the implosion of this post-war economic system, but, in other accounts, it is a function of the recognition at the level of power that new risks have emerged in the world - for example, in respect of environmental developments, in dangers to human health (HIV/AIDS, BSE), in the new risks produced by ever-advancing medical technology (for example, in genetics) or in the ever-speedier developments of computer technologies - which, individually and collectively defy the capacity of any one government to control: the challenge instead is that of knowing how to live with risk (Beck, 1995). In accounts of this shift to societies of risk, there is no pretense that the new forms of risk can somehow be sealed hermetically within the geographical boundaries or the legal jurisdictions of nations. The speedy development of ideas of cross-border free trade as an answer to the exhaustion, and loss of competitive edge of modernist, or Fordist, industrial economics in North America and in Europe adds further impetus to the ongoing development of a "common sense of government" in which the project of government increasingly is the management, and certainly not the elimination, of risk. This new governmental common sense cannot reduce to a counsel of despair, but is instead articulated - often through the "evaluation and audit" language of business schools - as a management science, committed to identification and dissemination of "best practice" by trained, and retrained, professional staff, checked via different systems of measurement (for example, performance indices) and framed in terms of an actuarial form of knowledge which highlights the types of risks and threats currently confronting any social or political institution, and the priority they should be given. No significant governmental institution has been immune from the development of this form of "knowledge" in the 1980s and 1990s, and the agencies "guarding the borders" of major nation are no exception.

But it is not only the emergence of the language and knowledge of risk which is common to most national border agencies, and the transnational partnerships with which they get involved. The "linguistic turn" involved in prioritizing "risk" over "welfare", for example, is closely associated with real social and economic transformations (the crisis of Fordist or modernist society and the return of mass unemployment), which in turn have placed enormous stresses and strains on welfare systems established in the earlier post-war period. So far as the border is concerned, prioritizing the general idea of risk over hitherto-existing systems of border-regulation involve a vast change from the kinds of customs and immigration regimes in place in the earlier post-war period. The individualistic attention given refugees or economic migrants by customs and immigration officials on the Canadian border was very widely known. The change in routine practices now demanded of border agencies, of course, comes at a time in which the wider post-war world itself is understood as being in a fundamental process of transformation - for example, in the return of genocidal wars in Central Europe and elsewhere- and, of course, the collapse of the old Soviet Union and the breakdown of the East-West security systems provided by the Iron Curtain. The desperate condition of that part of the world is seen throughout international police organizations and customs authorities as one of the primary sources of risk for "the west", in respect of the numbers of highly organized and professional criminals, successful survivors in the world of orthodox Communism, who are now free to leave Russia or other Eastern European countries in order to expand their sphere of operations in freer circumstances. So also is it widely thought in such circles that the successful institutionalization of large new transnational economic markets constitutes a temptation and an opportunity that any entrepreneurial figure (for example, at the production end of the drug trade) - whose markets had hitherto been more limited by modernist systems of immigration control and policing and who could only establish status in one country at a time - could not resist. So the broader set of world conditions are seen as rapidly filling up the gallery of Undesirable Others or High Risk travelers (Russian "biznessmen", Colombians, Nigerians, South East Asian business people of certain provenance and background etc), whose collective or individual movement throughout "transnational space" must be monitored as effectively as possible. At the level of each transnational partnership, there will be a detailed risk assessment of not just of "types of traveler" (inter-preted in terms of the gallery of Undesirable Others) but also an assessment of risk in relationship, for example, to particular airline routes, airlines, back roads or major highways (in the case of Customs Canada, for example, the "I-5 corridor", the Interstate Highway 5 in Washington State, between Seattle and Vancouver). We think it likely, from our conversations in the United States and Canada in 1996, as well as from other research in which we have been involved, that these conceptions of transnational (or global) threat will have a particular local character in different regions of the world. There is no sense amongst Canadian border agencies, for example, that American citizens constituted any kind of threat, but there was a strong sense that movements of other peoples (Mexicans, West Indians, Colombians and various other Latin Americans) northwards through the United States into Canada was seen as a threat, and there was also some suggestion that American officials saw the Canadian border itself as a potential source of threat in terms of people trying to enter the Unites States from North to South. The taken-for-granted phenomenology of threat in Canada, in that sense, is always along the North-South axis rather than on an East-West dimension. In other parts of the world, the phenomenology of risk will take different forms (for example, in the considerable emphasis in many European jurisdictions on Amsterdam as an entrepot in the international drug trade).

Global Tendencies in Border Regulation

The ever-increasing emphasis on "risk assessment" is just one defining feature of the convergent strategies of being adopted by advanced societies across the world in the regulation and surveillance of cross-border movements of people and goods. Another definitive development is the increasing number and range of inter-governmental agreements (memoranda of understanding, mutual assistance treaties etc.) which are being signed, at many different levels of political and economic activity and policy-implementation. In February 1995, for example, the federal Government in Canada announced the establishment of a joint border "management Accord" with the US Government, underwriting the two countries' friendship and participation in "the world's largest trade partnership". Another definitive aspect of the increasing salience of transnational economic and political relationships - namely, the enhanced influence, and expanding powers, of international policing organizations, like Interpol: a phenomenon that has already attracted both sympathetic and critical attention (Anderson, 1988; Bunyan, 1991; Walker 1994). A further development in the 1990s has been the increase in the number and range of partnerships struck by police agencies, both internally within nation-states and externally within different regions of the world, with other organizations in the public sector (customs, immigration, and many other similar agencies)[3] as well as in the private sector (airlines), in the name of one or other project of "policing", very broadly defined. A still further development, which we believe to be under-researched, is the parallel shift in the direction of "partnership" and "cooperation" on the part of these other non-police public sector and private sector organizations dealing with the public at large i.e. in some senses, in what would now be seen as a "public service market" (a sphere of consumption).

A prime example on this process are the developments that have occurred in the customs service in many "advanced societies" over the last decade. In 1994, for example, the United States Customs Service completed a major review of it own organization and practices, and released a public document *People, Processes and Partnerships*, outlining a new vision of the service for the 21st Century (United States, 1994). This report frankly outlined the sometimes "antagonistic relations" that had existed, historically, with "the trade community" and insisted that, in particular because of NAFTA and the General Agreement on Tariffs and Trade, a renewed Customs Service would be positioning itself more appropriately to meet "increasing demands for service" (Ibid, p. 12, 15). Internationally, the World Customs Organization (WCO) is in the meantime described as being centrally involved in, "look(ing) for ways to simplify and harmonize customs procedures throughout the world to help ease the flow of international trade and travel".[4]

In May 1997, indeed, the WCO, the World Trade Organization (WTO), and the United Nations Conference on Trade and Development (UNCTAD) announced a timetable, resulting from their particular collaboration, for the abolition of customs inspection altogether at national borders, in place of advanced electronic declaration of goods, and regular company audits.[5] In this sense, moves taking place towards the harmonization of customs practices within the North American Free Trade Area - like the establishment of the Trilateral Heads of Customs Conference established in 1992 working on harmonization of customs procedures within NAFTA as a whole - are entirely consistent with similar developments occurring elsewhere in a world moving generally towards "free trade", though it is arguable that such a formal framework is rather stronger a partnership that the Mutual Assistance Agreements that Canada has also struck with several other countries.

The Specificity of the North American Free Trade Agreement

Recognition of the world-wide movement in the direction of free trade and, in particular, to the creation of international free trade unions (or cartels) in different regions of the world should not lead us to ignore the specifics of different transnational trade agreements. The North American Free Trade Agreement is quite clearly an agreement specifically about commerce and trade on the North American continent. In no sense can it be seen as a prelude to any broader federal arrangement in terms of movement of labor or transformation in the definition of rights of citizenship. What NAFTA does involve, as we have already indicated, is a renewed commitment to what is now called "the trade community" (the world of business), especially in terms of easing the passage of trade across international borders. From the point of view of much of the Canadian "trade community" of course, this enlargement of markets is of vital importance, especially with the progressive reduction taking place in tariff walls: in 1992, about 40 percent of the overall output of private business and industry in Canada was exported and the total value of that export trade amounted to some (Can) $157.5 billion, with one in five Canadian jobs being dependent on that trade.[6] So also, of course, does NAFTA create significant extra opportunities within Canada for American (and Mexican) business, though it is important to recognize that NAFTA is probably of less strategic significance for American and American-domiciled companies than arrangements under negotiation to break down barriers between the Unites States and the "tiger economies" of South East Asia. Importantly, the North American Free Trade Agreement is a partnership, not between equals, but between two smaller economies and an economy which, until recently, was the most powerful and successful economy in the world - what Sklair refers to as a "hegemon" society (Sklair, 1991, p. 6) i.e. a society with structured and definitive advantages in the ongoing struggle for global resources.

There are at least two important implications to this new economic reality. First, as we have already seen in our discussion of economic migration, there is a real sense in which Canada's role as a kind of "port of call" for economic migrants into the heartlands of the job markets of North America, most of which are located in the United States itself. Second, there are political implications of another kind, problematizing a nation's claim to be sovereign in field of foreign policy and in some domestic areas as well. The "asymmetry" in Canada's relationship to its massive Southern neighbor has been at the core of anxiety in Canada for some time, but it is now underpinned by a concern that the United States effectively has a permanent majority in the transnational policy field in North America as a whole, especially when such transnational matters present themselves in economic terms. One prime example here is the Helms-Burton law, signed by President Clinton in March 1996: the following July, nine executives of the Toronto based nickel mining corporation Sherritt International were denied visas for the United States on the ground that they were guilty of "trafficking" in confiscated American property in Cuba.[7]

The Stubborn Play of Canadianicity at the Border

The generalized movement towards "harmonization" of customs practices within free trade areas and its specific expression in NAFTA has, however, encountered some limits in Canada. In the extended report on which this chapter was based, we pay attention not only to the distinctive facts of Canada's geography (27,000 kilometers of coastline and over 6,000 kilometers of land border) but also to the presence within Canada of areas where the jurisdiction of the Canadian state has become problematic, either because it is contested or because there are uncertainties about its delegation. The most well know example of a "contested jurisdiction" is the Mohawk reservation of Akwesasne, near Cornwall, Ontario, now firmly established as a "hot spot" of cross-border crime, especially in the smuggling (and manufacture) of contraband cigarettes and alcohol on quite an enormous scale. Akwesasne is also widely thought to be a primary border crossing point for illegal immigrants as well as a conduit for the smuggling of firearms.[8] In addition, however, there is the vast and remote expanse of the Canadian North, also identified by many law enforcement agencies in Canada (and the United States) as a relatively easy frontier zone for all kinds of trading in commodities and people. In the late 1980s, an extended area of aboriginal settlement in northern Canada, Nunavut, was granted self-improvement. The writ of the Canadian common law still formally runs Nunavut - enforced, as in many other Canadian provinces, by the RCMP on a contractual basis - but little is known about substantive policing practices in Nunavut or, indeed, about the policing of other subordinated aboriginal communities, like the Indian populations in northern British Columbia, the North West Territories and Alberta, and any relation this might have to regulation of transborder movements of people or commodities. The existence of these areas of contested or problematic jurisdiction in Canada has certainly been an irritating issue for law enforcement agencies in the United States, interested in the overall harmonization, and efficient good transnational practices, in the sphere of border regulation. The stand off between the RCMP and the Mohawks on the St Lawrence, and the continuing trades in cigarettes and alcohol has been a serious irritant for such authorities at quite a senior level.

"Akwesasne" has been quite a public source of friction between the Unites States and Canada. Some of the other frictions within NAFTA over "the border" have had less public purchase, being the subject instead of relatively less visible wars of position between law enforcement and custom agencies, on the one hand, and Ottawa and the provincial capitals, on the other. But the impact of these struggles on symbolic aspects of "the border" have had less public purchase, being the subject instead of relatively less visible wars of position between law enforcement and custom agencies, on the one hand, and Ottawa and the provincial capitals, on the other. But the impact of these struggles on symbolic aspects of "the border" and its relationship to Canadian identity is unmistakable. One of the most well-known areas of "resistance" on the part of the Canadian political class has been in the field of immigration and "asylum seeking". From their first days of settlement, the United States and Canada both have had a history and reputation as "immigration countries" - "new worlds" available to migrants from old Europe and other parts of the world. But, over time, the policies adopted towards new migrants in these two countries have diverged significantly: in Canada, in the period from Confederation right through to the second war, the operative concern being with the preservation of the two pioneer cultures (of France and England) and securing a loyalist and non-republican culture, set off against the radical and violent potential of its southern neighbor. The history of immigration into Canada in the aftermath of the second world war shows significant development, particularly in respect to the needs of the labor market and, more recently, the need to attract foreign capital investment, especially from the Pacific Rim. But there can be no escaping the continuing concern of Canadian immigration authorities to maintain some kind of control over the character of immigration into the country. Set against this concern, especially under the Premiership of Pierre Trudeau, was the role that Canada tried to play "on the world stage" as a kind of spokesperson for Third World Development and also on human rights. Pressures that have emerged in the 1990s from the Unites States for the "harmonization" of refugee policies have so far been quietly resisted, and, certainly at the time of writing, there is no prospect of Canada adopting what might be called a common border with the Unites States in this respect.

One key obstacle in this respect is the Canadian Charter of Rights. Legislated in the early 1980s, as the foundation for the repatriation of the Constitution from Westminister, the Charter can be seen as defining Canada's post-colonial independence and maturity. In contrast to the unwritten Constitution of the "mother country" - a society in which there is still no Bill of Rights and a society in which most aspects of government continue to be marked by extraordinary levels of secrecy and mystery, the Charter attempts to outline the elements of a contract between free and independent citizens and a modern State. This involves the construction of a very different balance that would be found either in the United States or in Europe. In a society in which the power of the State is not feared, in part because of the due process enshrined in the common law tradition, the State shares its sovereignty with citizens. But in a society whose present political form was constructed by immigrants and pioneer settlers on the land,[9] the independence of free individuals (and the limits imposed on the State in terms of interfering into the private lives of all citizens [or potential citizens]). It is only by understanding the pivotal role of the Charter in defining Canadianicity in the late modern period (from around 1980) that one can understand the continuing resistance of Government in Canada to the kinds of reforms demanded by so many law enforcement agencies in the existing system of refugee claim determination. So also, we would argue, is this kind of analysis important in understanding the resistance that has been shown in political circles in Canada to the enactment of equivalent legislation to the American Rackets Influenced Organizations statute (RICO), requiring disclosure of the details of the private bank accounts held by individuals or corporate bodies suspected of involvement in organized crime. What is at issue here is not necessarily the observation of the specific clause of the Charter (which, although widely displaced in many a public place in Canada, is not necessarily well know or remembered by most Canadians): what is at stake is the space the Charter creates for some notion of "being Canadian" to be articulated. In that sense, it has a similar (even if merely token) significance, in the ongoing play of symbols of identity and belonging, to the pride with which law enforcement agents themselves, when encountering American hunters at the border, gleefully and proudly confiscate those guns and ammunition "we don't allow in Canada".

Notes

1   This research was made possible by a Canadian High Commission Institutional Research Program grant, awarded in February 1996. We would like to express our appreciation of the support of the Commission, and to the many individuals who helped us during our research visits to Canada and the US in the summer of 1996. The names of these individuals are listed in the full report (Jamieson, South and Taylor, 1997).

2   Revenue Canada *News Release*, with back grounder, 5 June 1996.

3   A good example of this in Canada might be *Project Return,* targeting abducted children from different parts of the world currently living in Canada - a partnership of the RCMP, Canada Customs and the Department of Citizenship and Immigration.

4   *Interaction* 22 (March-April 1996)

5   Tony Snape "Customs set to become 'a formality'" *The European,* 1-7 May, 1997.

6   *Trilateral Customs Guide to NAFTA* Ottawa: Customs and Excise Canada n.d. Preface.

7   *The Guardian,* 11 July 1997. This report indicates that the Helms-Burton law has been condemned in London "as a violation of the GATT world trade agreement and as an illegitimate interference in the sovereignty of other nations." But that does not mean that it cannot be imposed by a "hegemon" nation within a free trade association over which it has effective domination.

8   These issues are extensively discussed in the chapter prepared by Jamieson for this book (Jamieson, 1997).

9   We have no intention here of ignoring the fact that the pioneers who settled Canada in the eighteenth and nineteenth century were not "the founding peoples" of civilized social life on the land that is now Canada. That distinction falls of course to the First Nations and the Inuit.

References

Anderson, M. (1988), *Policing the World: Interpol and the Politics of International Police Cooperation,* Oxford: Clarendon Press.

Beck, U. (1992), *Risk Society,* London: Sage. Ewald, F. (1991), "Insurance and Risks," in G. Burchell, C. Gordon and P. Miller (eds) *The Foucault Effect: Studies in Governmentality,* London: Harvester-Wheatsheaf.

Jamieson, R. (1997), "Borders, 'First Nations' and the problem of jurisdiction: the case of Akwesasne", Paper prepared for the International Conference on Global Organized Crime and International Security, International Institute for the Sociology of Law, Oñate, Spain.

Jamieson, R., South, N. and Taylor, I. (1997), "Market Liberalization and Cross-Border within NAFTA; the U.S.-Canada Border," Research report presented to the Canadian High Commission, London, under the Insitutional Research Program.

Sheptyycki, J.W.E. (1995), "Transnational Policing and the Makings of a Postmodern State", *British Journal of Criminology,* v. 35, n. 4, pp. 613-635.

Simon, J. (1987), "The emergence of a risk society: insurance, law and the state",*Socialist Review,* v. 95, pp. 61-89.

Sklair, L. (1991), *Sociology of the Global System,* London: Harveser-Wheatsheaf.

Walker, N. (1994), "European Intergration and European Policing: a Complex Relationship", in Malcolm Anderson and Monica de Boer (Eds), *Policing Across National Boundaries*, London: Pinter.

8 "Contested Jurisdiction Border Communities" and Cross-Border Crime: The Case of the Akwesasne

RUTH JAMIESON

Introduction

Conventional discussion of the threat of transnational organized crime by politicians, by senior police officials, and applied criminologists is characterized by an unswerving but generally optimistic pragmatism, usually extolling the merits of transnational partnerships (for example, between national police forces and/customs organizations). The object of this paper is to raise some questions about such a pragmatic and optimistic stance, particularly in respect of the circumstances obtaining in what I will want to call "contested jurisdiction border communities" (types of "locales" which appear to be increasing in number in different parts of the world at the end of the twentieth century). This paper will focus on one particular such border community, located on what most observers would identify as the American-Canadian border -the Mohawk community of Akwesasne - which has been the site of increasingly agitated discussion (especially in governmental, customs and policing circles) over the last ten to fifteen years. I will want to argue that the case of Akwesasne is one particular example of a much more general phenomenon. Within the European Community, in the 1990s, there has been quite active interest in police and customs circles over issues of "cross-border crimes" (or what, in some cases, might more accurately be called near-border crimes) in a variety of locations within the Community where political or legal jurisdictions are ambiguous or where they are actually contested. There are many examples of "contested jurisdiction border communities" throughout the developed world - each exhibiting rather different characteristics in respect of the claims they might make with respect to defending themselves against the jurisdiction demands made by powerful local nation-states, inter-governmental organizations or transnational policing or customs partnerships. For the purposes of the argument here, it is important to note how these particular locales are the sites not just of such contests over jurisdictions but also, importantly, the claims on the part of police and government officials, journalist and many local citizens, that these border community areas have become ever more important points of trans-shipment of illegal goods and persons - key "trading posts" or entrepôts in the current escalation of transnational forms of organized criminality. This chapter obviously suggests that these two different dimensions of "contested jurisdiction border communities" - the fact of ambiguity or problematic coordination of state efforts in respect of jurisdiction claims, and the fact of increased flows of illicit traffic - are connected, and not merely accidental. More than that, I will want to argue that students of these particular forms of "international crime" (in criminology as much as in political sciences alike) cannot ignore the specific cultural, economic and political process which, on the one hand, lead to the contested definitions of such forms of trade, and, on the other, contribute to the current (and growing) significance of these kinds of cross-border trading activities, no matter how urgently national or international governments try to define them as criminal.

Akwesasne

The "Mohawk Territory of Akwesasne" occupies a strategic location on the St. Lawrence Seaway, astride the border between Canada and the United States, about 95 km southwest of Montreal.[1] The geographical location of Akwesasne alone would have always rendered it a likely site for illicit cross-border trading (smuggling) irrespective of which community live there. As it happens, the Mohawks do. The claims of Canadian and the American governments over this particular stretch of the border have always been contested by the Mohawks themselves,[2] and the Canadian and U.S. governments have de facto conceded border-crossing rights to the residents of Akwesasne.[3] As I will want to argue later, much of what would be identified by established police and government authorities in Canada or the U.S. as "smuggling" is seen by the Mohawks of Akwesasne as routine, legitimate trading - a part of the normal everyday business of survival in Akwesasne. The Akwesasne Mohawks claim the right to travel freely with personal, community and trade goods "unrestricted by borders established by non-Aboriginal societies" (Mitchell n.s., p. 1). They regard Akwesasne as an unpartitioned sovereign territory over which they claim never to have conceded jurisdiction (whether to the British or French colonial states, or to Canada or the United States). They will also point to the colonizers' recognition of the sovereignty of the Mohawk Nation ("Kahnia'kehaka") in the Treaty of Utrecht 1713 and Article III of the Jay Treaty of 1794 between the United States and Great Britain. All Aboriginal spokespeople claim the right to cross the Canadian-US border as an "Aboriginal right" pertaining to all First Nations. Akwesasne Mohawks' contested relationship with the two nation states of Canada and the United States is one aspect of the local jurisdiction issue. The everyday governance of Akwesasne is also complicated by the jurisdictional claims of three sub-national systems - the provinces of Ontario, Quebec and New York State. Nowhere is this more apparent than in respect of policing which at various times has involved the RCMP, the Canadian Army, the FBI, the Ontario Provincial Police, the Sureté du Québec, the New York State Police, the Akwesasne Mohawk Police and latterly the self-appointed Mohawk Sovereignty Security Force.[4] In addition, Akwesasne is home to three separate Aboriginal councils claiming jurisdiction over its territory or particular parts of it. The St. Regis Mohawk Council, set up by the New York State government in 1802, assumes jurisdiction over the American side of the reserve and the Mohawk Council of Akwesasne, set up by the Canadian government in 1899, claims jurisdiction over the Canadian side, whilst the Mohawk National Council (the traditional form of Mohawk governance based on "The Great Law of Peace" of 1539) claims jurisdiction over the whole community. So Akwesasne is a border community where, on the one hand, the exercise of jurisdiction by nation states over their external borders (for example, in respect of the flow of goods and people) has been under dispute for some considerable period of time and, on the other, where internal arrangements of governance are both complex and sensitive to longstanding local customs. As will be seen later in this chapter, the jurisdiction divide between the nation states of Canada and the United States has assumed a particular importance or expression during the 1980s and 1990s in the unfolding of contrasting fiscal policies in the two countries - notably in respect of the level of taxation on cigarettes, alcohol and fuel[5] - with important consequences in terms of the volume and character of the trading of these commodities in and through Akwesasne. The "sub-national" levels of jurisdictional divergence have had a separate importance in Akwesasne, in respect of the struggles that have occurred over the management and policing of new commercial activities of some Akwesasne Mohawks - in particular the rapid development of a number of casinos in Akwesasne, closely involving leading figures of the local Warrior Society.[6] The opening of gambling operations in Akwesasne has been the subject of intense conflict, resulting in 1990 in an armed stand-off between pro- and anti-gambling factions.[7] In 1996, the St. Regis Tribal Council (which claims jurisdiction over the American side of the reserve) split into two factions - the "People's Government" and the "Constitutional Government", each with their own chiefs, largely on the single question of gambling regulation.

In a recent paper, Petrus van Duyne (1996, 342) has argued that transnational crime should be understood as a more or less direct reflection of the prevailing international market relationships of supply and demand. While this is an important recognition (of the overwhelming power of markets in determining the character of international criminal trade), I want to argue here that the specific forms assumed by transnational criminal markets must be understood in terms of the specific conjuncture of *geography*, the *divergence* of regulatory regimes across adjacent jurisdictions and the *contested sovereignty* of overlapping or neighboring nation states. I want to illustrate this argument through closer examination of these different dimensions of "cross-border crime" in Akwesasne.

I am suggesting that there are three connected, but distinct, issues involved in the analysis of "transnational crime", and illustrate it in the case of Akwesasne. The first focuses on the issue of sovereignty - the questioning of the capacity of either of the two connecting nation states to exercise its jurisdiction over territory which different Mohawk groups claim as their own, making no concession to the claims of the colonizing nation-state. The second focuses on the divergence of national practices in adjacent nation-states and the different taxation regimes being developed in each nation-state in respect of key commodities pursued with respect to trading markets. Anderson et al. (1995, p. 21) in their study of policing in the new Europe neatly refer to this as the "adjacency of opportunity". The third issue is the most complex of these analytical problems. It concerns the complex relationship between cross-border jurisdiction ambiguity or contest and the particular logic of development of cross-border trading in border communities in different specific circumstances of opportunity, as well as particular economic or geographical limits. Each of these distinct issues will be addressed in turn.

Sovereignty and the Myth of the Border

National borders have always been permeable to a greater or lesser extent, despite the best efforts of nation-states to exercise jurisdiction over them. But a distinctive and defining of the "smuggling" taking place through the border community of Akwesasne in the 1980s and 1990s has been the fundamental clash of perspective as to the legal status of these trading activities. The Warriors of Kahnawake (another Mohawk community located nearer to Montreal who trade with the Akwesasne Mohawks) describe their own trade in smuggled cigarettes, fuel (kerosene, gasoline, heating oil), building materials, alcohol, firearms, etc. as "international free trade" on the grounds, outlined earlier, that the Mohawk Nation claims sovereignty over its own territory (Hornung, 1993, p. 22). Although the Warrior Society takes the most radical and tribal nationalist stance on trade - in some instances more akin to "enterprise nationalism" - there is actually an overwhelming consensus in the whole Mohawk community with respect of their sovereignty and border-crossing rights. The Mohawks argue, specifically, that the right of First Nations to free trade and travel across the Canada-US border is recognized and preserved under a series of treaties (*inter alia*, Article XV of the previously mentioned Treaty of Utrecht 1713, Articles II and III of the Jay Treaty, Article IX of the Treaty of Ghent 1815 and Section 35 of the Constitution Act of 1982), but they also insist that these treaties are not the *source* of those rights. For example, Article II of the Jay Treat recognizes the right to free movement of Aboriginal peoples for trade and diplomacy, while Article III exempts them from payment of excise duties on imported personal and community goods.[8] Consequently they do not regard the transhipment of goods which are ordinarily subject to customs duties and/or excise tax (e.g., cigarettes, heating oil or alcohol) as being subject to such charges. They see it simply as a domestic form of "trade" - "no more of an issue than buying and selling peanut butter". The Mohawks' refusal to pay an excise tax (or any tax) on cigarettes is also justified in terms of the First Nations' "spiritual ownership of tobacco" a product to which they introduced to Europeans (Powless, 1996). Some distinctions are, however, drawn between the legitimacy of trading different types of commodities.

Van Duyne (1996, p. 342) wants to distinguish between two types of cross-border criminal market - markets in *permitted goods* which are illegally traded (for example, contraband alcohol) and markets trading in *forbidden goods* (for example, illegal firearms). But this distinction between the "permitted" and the "forbidden" can only be sustained in practice in circumstances where the authority of the particular state to impose these controls on commodities and their trade is uncontested. The Mohawks' assertion of their right to trade in goods which would otherwise (i.e. in Canada or the United States) be subjected to excise tax and duties has never been in question. But this consensus does begin to fracture on the question of trading in "forbidden" items like drugs and firearms - but, not because they are prohibited, but because of their potential social harm.[9]

One former chief observed, however, that although there was complete consensus on border-crossing rights among the people of Akwesasne, it was also the case that: "as it [the trade] gets more lucrative, so does the degree to which people rationalize it using the sovereignty argument" (Tarbell, 1996).

The sovereignty argument can serve as a rhetorical justification, not only for large scale smuggling, but for a host of other on-reserve activities like unregulated high-stakes gambling. The sovereignty argument is sufficiently abstract and elastic to stretch to the more extreme necessitarian arguments marshaled by the Warriors and entrepreneurs for the acceleration of economic development through the designation and use of reserves as unregulated free trade zones,[10] in order to provide an "economic arm" to the Warriors' political and military (Hornung, 1993, p. 79).

Jurisdictional Divergence and "the Adjacency of Opportunity"

The border between Canada and the United States is not only the longest undefended land border in the world. It has also been seen historically as one of the most "porous" of such land borders, and, as I have argued with others in a recent research report, the overall openness of this border has been considerably enhanced by the new discursive priorities of the North American Free Trade Agreement (that is, to "ease the transnational movement of people and goods" (Jamieson, South and Taylor, 1997). Throughout the 1990s, however, particular points on this border have become the focus of a considerably heightened level of concern over illicit trading - notably, with respect to the smuggling of cigarettes and alcohol, and, to a lesser extent, of people. At Akwesasne itself, the level of activity of the two national governments (as expressed in the activities of local of customs agents and police forces) has been at its most intense since the introduction of prohibition in the United States (the Volstead Act) in 1920. Nearly all commentators, in the press as well as in the law enforcement institutions on both sides of the border, identify recent growth of these trades as an effect of the recent rapid divergence of Canadian and American excise tax regimes, coupled with the difficulties of policing a border in a community where most key jurisdictional claims are under dispute. There is, however, a local history to these border practices well-known within the Akwesasne community: in the 1970s when gasoline (petrol) was cheaper in Canada, for example, many thousands of residents of upstate New York took to buying their gas from stations on the Akwesasne reserve. Although the direction and volume of illicit trade is largely driven by the price differential on given items, the particular routes and the nature and extent of the involvement of criminal or Aboriginal groups is also determined by the local context - especially the availability of large local markets. Hence the primary markets for smuggled cigarettes until the mid-1990s have been the densely populated conurbations around Montreal, Québec and Toronto, all within relatively easy reach of Akwesasne.

"Buttlegging"

At the height of what had come to be defined in Canada as a smuggling crisis in 1993-94, the Federal Government estimated that some 40 percent of the Canadian tobacco market (worth Can. $12.4 billion) consisted of cigarettes that had been smuggled across the border. The market share of smuggled tobacco ranged from a low of 15 percent in the Western Provinces to over 60 percent Quebec - with a mid-point of 35 percent market share in Ontario. The overall share of the tobacco market in Canada that had been captured by smuggled cigarettes had exploded from roughly 2.5 percent in 1985 to 38 percent in 1993. About 80 percent of smuggled tobacco products were made in Canada[11] and exported tax-free to the United States where, it is thought, they were purchased from American wholesalers and smuggled back into Canada via Akwesasne or other entrepôt locales (Office of the Prime Minister, 1994a, p.3).

Apart from its obvious concern about lost tobacco tax revenue (a substantial $1 billion), the federal Government was also concerned about "a general lack of respect for the law" by Canadians from all sections of society (Office of the Prime Minister, 1994b, p. 1) as well as by Canadian Tobacco manufacturers who were directly benefitting from this contraband trade. Products were being retailed at corner stores, on-reserve "smoke shops" (one Quebec reserve - Kahnawake - operated 70 different smoke shops) and in suburban high school corridors. The single biggest factor driving the growth of the illicit tobacco market between 1988 and February 1994 (when the

Canadian government was finally forced to "roll back" taxes on tobacco) was the difference in the average retail price of tobacco sold in Canada compared to the USA. It should also be noted that the adjacency of opportunity afforded by a significant price differential between jurisdictions also structures the internal contraband tobacco market operating in various American states (Michigan and California) and also between US and Mexico.

Table 9.1 Average Wholesale Price of a Carton of Canadian Cigarettes (Canadian dollars)

	Canada	USA
1988	$25	$15
1993	$48 ($35 of which was federal/ provincial tax)	$15

Source: Office of the Prime Minister, *Government Action Plan on Smuggling* (Feb. 1994)

Local involvement in this kind of "free trade" or "smuggling" (participation in the cash economy) has actually been pervasive at Akwesasne, as I have already suggested, at least since the 1950s, and a number of different local border practices were well-established, well in advance of the penetration into Akwesasne of any more national or international criminal organizations (Tarbell, 1996). The organizers of this "cross-border trade" are usually middle aged men who employ younger men as runners, but the trading may also involve either whole families or individuals acting alone. Cigarette smuggling is pervasive. The scale of the activity ranges from "spur of the moment opportunism" to "well organized, computerized enterprise" (Hornung, 1993, p. 22), the latter entailing a significant capital investment not only in "inventory", but also in infrastructure in the form of access roads and docks on the south side of Cornwall Island along with speed boats and transport vehicles. An indication of the size of some of these operations is the interception in November 1995 of a cigarette smuggling operation involving Canadian-produced tobacco being shipped into the US and re-imported into Canada via Akwesasne which is said to have netted the Mohawks a profit of $25.5 million Canadian on an initial investment of $20 million.[12] This seizure came at a time when cigarette smuggling was reported to have "slowed to a trickle" (Lindquist and Avey, 1996, p.1). However, the RCMP suggest that one reason for the enduring attraction of tobacco as a contraband commodity is that it can be used as medium of exchange in the drugs trade (Lindquist and Avey, 1996, p. 13). It is not surprising, in these circumstances, to hear talk in Akwesasne of the recent penetration of the trading activities at the border by "organized crime" groups with no previous involvement with the Mohawk nation itself.

The scale of these new cross-border trades provides a serious opportunity and encouragement to such serious criminal operators, and this "struggle for position" within the mushrooming local market in smuggling goods has its own effect on the local Mohawk community (not least, for example, in the advantage it gives to young men associated with the Warriors Society, willing to carry arms, to enforce control over particular routes or particular chains of supply and demand). This struggle over markets also plays into claims made by different organized groups in Akwesasne over the customs and rules defining what goods and services can be traded under the rubric of the sovereignty of the Mohawk Nation. But these appeals to traditional and established practices may be losing their moral force in a situation of escalating opportunity. One Mohawk commentator observed: "People make their own choices about what is morally appropriate. . . Some will do cigarettes, but not drugs" (Tarbell, 1996).

Others, no doubt, do drugs but not cigarettes. To the extent that jurisdictional divergence constitutes resource (Jamieson et al., 1997; Sheptycki, 1996, p. 1), it is also, of course, available for exploitation by all players in the transnational crime game - criminal organizations, manufacturers, border communities and border police. Few Mohawks will openly admit that there is Mafia involvement in gambling or other "trading" on Akwesasne. But, one informant did confirm that there were still organized crime connections, for example, where Akwesasne "businessmen" were provided with "set up" money in the order of $250,000 (US) from the Mafia in Las Vegas.[13] Importantly, there are other big players in the cross-border contraband trade at Akwesasne who exploit the divergence of US and Canadian fiscal and regulatory regimes to export their products into illicit markets - the cigarette manufacturers and distillers themselves. The contraband trade would collapse without the collusion of these "legitimate" businesses.

Conclusion

This chapter has attempted to advance an analysis of the escalation of a particular kind of cross-border trading activity that developed very rapidly in one particular community in North America in the late 1980s and early 1990s. With van Duyne, it recognizes the broader context that makes sense of the scale and intensity of this kind of activity includes the deep changes that were taking place in theeconomic market-place (including, here, the decline of opportunities for employment in legitimate local labor markets and in agriculture). But it also wants to recognize the importance of a set of long-established disputes between the Aboriginal peoples of this particular border community and the nation-states (and their various institutional representatives, like the police) which surround it, and a set of local practices that have developed in defiance of these intrusive attempts at transnational governance of the local community. It is a commentary on the resilience of these local practices, perhaps, that the Canadian government was forced, in 1994, despite all protestations of the public health community, to reduce the level of taxation it was imposing on cigarettes, as a key element in its Anti-Smuggling Strategy. The continuing attempt, in the international criminal justice community to argue that the war against transnational crime "can be won" *without regard* to the resilience of the local practices that characterize the border community where jurisdiction is actively contested is in this sense naïve.

In the meantime, I cannot conclude without commenting on the broader contexts within which these struggles between national and potentially criminalized local Mohawks are played out. For some, the Mohawks serve as convenient folk devils and an exotic species of criminalized "others" for law enforcement agencies. But, at the same time, the achievements of General Motors in polluting the territory of Akwesasne is not itself a candidate for the intervention of law by the Governments of Canada or the United States. Nor either, apparently, are the large "exporters" who profit from the existence of the international contraband market. Of all the players in the transnational crime game, they are uniquely placed to remain in a "win-win situation" whatever else happens in the "war on crime".

Notes

1   Other "entrepôt locales" on the border between Canada and the United States not occupied by Aboriginal communities would include the Windsor - Detroit bridge and tunnel and the customs post between Blaine, Washington and Douglas, B.C.

2   The Aboriginal rights at issue here concerns the movement of goods and people in general, but more particularly, matters of immigration (*United States ex rel.Diabo v. McCandless*, 1928), trade (*Francis v. The Queen, S.C.C. 1956; Mitchell v. MNR*), and customs and excise (*United States v. Garrow. 1938*).

3   As it is by the First Nations of North America. As regards the Mohawks' particular border-crossing rights, the Canadian government rather begrudgingly issued the "Akwesasne Residents Remission Order" in 1991 by which the residents of the community are entitled to bring certain personal goods over the border without paying taxes or duties and to bring goods over for re-sale to Akwesasne residents - an entitlement which they claim derives from their sovereignty as nation as well as from Treaties with and between colonial governments (Mitchell, 1995, p. 18). The Canadian Federal Court recently found in favour of the Akwesasne Mohawks (Mitchell v. MNR) where it was found that they had an existing aboriginal right to pass and repass freely across the boarder including the right to bring goods (excluding firearms, prohibited drugs, alcohol, plants and the like) from the US into Canada for personal and community use.

4   There is a tripartite agreement on First Nations policing between the federal and provincial governments and the Mohawk Council of Akwesasne for policing the Canadian side of the reservation. The agreement between the St. Regis Mohawk Council and New York State for policing the American side broke down in the mid-1980s and, despite efforts to re-institute a policing agreement in December 1989, no arrangements were agreed or in place before the conflict over gambling escalated into an armed stand-off in 1990.

5   The impact of the North American Free Trade Agreement (NAFTA, first signed by the Canadian and US governments in 1989) on the illicit cross-border trade at entrepôts like Akwesasne is beyond the scope of this chapter. In a research report prepared for the Canadian High Commission, we have examined two contradictory aspects of this process - the concern of customs authorities on both sides of the border to facilitate cross-border trade through a series of inter-agency agreements and new partnerships arrangements with private business, coupled with the heightened interest in the identification and policing of "risky" trade in goods and people (cf. Jamieson, South and Taylor, 1997).

6   The Mohawk "Warrior Society" emerged in Akwesasne during the late 1980s and allied itself to the pro-gambling faction on the grounds that gambling was

a sovereignty issue. By 1990 they had formed the paramilitary Mohawk Sovereignty Security Force (MSSF) and declared themselves to be the legitimate police force in the community. They issued a press release to the effect that any attempt to intervene in the gambling dispute by outside police forces (the New York State police) would be considered a "military expedition" against the Mohawk people (Johansen, 1993, p. 25).

7   For extended accounts of the 1990 crisis in the conflict over gambling at Akwesasne, referred by some as the Mohawk "civil war", see Hornung, 1991 and Johansen, 1993.

8   For example, the Mohawks can buy unlimited quantities of untaxed cigarettes in the US for their "personal use." See Mitchell (n.d.) for a concise statement of the Mohawk position on their border-crossing rights.

9   The smuggling of *people* across the reserve represents a form of cross-border crime which lies outside both types of criminal markets described by van Duyne. The justification for it is based on Mohawk sovereignty claims over transit of people through its territory.

10   An extreme example of the external exploitation of Mohawk sovereignty is use of the Kahnawake reserve as a venue for the staging of "human cockfights" or "extreme fighting" matches (which are banned in Canada and the US) for broadcasting on pay per view satellite television (*The Independent* 29.4.96).

11   The opposite is true for contraband "generic" alcohol which is distilled in the US.

12   The scale of smuggling of cigarettes across national borders in Europe in the late 1990s, and the increasing involvement of serious criminal enterprise in such trade, has led to several forceful (and self-serving) demands from manufacturers for the harmonization of tobacco excise duties across the European Community cf. for example, "Cigarette Ruling May Stub Out Revenues" *The European* 10-16 April 1997; Clive Turner "Why We Must Cut the Price of Cigarettes" *The Observer* 22 June 1997. European Community sources estimate that some 3.7 billion cigarettes worth 380 million ecu were smuggled in 1995 (European Community: *The Fight Against Fraud, Annual Report 1995*).

13   The FBI have also tracked shipments of bootleg slot machines from the Mafia onto the reserve (Johansen, 1993, p. 128).

References

Alfred, G.R. (1995), *Heeding the Voices of Our Ancestors: Kahnawake Mohawk Politics and the Rise of Native Nationalism*, Toronto: Oxford University Press.

Anderson, M.; den Boer, M.; Cullen, P,; Gilmore, W.C.; Raab, C.D. and Walker, N. (1995), *Policing the European Union: Theory, Law and Practice*, Oxford: Clarendon.

Beare, M. E. (1996), *Criminal Conspiracies: Organized Crime in Canada*, Toronto:Nelson Canada.

Office of the Prime Minister (Chrétien, Jean) (1994), *Government Action Plan on Smuggling*, Speech to the House of Commons, February 2, 1994, Ottawa: Office of the Prime Minister.

Duyne, Petrus van. (1996), "The Phantom and Threat of Organized Crime", *Crime, Law and Social Change* n. 24, pp. 314-377.

European Commission. (1996), *The Fight Against Fraud Annual Report 1995*, (Press Release), Brussels: E.C.

Fadden, John. (1997) *Divisiveness at Akwesasne: Legacy of 19th Century Colonialism*. www.peactree.com/akwesasne/division.htm.

Hornung, Rick. (1991), *One Nation Under Under the Gun: Inside the Mohawk Civil War*, Toronto: Stoddart.

Jamieson, R., South, N. and Taylor, I. (1998), "Economic Liberalization and Cross-Border Crime: Canada's Border with the United States," Parts I & II, *International Journal of the Sociology of Law*, June 1998 (21:2) and September 1998 (21:3).

Johansen, Bruce. (1993), *Life and Death in Mohawk Country*, Golden, Colorado: North American Press.

Lindquist Avey MacDonald Baskerville, "Forensic and Investigative Accounts", 15 August 1995, *Cigarette Smuggling in the United States*.

Lindquist Avey MacDonald Baskerville, "Forensic and Investigative Accounts", 15 August 1995, *Contraband Liquor in Canada*.

Lindquist Avey MacDonald Baskerville, "Forensic and Investigative Accounts". (1996), *Contraband Tobacco and Organized Crime: An International Perspective*, paper presented to the Conference of the International Association of Law Enforcement Intelligence Analysts, 26-28 June 1996.

Liquor Control Board of Ontario. (no date), *Illegal Alcohol: Not a Victimless Crime*.

Mitchell, Michael W./Mohawk Nation. (1995), *Border Crossing Report*, Cornwall Island, Ontario: Mohawk Nation.

Mitchell, Michael W. (no date), *Mohawk Viewpoint on Relations with Canada Past, Present and Future*, Cornwall Island, Ontario: Mohawk Nation.

Sheptycki, James W.E. (1996), "Law Enforcement, Justice and Democracy in the Transnational Arena: Reflections on the War on Drugs", *International Journal of Sociology of Law*, no.24, pp. 61-75.

9 The Use of the "Shining Path" Myth in the Context of the All-Out War Against the "Narco-Guerilla"

RODOLFO MENDOZA NAKAMURA[1]

Introduction

The Cuban revolution of "Che" Guevara and Fidel Castro set the tone of political argumentation in Latin America for the quarter of a century that followed: the assumed threat that the various armies and police forces of Latin America had to deal with was defined not in terms of a frontal attack by some clearly identified foreign "enemy"; rather it was defined in terms of a long, drawn-out subversion of the main institutions of state by "ideological" allies of the power in question within the country.

In the global context of a fight between capitalism and communism, the main job of police and army was to root out any trace of "communist" -inspired "armed insurrection"(Debray, 1967).

When political attention in North America started to turn toward the global threat of drug-trafficking, other tasks were added to the usual "subversion control" against "communist-inspired" movements: these were drug control and the fight against the illegal production and commercialization of narcotics, which took place in those states of Latin America which were perceived as being the main sources of supply for the drugs entering North America. In Peru, starting in the early 1980s, the army and police forces were assigned the formal task of fighting against the "communist-inspired" "Shining Path" and "Tupac-Amaru" (MRTA) "revolutionary movements", as well as against the drug-traffickers controlling the production of coca in the Upper Huallaga and Aguaytia regions of Amazonia. The three were considered as constituting the main threats to the existence of the state as a "democratic" and "moral" entity.

99

"Narco-Guerilla": Myths and Reality

The official thesis of the government of Peru is that the "Shining Path" and "MRTA" "revolutionary movements" in the Upper Huallaga and Aguaytia regions are authentic "revolutionary movements" which happen to owe their survival to the financing they are able to secure from the drug-trafficking overlords that inhabit the two regions. The idea of "narco-guerrilla" as an "alliance between drug smugglers and arms dealers in support of terrorists and guerrillas" and as an instrument of Soviet influence in Latin America originated in a 1985 U.S. government report (Clawson and Lee, 1996). My thesis, which I have been working on since 1989, is that both the "Shining Path" movement and the "MRTA", as they exist in these two regions, are original, full-fledged creations of the local drug lords, who set the movements up as "armed insurrection" organizations to help them fight against the 1982 plant-eradication and anti-drug policies of the then President Fernando Belaunde Terry.

In denying any "authenticity" to the "revolutionary" denomination of the two movements as they exist in the coca-producing regions of Amazonia, what I am bringing to light is the basic collusion that exists between the law-enforcing institutions of the Peruvian state, on the one hand, and the law-breaking forces they are pursing, on the other, in that both espouse the same structure of myth, which each is able to turn to its own moneyed interests.

The myth[2] of the existence of two politically-oriented "armed-insurrection" movements in the two coca-producing regions of Amazonia serves to clothe the self-interest of a number of local drug lords in the respectability which is accorded in the thinking and popular culture of post-Cuban revolution states in Latin America to "leftist", anti-establishment causes. It thus serves to hide from view, if not the very real crimes perpetrated by themselves against the local populations of farmers and farm-hands, at least the no less real practical collaboration they were able to develop "on the ground," as it were, with the army and police forces sent to control them.

What the myth does for the army and for the state is to allow them to proclaim urbi et orbi their prowess and the successes they may have encountered in the global war against "leftist" subversion and drug-trafficking. At the very same time, in 1989, when General Alberto Arciniaga proclaimed the success of his "revolutionary strategy" against the "Shining Path" and "MRTA" movements on the Upper Huallaga front, the drug traffic itself was literally liberalized (González, 1990, pp. 89-90). As the accent was once again placed on the anti-"communist" war, eradication of the illegal coca production was stopped, arrested "traffickers" and accomplices were heavily taxed, as was the transport out of the area by small airplanes which now flew out of airfields under the close supervision of the army.

What the myth does in practice is to legitimize the use of violence on both sides: by the traffickers, when, as was particularly the case early in the process, they need to intimidate the local population and thus force local farmers to flee the area and others to step up the production of coca; by the army, when they need to make a showcase of their aggressiveness, or when they want to put pressure on the traffickers, or when they decide to do part of the traffickers' intimidation job themselves. The names of the "Shining Path" and "MRTA" were from early on labels given to competing groups of drug traffickers in the region; as the price of coca has declined over the last few years, however, the "mythically" charged names have also tended to disintegrate locally, and people revert to calling the groups simply "firms".

The official myth of a "narco-guerilla" movement saw its inception under the reign of ex-President Alan Garcia Perez and it gained international recognition through the work of French researcher Alain Labrousse (1989). In 1989 an official of the US Narcotics Assistance Unit said that the US assumes "a marriage of convenience" between "drug lords and Shining Path" and "no total alliance"(Cavanagh, 1989, p.26). By the late 1990s, this concept of "alliance" gained credibility in the US (Palmer, 1992).

Sentences are served in courts of justice based on that myth. Myths, to be sure, are probably needed in all societies. But no society can live with myths specifically designed to blind people to the reality of official corruption.

First Problems of Eradication

The Peruvian state first came to deal with the problems attending the production of coca leaves through the consumer end. The stated function of ENACO, created in 1949, was not to control the production of coca in the high forest of Amazonia, but to manage its private consumption, for purely personal comfort, in the Andes Region. The organization argued that the mastication of coca leaves, which was common in the Andes, could lead to drug addiction. The medico-psychiatric bent of this approach was made to serve the personal political ambitions of a famous Lima doctor (Ruggiero, 1983).

In signing the Geneva Convention of 1961, Peru agreed to limit the production of coca to purely scientific and medical ends after a trial period of

25 years (ONU, 1987). It agreed by the same token to put an end to what was an ancestral practice among the Indian population of the Andes: the chewing of coca leaves. It was through ENACO that the state began in 1964 to control both the production and commercialization of coca in the Upper Huallaga. Functioning under an international mandate, two other state authorities were put in charge of limiting the expansion of coca crops and of dealing with the drug traffic: the intelligence police (PIP) and the civil police forces (GC).

ENACO chose to follow a policy based on tolerance and on the relativisation of the problem: aware of its social aspects, it registered producers under the simple denominations of "authorized" and "unauthorized" (Alvarado, 1974). In 1973, ENACO registered 115 "unauthorized" and 0 "authorized" producers in José Crespo y Castillo district (known as Aucayacu).

Coca producers in the Upper Huallaga live mainly on the high grounds above the villages close to Tingo Maria. In the 1960s and early 1970s these producers were relatively privileged. The new policy seemed to be largely designed to protect the well-established, older producers of coca.

However, the sharp rise of cocaine consumption in the United States during these years created a demand which unsettled the social and agricultural equilibrium in the region. Coca production has become highly profitable and thus has tended to replace the growing of other crops. This has nothing to do with the alleged poverty of the local peasants.

An uneasy balance among producers was nevertheless maintained, due in part to the development under state supervision of a large cooperative project designed to "boost the production of rice, maize (corn) and bananas".

The coffee and cacao producers, who had settled in the plains, organized themselves into service-oriented cooperatives, with a focus on the commercialization of their products. The coca producers, on the other hand, given the high profitability of their specific production, tended to keep away from such forms of organization.

The Origins of the "Shining Path"

In the 1960s coca was merely one crop among many others in the Upper Huallaga. But it was mainly in the hands of landowners functioning on the model of the large Latifundia of the Andes. The Pratto and Esquivel families owned about 40 hectares of coca each. The drug traffic thus began to develop in the 1960s out of large crop-growing facilities of this sort. In 1978, in

Aucayacu the "unauthorized" producers were cultivating 1,274 hectares of coca.

The situation began to get out of hand in the early eighties. The progressive militarization of the region occurred in an evolving situation and did not owe much to the theoretical formulations of Abimael Guzman's Ayacucho "Shining Path" Communist Party. At this time, the local drug-traffickers and producers of coca were threatened by the new policy of crop eradication which was set into motion under the Upper Huallaga Valley Coca Reduction Program (CORAH), funded in large measure by the United States government.

The Mobile Rural Patrol Unit (UMOPAR), a police force specially designed to fight against drug-trafficking, and which was also partially funded by the US government, developed a policy of rigor in its fight. Masked collusion between prominent members of the police force and the drug-traffickers themselves was allowed to develop nevertheless, as could be seen when "Commandante Chino Cano" of the UMOPAR left his post at Tingo Maria in 1984: guests invited to the big party he gave on the occasion included not only the main local authorities and the directors of the main local banks, but the big shots of the local coca drug traffickers as well. In January 1987, the GC under pressure of the DEA, captured five polices of the PIP which offering protection armed to traffickers in return money.

As the international community put on pressure for an all-out "war on drugs", the two state institutions mentioned above acquired many repressive powers and a knack for secrecy. Their public image was one of political immorality, and they consequently lost any credibility.

With the suspension of constitutional guarantees in the Upper Huallaga region in 1982, the government of President Fernando Belaunde was practically encouraging the UMOPAR and the PIP to use excessive violence in the region. The situation skidded out of control when these police forces started to perpetrate theft among the Huallaga producers without distinction. The social and economic situation in the region was so bad that it became a fertile ground for added violence. Concomitantly, a new generation of drug-traffickers developed, and it took on a decidedly anti-state bent.

The strike movement which developed at the call of the "Tingo Maria Defense Front" in the High Huallaga in December 1982 was non-violent. It lasted for ten days and was followed by the organization regrouping all the various producers of the region coffee and cacao growers as well as producers of coca down to and including the store owners. This shows the high degree of solidarity and social dynamism the population of the Upper Huallaga had at the time (Magallanes, 1989).

The new "Shining Path" myth that developed in the High Huallaga during the early eighties was in many ways similar to the "Pyshtaco" myth that developed in the early sixties in Tingo Maria-Aucayacu.[3] Both acquired the habit of striking during the night. During 1983-1985, a number of civilian authorities assimilated to "lackeys of the state" were executed during the night, as were workers working for the new crop eradication project under the slogan of "Yankee Out". Peasants accused of informing the UMOPAR police were also murdered.

The period in which such clandestine violence developed in the most strategically situated coca-producing areas of the Upper Huallaga culminated in February 1985. At this time the main road between Tingo Maria and Aucayacu was effectively closed by the summary execution by rifle-fire and machetes of eighteen persons accused by the new "compañeros" (comrades) of being "informers of the UMOPAR". According to the local population, as can be determined from interviews, this was clearly perpetrated by the "narcos", the drug-traffickers. For the personnel of the main governmental projects, most of whom came from the coast, it was a feat of the "Shining Path", who had come from Ayacucho.

A number of executions were thus perpetrated during the single year of 1985 in the Upper Huallaga which give us a general idea of the trend taken by increased violence in the region. The list of victims include:

55-year-old X Cavero, who owned 70 hectares of land distributed between La Roca and Venenillo, on which he grew both cacao and coca and raised some cattle. He was hanged and his tongue cut out for "non-participation in local meetings".

35-year-old X Mancini, former buyer of coca production in the areas of Pueblo Neuvo, La Roca and Venenillo, was also hanged and had his tongue cut out for "wishing to quit the 'filas' ('groups')".

24-year-old X Anatolia M., also a buyer of coca, was killed by bullets and had her tongue cut out, as well as her breasts. Her shaved body was discovered with a sign on her saying: "This is how informers die." She was accused of being on friendly terms with the UMOPAR.

As we can readily see from this list, all the declared "motives" were in one way or the other related to the drug traffic.

In the Cavero case, we can easily assume that what was of prime interest for the so-called "compañeros" was his strategically situated lands near Venenillo, where the new intermediaries in the drug traffic were implanted. Killing Cavero served as a sign for the old coca producers of the area that they had to leave and let their lands be redistributed among more amenable "new" producers.

It should be noticed that during this period, the PIP, like the UMOPAR, was supposed to lead the fight against drug-trafficking. They were not supposed to deal with "Shining Path" terrorism. It was thus easy for the new generation of drug-traffickers to pass off as "Shining Path" terrorists when confronted with easily-corrupted police officers.

Not long after being installed in 1985, President Alan Garcia Perez turned in July 1986 to the Lima-based "Research Center on Peruvian Amazonia" (CIPA) for an evaluation of the various Upper Huallaga "special projects", in order to profit from renewed US Agency for International Development (AID) financing of projects designed to control coca production. In its evaluation, the CIPA singled out the "Shining Path Movement" as deserving closer scrutiny. It based its report on outdated evidence furnished by technicians who had been living in Tingo Maria since the beginning of 1986, that is, precisely at the time when the drug-lords-inspired terrorism was shedding its anonymity.

Having monopolized violence in the area, the terrorist groups were by then coming out of hiding. They started to organize "the people" in associative structures encompassing the whole coca and *pasta básica de cocaína* (PBC or "pyschicata") producing territory of the Upper Huallaga. These organizations were directly inspired by the former organizing structures set up by the old coca producers, as well as those set up starting in the late seventies by the bigger Huallaga drug traffickers.

By the end of 1986, there were no other formal organizations in the region but that "of the people": these "people's" organizations are not unlike the producers' "cooperatives" that were first set up in the region at the time of the first colonization drive in Huallaga, but with an important difference now, all contact with the outside was severed, and the "organizing" was accomplished through the use of violence. The shift became all the clearer in January 1987, when President Job Orlandini and the last of his associates within the Arequipa Production Cooperative were executed by the "compañeros". A total of 500 hectares were thus freed for redistribution among new migrants willing to produce coca and be put under the control of "intermediaries" ("heads" or "chiefs"). The 400 heads of cattle belonging to the cooperative were then served as a repast to the "chiefs" and their families.

The "Shining Path" Center

The "compañeros" active in Upper Huallaga let it be known that they acted under the strict orders of a "Shining Path" "Center" situated in Ayacucho: they called it the "Mohene 'Shining Path' Center". The execution of individuals, or whatever needed to be implemented through the use of force was done in the name of that entirely fictive "Center".

Here again, this seeming "originality" of the terrorists tied to the drug-traffic actually copied the prior practice of the old Huallaga agricultural cooperatives: when they still existed, they were hierarchally tied to the "Aucayacu Central of Cooperatives".

When in 1986 a married couple of primary school teachers were executed in public for the first time in Pueblo Nuevo, the "comrades" perpetrating the deed justified themselves as doing it in observance of orders from the "Center in Mohene". The hamlet of Mohene was the place where people had been murdered during the phase when the drug-related terrorism was still "anonymous" and clandestine. It had since become a key area for the illegal production of coca. Its very name meant danger, and induced instant fear. In the same manner, and for very much the same reasons, "Venenillo" could be cited as a place where the "Center" resided. Still later, for the Uchiza and Aucayacu "compañeros" Pueblo Nuevo became the "Center" (or "Central"), that is, the mythic place where the "Shining Path" "High Chiefs" where said to reside.

During the whole of 1987, when the drug - traffickers' influence was not yet felt in Sortilegio and San Isidro (known as Hermilio Valdizan) the "Central" for the producers of both coffee and coca was situated in Pueblo Nuevo and in Aucayacu. But when the terrorists tied to drug trafficking finally established themselves in the area by executing the woman president of the school children's parents association, they legitimated their act as being done "on orders" from the Locro "Central". The President's son identified the murderer of his mother as being one of the "intermediaries" working for an important Locro drug lord. Presently, Sortilegio and San Isidro are places where "Shining Path" "High Chiefs" are said to reside.

In the so-called "liberated - zones", the population is forced to enter totalitarian organizations which are totally independent from the state. The "terrorists" under the whims of whom they have to live are but "intermediaries" for the big overlords, whose specific job is to collect the drug.

In December 1986, two rival gangs for the control of the local drug market came to heads in an open fight in Uchiza. One was the E. Calvo gang, which had taken on the "Shining Path" name, and the other, a group of new drug traffickers who had taken on the name of the "MRTA". It was E. Calvo's "Shining Path" who won. Escalante Calvo had a long history, which serves to reveal the very roots of the movement. He had not only under him a full network of drug collectors; he had also built up a small army of bodyguards made up of Peruvian as well as Colombian nationals ("Sicarios"). Armed self-defense organizations of the traffickers with influence "Sicarios" had operated in Uchiza⁴ and Aucayacu. Escalante Calvo's organization may serve as an example of all the other "Shining Path" organizations in the Upper Huallaga. Through such organizational structures, the local population was controlled and made subservient to the main actors in the drug traffic.

For example, in Tocache an ancient town of trafficker of cocaine and "red areas", the terrorism of drug dealers is as an act against the Police and the Army. A January 1989 article in Debate magazine outlines the trend of terrorism in Tocache in the following terms: "here, terrorism is only the total displeasure of the population" against "the State"(Umberto, 1989, p. 18). The terrorism is thus an act which results from a broad feeling, but the "population" is still confused with it. Peruvian anthropologist Luis Roman Villanueva once remarked that "the armed actions may be to see a war by the officers of the State or of the DEA" (Villanueva, 1989, pp.1-2).

The concept of an "armed strike" was designed to isolate the whole drug producing territory from anything which might be taken in the Upper Huallaga as representing the repressive state: bridges were thus destroyed, main roads were blocked, fire was set to the local offices of the main state projects. The first such official "armed strike" was launched by the terrorists tied to the drug-traffic in January 1987, with the participation of the "people".

"Popular justice" was dealt with during "popular meetings" to which the population was summoned to follow and participate in the whole ritual of trial followed by the immediate execution of the accused victim, a death- ritual where the people were in fact taught, first and foremost, to hold their tongue, (if they really wanted to hold onto them).

People who were merely opposed to violence, people who were opposed to the production of coca, as well as the new buyers of coca production who wanted to get a piece of the market were accused of being "traitors", "informers", or "latifundists". It so happens that a "Chato" - a "High Chief" - from Aucayacu, who was himself responsible for the death of 140 persons since he had begun his own reign in 1987, was caught in 1990 and publicly condemned and executed by other "Chiefs" and the "People".

The notion of "punishment" (or "just retribution") came to be widely used in this period, and was later used with the same connotations by the Army. It implied fault on the side of the victim, and reason or justice on the side of the persecutor. It came to be closely tied to the sense of death - "chifado" (from a word used in the Chinese restaurants of Peru to name a dish of chopped food).

A so-called "delegate" was present at the trials. His function seems to have been of a mediator. He did not belong to the higher echelons of the "Shining Path" movement, and his power was hence very limited. He could save the life of a designated "victim" by arguing, for example, that he or she needed to be judged within his or her own jurisdiction. The "delegate" often did restore, at the risk of his own life, the corpses of victims of the "terror" to their families, as no one was allowed to retrieve them after an execution.

A "popular participation" tax which amounted to US $975 in 1987 was forcefully imposed on the members of the different organizations, and were used by networks infiltrated within the army and police forces to buy arms of to help the release of "comrades" arrested by these same forces.

A "Comrade Maico" was officially arrested in 1989 by the army on the grounds that he was an important drug dealer. The local rumor had it that he was a "High Chief sent from Ayacucho by Abimael Guzman". Together with a woman accomplice known as the "Indian", he had used money raised through the local "people's organizations" to buy arms from the police and drugs for their own profit. He was soon set free. In October 1992, disguised as "terrorists", a group of soldiers from the army entered a village in the Aucayacu region and killed "Maico", The money the army was said to have seized on that occasion was fairly modest: US $3,000. Starting in the early nineties, a "Maico" myth developed nevertheless, representing him as a new "mando" of the "Shining Path" in the new drug trafficking hub of Aguaytia.

Relations Between the Army, "Shining Path" and "MRTA"

When the army started to intervene in Upper Huallaga in 1987 as the main representative of the state, tolerance for the narco-traffic began to prevail and total rejection of the state declined as a working propaganda issue.

After having established bases in Aucayacu and Tulumayo, in November 1987 the army led a sweeping operation in the villages of Huallaga with the help of eight helicopters. The army detachment, after ransacking the larger mansions, captured three "High Chiefs", "Mercado", "Trompa", and the "Professor". They were freed a few weeks later for $10,000 each. Money was also robbed from individual's and more modest houses. This was the army's way of retaliating against the "Shining Path" ambush at the end of the previous month, during which the army had killed more than 30 of the 200 young peasants who had been forcefully recruited for the task.

When the army got hold of the "Chato" in 1988, the local population was glad to see a prominent local dealer and murderer arrested. He was soon freed however on a $15,000 bail. The army did not hesitate, on the other hand, to execute in 1989 an Aucayacu radio journalist on the grounds that he was telling "too much truth". Amauta magazine cities the example of an engineer and various peasants killed by the army in Tocache (*Amanta*, 1989).

With the presence of North American DEA and Peruvian anti-narcotics police at the Santa Lucia base close to Uchiza, clandestine operations by the drug-carrying "avionettes" were moved out of fields close to Uchiza and Paraiso and relocated to a new site close to Aucayacu: at a time when the kilogram of PBC was worth between $150 and 200, each sortie by an "avionette" was taxed by the local army and police forces between $15,000 and 30,000.

Since 1989, the army has adopted the habit of chasing "terrorists" and drug traffickers in clandestine operations where soldiers are disguised as "terrorists". People caught during such operations could be released on the spot against $1,000 to 3,000 fines. When they were brought to the base camp, the so-called fine would be propped up to $10,000 to 15,000 per head. English journalist Jonathan Cavanagh has reported that in March 1989 the current UMOPAR Chief told him that drug dealers routinely offered him "about $10,000" for their immediate release (Cavanagh, p.25). In December 1991, the Tulumayo base police's "Los Sinchis" captured three people accused of being "Shining Path spies"; they were released on a payment amounting to US $5,000.

During this same year 1991, the army massacred seven peasants with stones and bayonets to encourage the people to believe in a "Shining Path" action. One peasant survived to tell the story. Two people caught during the action simply disappeared, as did somewhat later a soldier who had testified to having brought their food to the prisoners. The one important drug dealer who was caught in the action was freed after having paid $20,000 and left to pursue his trade in the Aguaytia region under another name. Massacres and kidnappings perpetrated by the Peruvian army in the Upper Huallaga during the years 1991 - 1992 have been well documented by Amnesty International's London office (1992).

These massacres served to reinforce the thesis of an opposition between the "Shining Path" and "MRTA" movements in the Upper Huallaga, and to confuse the peasants and farmers of the region in forcing them to hold their tongues or in dealing with them in the most gratuitous ways. "Delegates" and "important 'Shining Path' High Chiefs" were of far greater worth. "Terrorists" and "traffickers" ended up lacking sufficient financial means. As a result of these confrontations, the number of murdered due to the anti-drug war and to terrorism in Upper Huallaga rose dramatically, from only 20 in 1983 to 392 in 1988 and 50 in 1996.

On the occasion of the National Day on July 28, 1992, an Army Captain from the base in Aucayacu, Esparza Salinas, organized a festive commemoration of it on the same lines as the "popular parties of the people" given in 1986 to 1989 by the so-called "Shining Path" party. The new National Day party was of course carried out in honor of the Army. The Army sought legitimacy by thus meeting the population for an entire week, donating nice presents to winners in the sports competition. A dancing party was organized which lasted for three days. All benefits from beer and ticket sales were pocketed by the Army Captain. A woman hired by the army sang the hymn: *"March soldier, go on soldier with force and courage. . ."* The whole parody of this exemplary National Day was broadcast on television.

Nevertheless, certain facts were left unclarified. Thus, one week before the 28th of July, Captain Esparza Salinas had urged the 600 businessmen of Aucayacu to "collaborate" by donating $50 per person for the organization of the party. During the week preceding National Day two lightweight aircraft transporting drugs left Aucayacu and were intercepted by a helicopter of the DEA. Captain Esparza had demanded 20 "cocos" for each aircraft departure. One "coco" is equivalent to $1000. Captain Esparza was linked to the drug trafficker William Alvarado Linares (known as "Champa"). He committed himself to executing some "trequeteros" (intermediate drug dealers) who were enemies of "Champa". Among those executed was a certain "Davila" who had quit "Champa". Under the orders of the latter, Captain Esparza captured him at Aucayacu and executed him there, despite efforts by his family to liberate him.

Another drug dealer, "comrade Magencio", was captured by the Army in Esperanza in November 1993. According to the population, "chief Magencio" had himself executed a father and his son in a fake "popular meeting". The Army used "Magencio" as an informer to capture other drug dealers. He was then liberated by the Army. Two other smugglers who had been captured through information provided by "Magencio" were freed after several days and only after having paid $10,000. Though they were by no means prominent figures in the drug cartel, both were nevertheless imprisoned at Huanuco. They were set free in 1995 after their families had paid large sums.

At the end of June 1995, the government promoted heavy media coverage of the capture of the drug trafficker Cachique Rivera, (known as "El Negro") of Upper Huallaga. He was depicted as having been wanted since the 1980s by the intelligence police (PIP) (Reyes, 1995, pp.22-29). This supposedly "notorious" drug trafficker lived in Locro, close to the Base of Tulumayo, which had been a UMOPAR base, before being used by the Army and the Police. "El Negro" was a member of armed organizations that fought against programs run by CORAH aimed at the eradication of coca plant cultures.

Cachique Rivera was given a life sentence by a "military tribunal with hidden faces". However, in August, 1995, the Military court of Lima commuted the sentence to 30 years in prison. How can one account for this sudden clemency on the part of the military judges? The answer is fairly obvious: the drug trafficker was forced to confess along the lines of the "narco-guerilla" indictment drawn up by the military judges. Cachique Rivera did not question the charges brought up by the military judges, according to whom he had set up an alliance with the terrorists of the "Shining Path" and the "MRTA". He did not contest that the drug traffickers paid large sums to the terrorists who controlled the clandestine airports which they used to fly out cocaine, and that they moreover handed over modern arms to the guerilleros (*Expreso*, 1995, A 12).

The Upper Huallaga drug trafficker known as the "Vaticano" testified from January to August 1996 at the trial of General Jaime Robles Araico and Eduardo Bellido Mora, two former heads of the politico-military Commando of High Huallaga, that he had entertained close relations with them during the years 1991 - 1993. The declarations he made on Peruvian television in June and July about these close ties could not but mark the beginning of the end of the official "narco-guerrilla" thesis.

"Vaticano" made many public statements to this effect on Peruvian television in June and July 1996. This of course was a clear rebuttal of the official "narco-guerrilla" thesis. One can therefore well imagine the kind of treatment that "Vaticano" had to undergo in high security prison in order to withdraw his former statements. He did indeed withdraw them at the end of his trial, and the military judges only condemned General Jaime Rios Araico (*Quehacer*, 1996, pp. 56-58). These facts, nonetheless, are clear evidence of the dubious role played by the Army.

From June to July 1995 in Aucayacu, two drug trafficker gangs led respectively by "Champa" and Claudio (known as "Cristal"), engaged in a shootout which left more than 40 dead. Both gangs were supposed to be "Shining Path" guerrillas. In actual fact, according to the local people, the two groups were fighting each other because one supported the Army and the other the Police. Meanwhile, the Police, disguised as "terrorists", got involved in the confrontation by hijacking some Aucayacu villagers and, while misled by the operation, killed and wounded some policemen which it took for real terrorists. The resulting scandal revealed that the Army and the Police were in rivalry to share in the profits of the two smuggler gangs.

This only added to the crisis of legitimacy which the government had to face since the exoneration of General Eduardo Bellido Mora concerning his links with "Vaticano". An operation was launched in August 1996, which led to the capture of the drug trafficker "Champa" in Ecuador. President Fujimori himself entered the fray. He described "Champa" as the heir of the drug "capos" who controlled the market of Upper Huallaga up to the border with Columbia. He was said to be closely linked to the Medellin cartel and to have exported more than 3000 kilograms of drugs per month; he was, moreover, accused of having ordered numerous executions in order to control the commercialization of narcotics. President Fujimori took the opportunity to congratulate the Chief of the intelligence police (PIP), Doctor Vladimiro Montesions.

However, the operation brought out three embarrassing facts. First, as the newspaper Expreso revealed, "Champa" himself had formerly been a policeman (*Expresso*, 1996, p. A12). Second, the clandestine airport of Aucayacu, supposed to be under control of the terrible "Champa", "Cristal", "Cachique", and others, was located a mere 200 m. from the Aucayacu Army Base. Third, "Champa" was only one among many other drug traffickers who instigated the terrorism in Upper Huallaga under the banner of "Shining Path" and "MRTA".

Fortunately though, not all the army officers were corrupt. It was an army General, José-Luis Morales Hidalgo, who convinced Cachique Rivera to acknowledge having paid, together with 10 other drug traffickers of Upper Huallaga, $100,000 a month to the military chief of the Mantaro front line, General David Jaime Sobrevilla, for the right to use the landing runway from 1993 to 1995. $25,000 were to be paid for each lightweight aircraft carrying a load of drugs.

Drug dealers from Aucayacu and Aguaytia who worked for large-scale drug traffickers had confirmed in 1990 the existence of an enormous clandestine airfield in Villa Coca in the central forest (Mantaro). It enabled the drug traffickers to circumvent Upper Huallaga and Aguaytia where the armed forces and the police were under severe surveillance by the DEA.

In response to these embarrassing revelations, retired General David Jaime Sobrevilla came up at once with the "narco-guerilla" thesis. He insisted that military operations against drug traffickers in the coca region of the central forest accounted for only 5% of all military operations. "And the rest of the military activity was directed against subversion, for this zone was the homeland of terrorism" (*La Republica Policial*, 1997). What General Jaime Sobrevilla was desperately trying to do was to carry on what General Alberto Arciniaga had begun at the Base of Uchiza in Upper Huallaga in 1989: organized corruption under the cover of a war waged against the armed movements for "national liberation". Others would call him the "anti-Sendero" general (or the general of the "revolutionary strategy" against "Shining Path").

Conclusion

To attribute prime responsibility for the violence in the Upper Huallaga and Aguaytia regions of Amazonia to entities such as the "Shining Path" and the "MRTA" merely serves to divert any serious study away from the criminal activities of the mafia in these regions; more seriously, it conceals the collusion between law - enforcers and criminals and thus cover up corruption and crime on the part of state institutions.

But one should also remain attentive to the other negative effects of the all-out war on drug production and trafficking, which was largely instigated on the international level by the United States government. It was because elite consumption of cocaine rose sharply in the wealthier nations of

North America and Europe that a policy of repression and plant-eradication came to be implemented in the poorer countries of the South where legal controls and legal institutions were weaker. In Peru's Upper Huallaga and Aguaytia regions, the fragile social order collapsed as crime, corruption and "revolutionary" movements such as the "Shining Path" and "MRTA" increasingly preyed on the local economy and made life terribly miserable for the average inhabitants of the region. With such a "top-down" form of blind repression resulting in an all-out "laissez-faire" towards all forms of unlawful behavior and exploitation, the resurgence of the "Pyschtaco" myth in the region can be seen as translating the reaction of the local populace to these new conditions.

Notes

1 The names of several people in this chapter, including the author's, have been changed for their protection.

2 My concept of myth is influenced by the concept of "technical myth" as used in the study of "Modern Myth" (Cassier, 1993).

3 "Pyschtaco" ("The Butcher"): Name of an ancient Andean Indian myth according to which a powerful but terrifying and "butcher"-like character going by that name preyed upon the people at night, cutting their throats in order to feed upon their (white) fat. The name was revived among Andean Indian farm-hands during the 1960s in the Upper Huallaga valley. At this time, the Peruvian government in Lima had just introduced a distinction between "lawful" and "unlawful" production of coca in the area, and part of the production of cocaine base paste (called "pyschicata", the "ground stuff", because it was obtained through the "grinding" of coca leaves), went "underground" to be produced largely under the cover of darkness. The name "pyschicatero" referred exclusively to these illegal "grinders" of coca leaves, who were still working for the large plantation owners. They drew the "fat" from the "people" in order to have it transported away during the night in small airplanes to other "powerful" people living in North America. The phonetic proximity between "pyschtaco" and "pyschicatero" was close enough for the ancient myth to be revived and play out its effects in a wholly new context. The new drug-traffickers came to be called "pyschicateros".

4 "Murió el colombiano traído desde Uchiza", April 7, 1989, *La República*, p. 16.

References

Alvarado, Jara, Antonio Eulalio. 1974. Diagnastico socio-econimico del cultivo y la comercializacion de la coca en la provincia de Leoncio Prado, Tingo María: UNAS.

Amnesty International. Secrétariat International. May 1992. Reprint. "PEROU Les droits de l'homme sous le gouvernement du président Alberto Fujimori." Londres: Amnesty International. Original edition 1992.

Amuata. "Crimen militar en Tocache creo que mataste un ingeniero", March 30 1989.

Cassirer, Ernest. 1993. Reprint. Le mythe de l'Etat. Paris: Gallimard. Original edition, 1946.

Cavanagh, Jonathan. Marzo 1989. "Negocios en la Selva narco - senderista." *América Economia* No 25. p.26

Clawson, Patrick L., Lee, Rensselaer W. 1996. *The Andean Cocaine Industry.* London: Macmillan Press Ltd.

Debray, Regis. 1967. revolution dans la revolution? lutte arme et lutte politique en amerique latine. Paris: Francois Maspero, cahiers libres no 98.

For a detailed of Shining Path of Peru, see: Mercado, Roger. 1982. Reprint. El partido comunista del Perú: Sendero Luminoso. Lima: Cultura Popular. Original edition, non data.

See: El MRTA en la Selva. 13 de Abril de 1989. Cambio. p. 1-24.

Expreso. "Justicia militar revoco cadena perpetua. Rebajan a treinta años de prisión condena a narco Abelardo Cachique Rivera," August 29 1995, p. A12.

Expreso. "Pobladores de la region solicitan ayuda. Dos 'firmas' se enfrentan en el río Napo: 23 traficantes muertos," October 16, 1996, p. A12.

González, Raúl. 89-90. "Las Armas de un General." *Quehacer,* diciembre 89-enero 1990: 38-43.

Jara, Umberto. Enero 1989. "Un poder que se expande." Contacto en el Alto Huallaga. *Debate,* p.18.

Labrousse, Alain, Hertoghe, Alain. 1989. *Le Sentier Lumineux du Pérou, un nouvel intégrisme dans le tiers monde.* Paris: La Découverte.

Magallanes, José. 1989. *Politica agricola del Estado y estrategias de las organizaciones campesinas: el Alto Huallaga.* Ginebra: IUED

ONU. 1987. *Las Naciones Unidas y la Fiscalizacion del uso indebido de Drogas.* New York, New York.

Palmer, David. "Shining Path of Peru." (New York Press 1992) in Bruce H. Kay. 1997. *Revolution, Inc: Guerrillas and the illicit drug business in Peru.* Duke-University of North Carolina Program in Latin American Studies.

Quehacer, julio-agosto 1996. "La corrupcion y las drogas. 56-58

Reyes, Francisco. 1995. Cachique lo cuenta todo. *Sí.* (12 June): 22-29.

Ruggiero, Romano. 1983. Deux fausses équations: coca bonne = cocaïne bonne; coca mauvaise = cocaïne mauvaise. *Cahiers Wilfredo Pareto.* Tome XXI.

Villanueva Roman, Luis. Agosto 1989. La coca violenta del Huallaga. Alerta Agrario, p.1-2

10 Organized Crime in Russ Domestic and Internation Problems

YAKOV GILINSKIY

Organized Crime as a Social Phenomenon

Organized crime is the functioning of stable, hierarchical associations engaged in crime as a business. These criminal organizations are most prosperous when they manage to create a system of protections from adversarial elements (such as governmental regulation and enforcement of criminal statutes) by means of corruption. Although some inherent features of criminal associations (e.g. the strict selection of staff, high labor discipline and the undivided focus on profit) would seem to ensure the great vitality of these organization, opportunities for the success of these criminal operations are largely dependent on external social factors (such as periods of economic and governmental destabilization, etc.). In the case of Russia, I will examine how the unstable, modern period of reform has heightened the opportunity for, and the spoils of, crime.

The members of criminal gangs are neither heroes nor villains. They are people engaged in a form of business which makes sense to them. Nobel Prize Winner in Economics, G. Becker, suggests that criminal activity is a recognizable profession which people devote their energies to, not unlike teaching or engineering. It is chosen when the profit (revenue minus costs) exceeds that of a comparable legal occupation (Becker, 1987). The criminological literature on organized crime echoes this blurred distinction between business and crime (Abadinsky, 1994; Albanese, 1995). In fact, many of the indispensable features of criminal organizations parallel those of corporations.

Criminal organizations feature:
* a stable association of people, designed for long-term activity
* financial pursuits dependent on criminal activity
* the goal of maximizing profit
* a complex and unambiguous hierarchical structure

- the goal of disabling, negating, or infiltrating agencies that hinder the growth of the crime agency.
- the aspiration to monopolize (its particular form of trade) in their territories.

Are we always in a position to draw a distinction between legal business and illegal business enterprises utilizing a criteria of morality and legal statute? In Russia it is hardly possible. Russia serves as an example of the internationalization of organized crime. The normal functioning of a major world-power has been infiltrated and is being influenced by crime bosses. The following section explains how and why this has come to be and reveals both the domestic and international fronts of Russian organized crime.

Organized Crime in Russia

Organized crime, after 1917, existed in the form of gangsterism. By the 1930s, these informal bands of criminals had evolved into professional swindlers and thieves. Living by the "thief's law", an honor code for those who chose crime as a way of life, these career criminals soon infiltrated the "legitimate" institutions of Russia. By the 1950s, a class of white collar criminals (known as Tyenyeveci or "shady dealers") were recognizable. Their stock in trade was misappropriation of collective property, participation and fueling of black markets and bribing party functionaries and state officials. In the modern era, with Russia's currency and government wildly unstable, these "white collar" criminals have become allied with the street-level criminal. This new mafia of businessmen and thugs is prospering in a smash-and-grab period of radical reform, privatization, liberalization and decentralization of economic bases.

The economic reform under way in Russia, the transition from a planned state-run economy to an open marketplace, is, with little doubt, of a progressive nature. Alongside of these changes, criminogenic activities are occurring. The redistribution of property is being undertaken with not only legal methods but with bribery, intimidation and murders. A sharp stratification of wealth and standing has occurred leading to a population of a pauperized majority and a newly prosperous minority (the so-called "New Russian"). For the mass of Russian people, underemployment is the norm. For the leadership of Russia, their efforts of economic reform, regardless of sincerity of intent, are accompanied by corruption, incompetence, schemes such as nomenclatural privatization, etc. (See: Handelman, 1995; Nisaco, Lamothe, 1995; Schmid, 1996). The prospects for true reform are dim.

Mafia tribute-seeking from legitimate commercial structures

In the public sector, the mechanism for corruption is infiltration, in the "private" sector it is tribute-seeking. There are two common forms of tribute-based rackets in Russia. The imposition of a tribute (pay-off) on small shops and extortion of tribute from commercial organizations. In the latter case, the mafia receives the tribute as recompense for undertaking the organization's debt-collections or for other "professional services". Criminals have a distinct niche in the "taking care of business" racket. Who better than strong-arms who are not legally allied with businesses to collect debt when the decisions of arbitration courts cannot force payment?

Since 1993, the Center on Deviance of the St. Petersburg Branch of the Institute of Sociology of the Russian Academy of Sciences has undertaken a study of the black market and criminal organizations in Russia. Findings demonstrate that most commercial structures are embraced by rackets. The informational network of mafia groups in St. Petersburg is well-organized and focused on scouting enterprises that begin to make excellent profits. At this point, the mafia penetrates the new commercial structure and exacts its tribute. The racket has infested all manner of enterprises with the possible exception of the military and some foreign firms.

Fields of criminal activities, other than shake-downs, in St. Petersburg include bank transactions involving forged documents, hijacking and reselling of cars, arms sale, money laundering and control over gambling and prostitution services. The Center on Deviance notes that criminal respondents are eager to move out of these more pedestrian criminal enterprises and focus their energies on emerging hi-tech domains for crime and in grabbing the spoils of privatization. Mafiosi obtain information on upcoming real estate auctions and intimidate prospective buyers into not bidding to "avoid trouble". The criminal organizations procure real estate at the lowest possible prices in this manner. Criminal organizations also overtake industries by purchasing shares from workers until the point of acquiring the controlling number of shares.

The criminalization of Russian business is hard to overstate. Respondents to interviews by the Center on Deviance claim, "one can not do business without illegal dealings...the medium of the businessman is extremely criminalized...one has to bribe for everything debts are collected through force...tax inspections are highly corrupt and accompanied with bribery...Mafiosi sit among members of the boards of banks, etc".

The threat to Russia's domestic stability

It is this corruption that is the main danger to Russia. Corruption is inescapable in all commerce, bodies of governance and law enforcement agencies. In recent years, Russia has been consistently ranked among the top ten countries in the International Corruption Ranking of Transparency International *(Moscow News*, 1996). It is hard to imagine, however, a country more totally corrupted. The war in Chechnya, total governmental corruption, massive human rights abuses, particularly in armed services and penitentiary settings where tyranny and torture dominate and the power of criminal capital bespeak the fact that contemporary Russia is a criminal state (see Handelman, 1995; Schmid, 1996). "Organized crime has controlled government since 1994-1995...the mechanisms of the State have been criminalized" (Dolgova, 1996). The reaction of the people is terror. The survey results from the Center on Deviance shows 56% of respondents stating that they are under threat from aggression or violence and 42% feeling under the direct threat of organized crime.

Fear of crime hardens people and demands to curb crime arise. Authorities typically offer harsher punishments as the main weapon to fight crime. Legislation rarely ameliorates the problem and in the case of the Decree of the President of Russian Federation No. 1226, urgent measures on the protection of the population from gangs and other displays of organized crime, legislation can trample on civil rights protections or contradict the Constitution of the Russian Federation.

Narcobusiness: Russian Organized Crime Beyond its Borders

The success of Russian organized crime abroad (especially in the narcotics trade) can be largely attributed to the corruption of law-enforcement agencies and authority structures at home. The political games that the Russian government plays with narcotic-exporting countries (such as Azerbaijan, Chechnia and the states of Middle Asia), further dilute the authority of Russian agencies to combat drug trade. Corruption of law-enforcement officials, assigned to stem narcotics trade, is common, although Russian police officers rarely become leaders of the Russian narcomafia. It is not rare, however, for officers to be low-level functionaries in the drug trade, or to comprise part of the consumer base. Clearly, the indirect indices of the scope of the problem, brought to public light by sensationalized drug raids and seizure of drugs by custom officials, suggest an increasingly menacing issue. As far as official data, there is 7.7 times more registered crimes in 1996 than 1988. The main body of crimes consist of drug dealing, manufacturing, purchasing and possession. It should be noted that Russian police prefer to arrest and prosecute cases involving drug *consumers*. It is easier to prove the guilt of users than to trace a path, and establish the guilt, of distributors. The massive amount of drugs confiscated by police and customs officials attests to the magnitude of trade across borders. In 1992 22,000 kilograms of narcotics were confiscated. A peak year for confiscations was 1994, with more than 80,000 kilograms. In recent years, the amount of confiscated narcotics have leveled off with 49,425 and 43,528 kilograms, respectively, for 1995 and 1996 (State of Crime in Russia, 1996, 1997).

Conclusion

The following traits of organized crime are typical in Russia:
- It is widespread, exerting control over a majority of the country's enterprises and banks.
- Its criminal activity yields an extremely high profit.
- Organized crime associations perform many of the traditional functions of courts and law enforcement agencies (i.e. enforcement of arbitration rulings, providing protection, collecting debt, etc.)
- A wide social basis for organized crime exists owing to underemployment and social anomie.
- Violence is the most common method for resolving problems and removing obstacles to profit.

Russia is moving farther along towards a state of general criminalization. The social, economic, political and moral condition of the country provides no basis for optimism. Domestic stability is threatened by organized crime groups that have effectively grabbed the reins of state leadership, through their powerful influence upon legitimate officials. Internationally, narcotics trade flourishes across Russian borders and compounds the country's domestic woes with growing numbers of addicts. Democracy and true economic reform, should they be the sincere goal of a new Russia, are clearly jeopardized by the current state of affairs.

References

Abadinsky, Howard. (1994), *Organized Crime*. Fourth Edition. Chicago: Nelson Hall.
Albanese, Jay. (1995), "Organized Crime: the Mafia Mystique." *In Criminology. A Contemporary Handbook*. Ed. By J. Sheley. Wadsworth Publishing Company.
Becker, G. (1987), *Economic Analysis and Human Behavior. Advances in Behavioral Sciences*. Norwood. (N.Y.): Ablex Publ. Corp. V.1 p.3-17.
Dolgova, Azalia. Ed. (1996), *The criminal situation and changes in Russia*. Moscow: Association for Criminology. (in Russian).
Handelman, Stephen. (1995), *Comrade Criminal. Russia's New Mafia*. Yale University New Haven: London Press.
Moscow News 1996. No. 5.
Nisco, Antonio and Lamothe, Lee. (1995), *Global mafia. The New World Order of Organized Crime*. Toronto: MacMillan.
Schmid, Ulrich. (1996), *Gnadenlose Bruderschaften Aufsteig der russichen Mafia*. Zurich: Verlag Neue Zuricher Zeitung.
State of Crime in Russia, 1996. (1997), Moscow: MVD RF (in Russian).

11 Regionalization and Expansion: The Growth of Organized Crime in East Siberia

ANNA L. REPETSKAYA

The present state of criminality in Russia is closely related to changes in the Russian government. The process of regionalization resulting from these changes have forced criminal organizations to focus their attention not only on large cities (e.g. Moscow, St. Petersburg), but on territories of separate regions of the Russian Federation. One of these regions is East Siberia. Situated in the center of Russia, East Siberia is the junction of transport roads from the Far East, North and South Eastern Asia and from central parts of Russia and Middle Asia.

Factors related to the criminalization of East Siberia

The resources in East Siberia attract the attention of criminal organizations. Enormous reserves of strategic and raw materials are confined in this region. Ventures for the processing of Siberia's natural resources- coal, gas, wood, fur, gold, aluminum, etc. necessitate financing, export and sales, institutions that further entice criminal agencies.

   The penal and correctional institutions that had been situated in Siberia have resulted in increased criminalization of the territory. One third of discharged prisoners from these institutions settle in Siberia.

   The creation of joint stock companies and privatization processes that are not always rational, as well as a depressed and unstable economy leading to unemployment both patent and latent, have lead to an increased level of population anxiety. In such a setting, it is not surprising that criminality in the region grows according to absolute and relative indexes. Unfortunately, the tendency towards increasing recidivist, group crimes, including organized crime, remains unchanged.

At the same time, the state of organized crime is not the same in different regions of East Siberia. A clearly defined tendency is observed here; the increase in industrial development, leads to higher indices of organized crime.

In comparing the indices of recorded crimes committed by organized crime groups in different parts of the region it will be noted that the greatest number of crimes committed by organized criminal groups (OCG) are in large industrial centers of the region. In 1996, there were 569 in Irkust Region; 369 in Krasnoyarsk Territory; 191 in Buryatia; 256 in Chita Region; 72 in Tuva; 156 in Khakassia.

The Irkutsk Region is the center of enhanced criminal activity of organized crime in Siberia. In 1996 the East Siberian Regional Board on Organized Crime (ES RBOC) revealed 99 criminal formations in Irkutsk that numbered 387 persons. According to official data the aggregate damage from criminal activity of organized crime groups is more than 10 million dollars.

The growth of crime in Irkutsk is phenomenal. At the present time, no fewer than 198 OCG's have been identified consisting of 918 persons. Nine OCG's have intra- and interregional criminal relations and 12 groups associate with criminals from the Countries of the Commonwealth and from China and Mongolia. Total cash income of criminal groups are no less than 20 million dollars. And this is in a single region (Irkutsk) of the territory.

Siberian Crime Groups and Their Specializations

The pattern of organized crime in Siberia is diverse: there are a lot of the so-called "Siberian" and ethnic groups which compete for leadership and associate with representatives of the underground world abroad. The East Siberian RBOC has discovered 4 such ethnically-based criminal communities which account for 75 organized criminal groups involving 556 persons. These are the "Bratsk", "Georgia", "Northern Caucasia" and "Azerbaijan" communities. These groups are constantly redistributing their spheres of influence and mastering new means of legalization of shadow capital. All this is accompanied by armed violence relative to competitors in criminal businesses, and intimidation and cooption of the leaders of financial and commercial structures.

Specialization of the criminal activity of groups is rather traditional. There are many types of criminal businesses such as: arms trade, narcotics trafficking, extortion, financial fraud, illegal operations with real estate. However, organized crime in Siberia has a modality reflecting its resources. For example, stealing and exportation of strategic fuel and energy resources, illicit gold turnover, illegal fur trade, driving the cattle abroad from frontier regions where cattle breeding is traditionally developed (Chita region, Tuva) are signature criminal pursuits of Siberia.

Arms trade is generally related to the presence in the region of a considerable number of military units. This is especially widespread in Buryatia, one of the stations of the Zabaikalian Military District. In 1996 an organized criminal group specializing in stealing ammunition from the arsenals of military units was discovered. Two hundred sixty eight live grenades were seized from criminals. A criminal group composed of former military personnel involved in stealing and delivering battle equipment and ammunition to Khubsugul (Mongolia) through "windows" in the frontier has been discovered in Ulan-Ude (Buryatia). Explosives were also stolen from military stores in Abakan (Tuva) and were delivered to China.

Almost 50% of OCG possess up-to-date fire-arms (Kalashnikovs automatic type). Criminal formations acquiring weapons within the region are importing them from frontier countries to be delivered and sold to other organized crime groups, individual firms and private persons. In particular it is known that the Azerbaijan OCG delivers automatic arms to the Irkutsk Region.

Drug business is another kind of activity of organized crime in the region. Organized criminal groups in Siberia have international relations that specialize in drug-trafficking and import to the region. During the last year the amount of confiscated narcotics reached 218.6 kg. Raw poppy, poppy straw delivered from Middle Asia, marijuana brought from Buryatia, and synthetic narcotics compose the major portion of imported drugs.

The regional economy is also infected with criminality: there are hundreds of criminal enterprises, fraudulent banking transactions amounting to billions of dollars, illegal currency transactions, tax evasion. In Irkutsk Region 79 pseudo-firms have been created for the purpose of committing such crimes; last year the official total damages from such enterprises was 5 million dollars. It should be stated that the majority of the above crimes are highly latent in that they are frequently protected by corrupted officers.

As indicated earlier, one of the specific directions in the activity of organized crime in East Siberia is the theft of strategic, fuel and energy resources, in particular, illegal operations on market of non-ferrous and rare-earth metals. The presence of cheap electronic power and rich deposits make it possible to develop production of non-ferrous metals; and ease of their sales and enormous profits result in significant growth of crimes related to their stealing.

China is the chief market for such goods due to its geographic proximity. However, similar deliveries to European markets take place. Thus, in 1995 ES RBOC together with associates from St. Petersburg seized 950 grams of rare-earth metal rhenium valued at 5 million dollars, and commercial silver valued at 22 million dollars. Strategic metals, namely: zirconium (22 kg.), beryllium (20 kg.), mercury (15 kg.), platinum (30 kg.) were confiscated in the Krasnoyarsk Territory. In a sensational confiscation, exportation to China of 6.5 ton of siluminum and 160 tones of aluminum (about $ 4 million) was prevented.

Fuel and energy resources are stolen mainly in the territory of the Irkutsk Region where one of the largest Russian Petrochemical Companies operates. In the summer of 1996 a train with 5000 tons of petrol departed for Vladivostok and vanished without a trace. Oil products totaling $4.600 million were stolen from a Mongolian-Russian joint venture by a swindle employing a forged letter of guarantee purportedly from the Angarsk Petrochemical Company.

The Role of Law-Enforcement Agencies in Organized Crime

Organized criminal structures gain protection by corrupting law-enforcement officers. Presently a number of top authorities, chiefs of the towns and districts of the region and officers are being prosecuted for their criminal activity.

Penetration of organized crime into legitimate businesses, credit-financial system is abetted by the inability of legislation to regulate many civil-legal relations, high revenue of certain enterprises, willingness to "launder" money earned by criminal means and success in getting significant weight and political influence to allow such dealings.

A major difficulty in combating organized crime are the defects in the law-enforcement system, in particular, by corruption and a low level of professionalism of the personnel in the system. The absence of a legislative base delineating the roles of law-enforcement bodies against organized crime hinders any progress in this field. It is also necessary to resolve the problem of victim and witness protection for prosecutions that do occur. Law-enforcement bodies cannot currently ensure their long-term protection due to the absence of means.

A major problem in the struggle against organized crime is the lack of readily available and reliable information about the members of organized criminal agencies. As there is no information regarding which persons constitute these known organizations, there is no basis for investigations and prosecutions of functionaries, let alone, criminal group leaders. Only an integrated information based solution will make it possible to attack organized crime.

12 Alienation and Female Criminality: The Case of Puerto Rico

ZULEIKA VIDAL RODRIGUEZ

Introduction

The manufacture, transportation and use of drugs is a problem without national borders. Due to the free range of this problem, drugs constitute a great concern to the world community and serve as an excellent example of the globalization of crime. To examine the full scope of drug addiction and trafficking it is necessary to do two things:
1) consider the problem using an interdisciplinary approach and,
2) consider the problem in terms of regional practices, while remaining aware that drugs affect the larger international community.

Central to this examination of drug addiction and trafficking is a focus on the gender-specific effects of these crimes. The dimensions of women's criminality have been rarely examined in social justice investigations in comparison with the male criminal. The current investigation is particularly valuable in that the criminality of females can be considered in the context of the drug trade.

Without the discussion of the gender framework, the problem of social and criminal deviant behavior of women cannot be understood. Social problems based in women's social alienation are a central part of the analysis of female criminality. This chapter will examine female criminality in Puerto Rico and will note the interweaving of other social and cultural problems, such as poverty, prostitution and social alienation with the problem of drug addiction and trafficking as they pertain to women.

Women in the Criminal World and Theories of Gender

Gender implies sexual, social and cultural differences which have been built into the structures of society over many years of socialization. Foucault (1960) explained these differences as being a way in which human power relations

129

are ordered along the lines of male and female. Joan Scott (1988) further explains these differences. She states that there are transcultural differences, within those sexual differences, depending on the referent of the social group and even in the developmental stage of human development. This develops in our most basic of social institutions, including the family, religions education and social class.

This issue was discussed at the Third Conference of Social Investigators in Relation to Gender. At this conference Milagros Bravo, Eileen M. Colgberg, Loida M. Martinez, Maria Soledad Martinez, Annette Mendez and Luisa R. Seijo (1992), contended that ". . .the identity of women and their subjectivity is built within a system of domination, where she is perceived as weak, and less prepared than men to exercise functions of leadership and competence".

In the context of criminality, recent research presents an interesting issue in relation to the understanding of the behavior of the female offender:

> . . .crimes defined as masculine seem to mean violent overt crimes, whereas 'ladylike crimes' are shoplifting. Women are neatly categorized no matter what kind of crime they commit: If they are violent, they are masculine and suffering from chromosomal deficiencies. . . [or] penis envy. If they conform, they are manipulative, sexually maladjusted and promiscuous. (Klein, 1995).

Noting this, it is not surprising that women cluster around the "ladylike" crimes of forgery, counterfeiting and fraud embezzlement or the "deviant" crime of prostitution.

Thus, when criminology seek to explain crime, female offenders generally are left out of the equation. Statistically, men commit crime at a much higher rate than women, yet it is important to make a differentiation between women's and men's crimes because the motivations differ dramatically. Nash and Safa (1988) explain the experiences of women as being driven by cultural expectations and the needs of their families.

Women in Prison in Puerto Rico

In November 1990 we conducted research as part of our academic course in the Federal Bail Program in Puerto Rico. We supervised two students, Madeline Gonzalez and Itza Sevoane, who assisted us in interviewing women imprisoned in the State Women's Prison in Vega Baja. The prison is located in a small town on the North coast of Puerto Rico, clustering together all women interned in the adult justice system.

Thirty women were part of our sample. The women were all awaiting trial without bail, mainly for the reason that they could not afford the amount bail imposed by the judge, commonly fluctuating between $40,000 and $50,000.

The economic and social profile of these women support our thesis that women commit crimes because of economic need. Women are in poverty conditions in terms of age, the median age was 23 years, civil status, most were single and not receiving the economic aid of others, they lived alone or with their parents (55%) and maintained a low level of education, usually between the seventh and ninth grade. The most striking finding is, however, the 83.3% unemployment rate among women at the time they committed their crime.

The type of crime committed also confirms our thesis that women's social alienation and their participation in illegal drug trafficking. The type of crime committed clustered in the sale of drugs at 30%. Furthermore, all of the crimes charged had some level of affiliation with drugs, either directly or indirectly. The women we interviewed were not charged with prostitution in the arrest, but a substantial number admitted involvement in prostitution at some time.

Furthermore, our interviews revealed the broader motivations behind the women's crimes, particularly the general social alienation of women. The women identified these major factors as being associated with their crimes,

- Drug addiction
- Selling drugs for own economic subsistence
- Selling of drugs or drug addiction related to partner
- Partner is drug addicted or in jail at present
- Deteriorated family relationships in past or present
- Poor relationship with her children
- Lack of effective networks
- Poverty
- Single mother

Social problems women associate with at the time of arrest, or at the time of committing the crime:

- Drug addiction
- Alcoholism
- Domestic violence
- Rape

- Sexual aggression
- Poverty
- Economic exploitation by friends or "pimps"

Furthermore, many women identified a past marked by social problems; these factors are identified as follows:

- Sexual abuse by parent
- Homelessness
- Child abuse
- Dropout from school or school deficiencies
- Father's absence
- Abuse by mother or isolation from mother
- Parents' divorce

The women in the study were very young. Our interviewers were also quite young. Two of the women interviewed observed this connection and made these comments:

"Oh! You are as young as I. Now I have children, poor education, nobody really cares or loves me. I have a legal case, I'm an addict, a criminal. I have no future."

These comments, sadly, represent the voices of our women in crime.

Female Criminality: Trends, Challenges and Future Policies

Each country has its special features regarding crime, illegal organized drug schemes and structural dynamics which impact female crime. When confronting the globalization of crime with regard to female criminality, the country's history and culture related to gender, as well as its social norms, values and ethnic identity must be considered within the framework for analysis. This formulation is essential in creating policies in the "war against organized crime". In the recent analysis of international illegal drug trafficking, trade and organized crime and drug enforcement task force agencies, the gender issues is invisible.

Lyman and Patter's (1996) excellent analysis of illegal drug trade routes in Latin American, the Caribbean, Asia, Europe and the United States does not consider a single factor in the gender discussion. The structural analysis of the trafficking organizations does not consider the role of male and female functions in the inner workings of these groups.

Allison Morris (1987) explains that the development of criminology focusses on developing crime theories based on the male validation process.

These theories interpret men's crime frameworks, ignoring women altogether. There is a need to create new theories in the construction of criminology which challenges the myths of male and female criminality and pursues a broader scheme of reference. For example, I propose an ecological approach to female criminality (figure 12.1).

Morris also addresses another problem faced by current criminology theory: that women are often misrepresented or stereotyped in a superficial manner. The "negative qualities inherent in all women were simply more apparent in criminal women for they had not been neutralized by such factors as piety and maternity" (Morris, 1987, p. 12).

We contend that the public policies toward criminality should contain responsive social and security policies in regard to organized crime. The lesser statistical incidence of female criminality should not be an excuse to ignore more humane policies toward this alienated population. Female criminality should be incorporated into the analysis when discussing the globalization of organized crime policies. We conclude that the complexities interweaving other social problems overwhelm women in our society, particularly in the context of female criminality. These problems are particularly reflected in drug addiction, which deteriorates women both physically and mentally in a rapid and inhuman manner.

The slavery of prostitution and sexual exploitation of women, usually connected with drug addiction and illegal drug trafficking has a great social cost for our world. Women's self esteem decreases when she is involved in alienating practices such as playing the role of the drug trafficking "mule".

The argument for improving women's quality of life as a method for the prevention of female criminality is further supported by noting that children are neglected during women's imprisonment.

Noting all of these reasons by which it is important to increase the quality of life of females in order to prevent the alienation which causes criminality, we make the following recommendations to the international community:

- Develop innovative strategies that are problem-oriented. Encourage educated policing and citizen-oriented policing sensitive to women in crime and their special concerns. This particularly concerns women victims of domestic violence.
- Enhance prevention programs as well as law enforcement strategies through organized crime and drug enforcement task force agencies.
- Develop awareness in the world community to motivate an increase in the quality of life conditions in poor communities. This

particularly must encompass education, self-respect and a total eradication of slavery, meaning prostitution and household slavery.

- Investigate the possibility of utilizing certain drugs so as to offer alternatives for women drug addicts.
- Approach drug problems as a public health issue, not a moral one. Treat women in treatment programs as patients; do not further escalate their feelings of alienation.
- Develop better labor conditions as to lessen women's vulnerability to crimes such as prostitution.
- Create policies in the "war on drugs" that are well balanced and take into account issues of human rights. Focus on the crime organizations, mafia and narco-traffickers.

Figure 12.1
Women, Gender and Criminality: A Social Ecological Approach

Society Values   Patriarchy Ideology Alienation
↓   ↓   ↓

Poverty
Patriarchal Social Structure
↓

•Drugs	•Gender Differences
•Drug Addiction	•Powerlessness
•Illegal Drug Trafficking	•Identity Alienation
•"Mules" Intermediate Level	•Slavery
	•Immigration
•Prostitution	•Race, Ethnicity and Social
•Slavery	Class
•Domestic Violence	
•Rape Sexual Abuse and	•Subjectivity Construction
Sexual Aggression	
•Family Desintigration	•Devaluation -Low Self
•Risk of AIDS	Esteem
•Children -Alienation	
•Custody of Children by State	

References

Albanese, J.S. (1996), *Organized Crime in America*, Cincinatti, Ohio, Anderson Publishing Co., Third Edition.

Bravo, Milagros, Colberg, Eileen et al. (1994), Genero y Mujeres Puertorriquenas: Tercer Encuentro de Investigadoras, Intercambio, City University of New York y Universidad de Puerto Rico, Centro de Investigaciones Sociales.

Erickson, P. & Murray, Glenn. (1989), *Sex Difference in Cocaine Use and Experiences: A Double Standard.* AMJ Drug and Alcohol Abuse, 15, 135-136.

Gately, W & Fernandez, I. (1994), *Dead Ringer: An Insider's Account of the Mob's Colombian Reaction.* New York: Donald I. Fine.

Leonard, E. (1982), *Lo que toda victima de violacion, sus familiares y amigos deben saber.* San Juan, Puerto Rico: Departamento de Salud: Centro de Ayuda a Victimased Violacion.

Klein, David. (1995), *Social Stress and Family Development.* New York: Guilford Press.

Morris, A. (1987), *Women, Crime and Criminal Justice.* London: Blackwell.

Patterson, O. (1991), "Slavery, Alienation and the Female Discovery of Personal Freedom." *Social Research* 58:1. 159-187.

Scott, J.W. (1988), *Gender and the Politics of History.* New York, Columbia University Press.

PART III:
PUBLIC POLICY AND
INTERVENTIONS

13 Criminal Financial Investigations: A Strategic and Tactical Approach in the European Dimension[1]

PETRUS C. VAN DUYNE, MIKE LEVI

Introduction

The past decade has witnessed a broadening of the attention on income from crime and what is done with it, particularly on the part of the various forms of what is commonly called organized crime. This development can be observed in the legislation on the confiscation and forfeiture of the proceeds of crime and anti money-laundering legislation in most industrialized countries (Meyer et al., 1989; Levi and Osofsky, 1995; Fisse et al., 1992; Gilmore, 1995) and in the growth of policing (including customs and excise) involvement in financial investigations.

Almost every country (including the Netherlands, Belgium and the United Kingdom) has instituted special financial units to carry out or direct financial investigations. This has been encouraged by the spread of anti money-laundering legislation, which has led to new investigations against individuals or organizations suspected of handling crime-money (Gold and Levi, 1994; Nachreiner, 1995). The objectives of these financial (organized) crime investigations are no longer confined to a) arresting and bringing the ringleaders and a few aides to trial and b) confiscating the sizable instrumentality of crime and assets, like cash, cars, houses and boats, but c) to crippling such "crime-enterprises" financially. One could argue that the classical fact-and-suspect investigation has been broadened to focus on the financial management of the crime-enterprise involved. This is allied also to the drift towards proactive investigation, encouraged in the UK by the Audit Commission (1993), but proceeding at a more cautious and variable pace in continental Europe, "paralyzed" as it is by scandals arising out of covert policing² and - for example, in Germany by constitutional principles and data protection regulations which inhibit the growth of undercover police work.

The tackling of profit directed (organized) crime-enterprise by means of the analysis and examination of their financial management (the flow of goods, payments and spending) can be indicated by the broad concept of "financial investigation". This orientation to the "crime-money connection" can serve several goals:

1. Financial investigations can contribute to the generation of evidence against individuals under suspicion, like payment for the acquisition of smuggling transport (boats, trucks), payment of bribes or the money-flow versus the invoicing in cross-border VAT-frauds (Aronowitz cs., 1996).

2. In connection with this search for evidence, financial investigations can add value by establishing databases which can help construct the suspected facilitating networks, including particular lawyers, accountants or seemingly legitimate investment companies which have so far escaped attention.

3. It can strip the criminal of his ill gotten assets and finance (directly or, more commonly such as in the UK, indirectly) the costs of the police investigation.

4. Financial investigations can have an added value to the actual prosecuted crime-enterprises by contributing to weaken or even disrupt the market network in which they are commercially situated.

Money-laundering investigations have not been mentioned as a separate investigative aim, because they have a contributory role in attaining most of these objectives. For example, the uncovering of a money-laundering scheme may provide the legal grounds for a confiscation order or, where legislation permits, a ban on a corrupt professional from continuing his or her profession. In a similar way, the mapping of a money-laundering network may reveal the underlying cooperation between crime-entrepreneurs and generate further investigations.

Although the financial approach has been acclaimed by various policy makers in the Netherlands and the UK as the new investigative tool, there isnot really much new about it (Van Duyne, 1996; Pheijffer c.s., 1997). Nor isit a clear and distinct "tool". Any proper police investigation of crimes for profit takes the financial aspects into its scope, because profit (as well as power) is often the leading motive of the perpetrator, whether it concerns the fencing of stolen goods or murder for money. However, such a financial orientation is not a general routine or firmly rooted in the daily practice of the CIDs in either country. Though in the UK, there is a once-and-for-all training course for financial investigators -which is a necessary condition for them to be approved to receive suspicious transaction reports and to deal directly with financial institutions about these reports- the financial analysis and the necessary skills are usually developed ad hoc, and not as an independent method of analysis which may also be used in pro-active investigations. When the crime has been solved and the suspect has been brought to trial, the accumulated knowledge and experience frequently "evaporates" because new tasks have to be carried out. This "reinventing the wheel" is hardly a unique characteristic of financial investigation: it is commonplace.[3]

In this chapter, we will elaborate the financial investigation approach in regard of the policy against "organized crime" by differentiating between its strategic and tactical form.

Strategic and Tactical Financial Investigation

In a money-laundering investigation, the aim is to unravel the paper trails in a labyrinth of money transactions in order to get a clear picture of the money-flows and prove culpability. When (or if) the investigation is directed at the elimination of the criminal network, the investigators will strive to get behind the money-flows and assets in order to uncover the working and power relations. The combination of such investigation can go beyond these tactical objectives and can be used for the more strategic aim of mapping the criminal landscape or market-section in order to find the weak spots which can be used for subsequent investigation. In short, the various forms of financial investigation can have both tactical and strategic purposes.

Before discussing these forms of financial investigation, we will first deal with the various crime markets which are the potential "hunting grounds" for the financial investigators.

Basic Acquisition Market

The phrase indicates virtually all the criminal activities which yield money through property crime or by trading in forbidden goods and services, usually investigated by traditional CID-means and financially oriented from the start.

The Financial Processing Market

Successful crime trade leads to an accumulation of money. Increased pressure because of the anti money-laundering legislation and law enforcement leads to a requirement for more professional handling of the moneys as has been observed by the Financial Action Task Force.[4] This increases the price for the money-laundering services, creating a secondary crime-market just as for any other service.[5]

The Precipitation of the Crime-Money

The accumulated and laundered money must finally show up somewhere in other financial or production relations; it must enter the legitimate world. It can be invested in some tax haven to provide against a rainy day or be "made to work" in legitimate activities, for example a restaurant, an art gallery or in the real estate market.

Strategic Financial Investigation

The aim of this kind of investigation is to map the financial processing market and the impact areas of the crime-money. One of the concerns about organized crime is that crime-entrepreneurs may have opportunities of purchasing respectable status with their laundered money. This would lead to increasing corruption and an intertwining of organized crime and the legitimate economy. Thus, the aim of strategic financial investigation is the disclosure of the money-management (money flows and the precipitation of the crime-money) in order to hamper the consolidation of the market position of crime-entrepreneurs and/or the acquisition of a sphere of influence or power in the upperworld.

This formulation focuses on the prevention of which is not only an administrative policy of the civil authorities, since the primary orientation of financial investigation is a criminal one. Strategic financial investigation should not be practiced at a distance from the tactical operational case investigations or hover abstractly above the daily CID-practice. Together they can contribute to the elimination of crime-enterprises and the disruption of criminal trading networks. This also helps the aim of preventing the consolidation of the market position and power of crime-entrepreneurs.

For example, the Dutch fiscal police (FIOD) collects the information of individual cross-border VAT violations in order to obtain the patterns of this developing crime-trade. These patterns are mapped according to region, the nature of the exported products (or documents) and perpetrators. At present this method is systematically applied to the huge problem of organized VAT-fraud. In individual cases the assembled information is used by the fiscal fraud squads and speeds up their investigations. In a more traditional crime area, the red-light district of Amsterdam, the police monitor the acquisition of restaurants, pubs and real estate by criminals in order to prevent concentration of certain crime figures or the extension of their sphere of influence in adjacent districts.

Spheres of criminal power

Another element of the prevention objective: "a sphere of influence or power" is at first sight open and vague. In its simplest meaning, "power" in a social setting is the capacity to influence the decision making of other people. One can differentiate between several forms of power in crime enterprise:

The domestic power   In the first place there is the traditional power of crime-entrepreneurs "at home", that is in their own criminal (underworld) environment. Their mental horizon is as limited as that of most entrepreneurial citizens or politicians, for whom their constituency is their power base. However, one should not underestimate the seriousness of such domestic power or its financial impact.

Commercial sphere of influence   A survey of the history of the big crime-entrepreneurs indicates that crime-entrepreneur of various countries are merchants, selling and buying from wholesalers or national or local central distributors (Van Duyne, 1997).   This may require bribing foreign law enforcement officials. The commercial sphere of influence can form the basis for power building in the legitimate world, though. This is particular the case with organized business crime, which implies an overlap with the following layer of power.

Economic power in the legitimate world   This kind of power development is considered the most threatening: crime-entrepreneurs who obtain bridgeheads and positions of influence and power in the legitimate trade, and industry and public administration. One has to differentiate between the various crime-markets and the crime-entrepreneurs involved: on the one hand there is the underground economy of forbidden goods (usually illegal drugs), and on the other there is the organized business crime which offers its legal goods and services to the legitimate world itself.

Concerning the economic power of crime-entrepreneurs in the upperworld, we have to differentiate between the commercial influence of the economic criminals (see b) and power as a consequence of the impact of the crime-money. The latter implies the investment and application of surplus capital in new production relations in the legal world; consolidating the entrepreneur's power. He becomes increasingly "untouchable" while the amassed assets and other forms of participation in the legitimate economy provide economic power there.

Strategic financial investigations should particularly be directed at these three social targets of power building:

- the elimination of the domestic power
- the disruption of the criminal trading networks
- the exposure and elimination of social-economic bridgeheads in the upper-world.

Money flows and the appearance of crime-money

In practice the flow of money and its appearance in the legal world are interconnected, as the ultimate aim is to have the money available as cleaned, legitimately earned capital and to use it in social life without awkward questions being asked. To attain that objective the moneys will have to make many peregrinations during which many temporary stops are made in the legal world.

The money currents Unless thoroughly laundered, crime-money is a floating and fluid form of property. What can be observed are repeatedly surfacing cash flows or bank-accounts. Such assets may be called "homeless money" (Naylor, 1987). There is probably a huge financial pumping cycle which is more similar to a sort of blood circulation than to a static precipitation involving the consolidation or amassing of the proceeds of crime. Like blood transports oxygen and food to the various organs, the financial circulation transports the money to the vital market participants. Part of the money is destined to pay the sellers of contraband, to buy means of transport, corrupt officers and to pay the executives. Another part may consist of a chain of transformations with the ultimate aim of a laundered surplus capital, which can finally be hoarded like a layer of fat.

The management of crime-money is no less a cross-border operation than the crime trade itself. In the industrialized world with its high degree of administrative and fiscal control successful criminal money-management in one jurisdiction is hardly feasible. The finely woven system of administrative and fiscal obligations in the national jurisdictions creates too many paper trails for a successful laundering system in one jurisdiction.[6] As soon as money-laundering grows in scale, risk avoidance requires a channeling of the money into an international money circulation. And the more respectable and important the criminal becomes, the more risk-averse, since the investment in respectability brings its own opportunity costs. Money flows are largely a flow of cross-border money transfers for which a chain of legal persons have to be created in many foreign jurisdictions in order to conceal the transactions from the prying eye of the law enforcement. The setting up and execution of such a money management service rendered by the numerous tax havens around the world has become a major source of income for countries with few other economic opportunities (Walter, 1989).

The disruption or interruption of this financial circulation has always a negative impact on the viability of other segments of the chain of underlying transactions and on the trading network of business relations: the payment of merchandise, transport etc. cannot be carried out, arousing dissatisfaction and distrust. In brief, such disturbances are hitches which act like a brake on the establishment of networks. In addition they hinder the building up of financial reserves so that less money is left for the investment of crime-money and the development of social status.[7]

The precipitation of the crime-money It may look trivial, but the only loss of capital in the organized crime trade is the destruction of confiscated contraband. For the rest, the ill gotten assets will always appear somewhere in the economy. Expressed in "value-free" terms, the crime money will always contribute to the Gross National Product of some national economy (Boeschoten, 1992), via its multiplier effects in stimulating firms, at least some of whom will also pay tax. A large part of the crime-money "trickles down" via internal expenditures on the criminal network. The "social costs" of the criminal enterprise consist of handsome payments to the accomplices like couriers, truck drivers and other executives. The distribution of these moneys does not leave many traces. The moneys disappear in the daily management of the criminals and usually enters the upperworld directly in the form of consumptive spending. Here contributing considerably to the income of many law abiding citizens, e.g. lawyers and the travel, entertainment and catering business.

At issue here is that part of the crime-money which can be considered surplus capital: not used for carrying on of the crime-enterprise or the own household. In which sections of the legitimate trade and industry does it appear in the sense that it is transformed into other means of investment or production relations? Does this transformation lead to power building in the legal world? And finally: which crime-entrepreneurs do succeed in transforming it into legitimate production and investment relations and achieve some kind of sphere of influence or power in the legal world beyond their previous criminal trading base?

The following have been mentioned frequently as suitable areas where crime-entrepreneur are supposed to invest their ill gotten profits:

a. the catering business
b. gambling, particularly gaming machines
c. the real estate market
d. the real estate development and construction industry
e. transportation

The catering business This economic sector ranks high as the favorite investment area of crime-money. The crime-entrepreneur who owns a pub has a higher status: the place is his hang-out where other criminals will come together for social or criminal purposes. Most criminally owned pubs or restaurants are operated normally or no more fraudulent than is usual in this field.

The gaming machine market Gambling is considered a vice. As vices are traditionally exploited by criminals (and the state, taxing the profits), it is not surprising that the police also investigated the potential penetration of this market segment by organized crime. Nor is it surprising that the police has found "alarming indications" that confirm its suspicions.

The real estate market Real estate is traditionally an attractive area for investment. It enables the investor to acquire assets which demand relatively little effort to manage, while the value of the investment usually increases or keeps pace with inflation. The only disadvantage of real estate is that it is a "registered good": the documents of the land register contain information about the acquisition price, the owner, whether there is a mortgage etc. Buying always entails paper trails.

If the crime-entrepreneur succeeds in buying real estate, the next question is whether these assets can be used as a power leverage in the legal world. The real estate market has a complex and opaque structure and is doubtful whether crime-entrepreneurs from the underground economy have the expert capacity to manipulate the relations in the real estate market for their own power building in the legal world. To do so one needs the long term cooperation of many intermediaries.

The real estate development and construction market Government and police sources have expressed their concern that crime-entrepreneurs have so much surplus capital that they might use it to obtain a sphere of influence in real estate development. One traditional sector in the construction market in which crime-entrepreneurs did obtain a longer lasting foothold is the underground labor market of the criminal (sub)contractors. It is thriving because the (sub)contractors do not pay the employer's social contribution to the social security authorities.

The transport business The transport business is frequently mentioned as a branch of industry which is supposed to be highly vulnerable to infiltration by organized crime. This is not surprising as a large part of the revenues of crime-entrepreneurs derives from the smuggling trade for which the transport forms the essential logistics (Bovenkerk and Lempes, 1996). The transport business is being abused indeed: hauliers frequently are not aware that their vehicle contains contraband and face the loss of ships or trucks while their truckers are being detained. However, many hauliers have also started a smuggling line of their own, without any seduction from underworld crime figures. Frequently the smugglers establish or buy small transport firms which were dismantled after they had fulfilled their purpose.

Only a limited number of crime-entrepreneur succeed in consolidating their social-economic place in the legal world, namely those who (a) do not make victims in their economic surroundings and (b) succeed in co-mingling their fraudulent trade with their legitimate enterprises. Organized tax fraud being no "plebeian" crime, such enterprises receive frequently only a fiscal slap on the wrist and continue their criminal affairs unabatedly (Van Duyne, 1997). However, most organized business criminals are incapable of establishing such a "sedentary" enterprise. They make too many victims, operate too conspicuously and lead a nomadic life: they are homeless crime-entrepreneurs with homeless money.

Reviewing the "state of the art" as far as it has been substantiated by hard evidence in the Netherlands and the UK, it is fair to conclude that the social-economic areas to which successful crime-entrepreneurs from the underground economy are able or willing to rise, are limited in most cases to catering and real estate.

The nature of strategic investigation

We have to deal now with the question, what kind of strategic financial investigation may have to be set up? What may be the reason to start such an investigation and what should be its targets?

Concerning the reason to start a strategic financial investigation there should be no misunderstanding: the reason must be of a criminal nature. If that is not the case, there is no task for the police. The financial-economic situation in a branch of industry must be such, that there is a reasonable assumption that criminal relevant acts may be committed. This means that the police should not engage in open fishing expeditions on the assumption that wherever one will closely examine an economic sector, one will always find some wrongdoing.

The second part of the question concerns the targets of strategic financial investigation. The general aim is the uncovering of the money-management of the crime-enterprises in order to prevent their consolidation of their market position. This aim concerns the financial processing market and the precipitation areas of the crime-money. When we operationalize these general aims to practical applications, we get the following operational targets.

Transfer of knowledge The first practical target is the transfer of knowledge to operational CID-investigations or the preparation thereof. A good transfer of such a kind of knowledge (already present in the police forces, but so scattered as to be virtually inaccessible) to an investigation unit and tailored to their special demands and targets may save much time and effort. One should not underestimate the time which is wasted in inventing new wheels by police and prosecutors.

Financial landscape supervising A second practical target is the supervising or monitoring of the financial criminal landscape. This implies the collection of signs, indications, warnings of experts concerning developments and changes in the financial landscape which deserve closer attention. The findings of such investigations may be of great practical value for a criminal investigation, and it can result in preventive policy based on administrative measures and legislation.

In summary the outcomes of strategic investigations can contribute to the general aim in two ways:

- they can yield information which can be used directly in an operational CID-investigations or can be used for the preparatory phase of it
- they can provide insights into the weak spots of the financial processing of crime-money in order to tackle it operationally or preventively by means of additional regulations.

Tactical financial investigation

With this side of the subject we enter the workshop floor of daily police practice. As has also been indicated by Levi and Osofsky (1995), financial investigation is also a matter of the "ordinary" profit directed property crime. At present the international accounting companies are developing forensic financial expertise, not just in fraud but also to act for the corporate defense, mainly in tax fraud investigations so far or for civil plaintiffs who are victims of fraud.[8] In addition the Dutch "Pluck units" (specialized forfeiture units to "pluck" the criminal's assets) have been established in the police forces and have developed their expertise in the framework of prosecutorial investigations. The British police, handicapped by fragmentation, have developed expertise at a less consistent pace, though the new Labor government promises to accelerate involvement in this arena, buttressed by even tougher legislation.

Apart from these ongoing developments there are two other forms of tactical financial investigating which we would like to mention:

1. the financial mapping of a crime-enterprise which does not only aim to uncover the basic criminal facts (the acquisition side) but also the structure of the correlated financial transactions and

2. the related Money-management of the proceeds. Put into simple words: the pattern of payments and transactions to operate the flow of forbidden goods and services and to veil and launder the proceeds. These forms of tactical financial investigation overlap considerably.

Fraud investigations Though organized business crime concerns usually well established "classic" fraud techniques (ranging from no bookkeeping at all to a deliberate complicated chaos of invoices) as a cross-border phenomenon it is hard to tackle. The main difficulty is the co-operation or operational tuning of the various national investigation units. Taking into account that even within a national jurisdiction the cooperation between law enforcement services is variable, one can imagine that cross-border co-operation faces a multitude of bottlenecks. This is certainly the case with international fraud schemes in which the various countries have different financial interests (Levi and Pithouse, in press).

A cross-border fraud scheme with numerous suspects is more than a seemingly intangible network of disappearing shell companies. For most of the transactions there are foreign counterparts, aides or a branch of the own organization. This can be observed with cross-border EU-fraud or VAT-fraud schemes. In most cases one succeeds in gathering evidence against the suspect but such evidence does not necessarily lead to the elimination of the criminal trading network. This requires an extensive analysis of the components of the network and a description of the operational links between these components. Such an examination cannot be carried out without close cross-border co-operation between the national investigating services.

Forfeiture investigations Investigations aimed at getting back ill gotten profits can be carried out during the normal CID-work, like house-searches and the confiscation of instrumentalities of crime, as well as during a painstaking examination of the paperwork of en enterprise in order to unravel the legitimate and illegal money flows.[9]

Rational wealthy crime-entrepreneur know the risks of being rich and try to avoid direct ownership of assets or capital, by putting new in the name of other natural and legal persons, preferably residing abroad. The investigation of such suspects requires the expertise of various disciplines, like company law, (international) tax law, commercial law etc. This implies that such an investigation will soon develop into a (cross-border) criminal network examination and require international law enforcement cooperation.

Money-laundering investigations Money-laundering investigation do not only encompass the gathering of evidence against persons who are involved in the actual handling of crime-money. Of equal importance is the tracing of the paper trails in order to uncover the whereabouts of the money or where the money has appeared, of course given proof of its illegal origin. A money-laundering investigation in a cross-border crime-enterprise can involve an extensive search through many jurisdictions and the scrutiny of numerous (shell) companies which seemingly are only at the periphery of the enterprise but are essential in the heart of the money processing section. The questions to be asked are frequently not of the typical who-did-what, but concern the legal and commercial relations between legal persons in order to unveil the unusual or deceptive character of the transaction.

If the unraveling of such cross-border money trails is already quite complicated, the investigation becomes extremely difficult (and expensive) when the moneys are temporarily intertwined with legitimate trade or businesses. Even more difficult for the investigation are the schemes which use the opportunities provided by the service and amusement industry, whose intangible turnovers make it difficult to demonstrate the falsity inflated claims of "good" (laundering) business.

Depth analysis of crime-enterprises Crime-enterprises are primarily a reflection of the nature of the unregulated crime market: they develop piecemeal and the longer a criminal remains successful the more complicated his "organization" becomes, not because of the smartness of the design but because ongoing organizations develop like a delta network of streams, brooks and creeks. The investigation of such enterprises is very demanding and costly. Financial investigation can be of great value for the normal CID-work. Because of the confidential nature of the crime trade, no financial relation is entered without a social connection. In brief, investigating such networks implies that a social subject and financial orientation go hand in hand.

Crime-enterprise analysis may be very complicated, but the basic principles for the detective work may be rather simple. The point of departure in seemingly complicated structures is the short term benefit principle: to whose advantage is this deceptive scheme and who are the pivots around which the wheels turn? In addition one must take into account trade habits and codes: what does a normal merchant do and where does this scheme deviate from what makes normal business sense? Such a way of investigating is (intuitively) based on commercial knowledge (what is socially and technically usual), psychological insight (what do I know about my suspects) and of course translating these insights into criminal law. A good interaction between financial strategic and tactical investigation, together with the classical police methods (following, electronic surveillance, informants), can yield an added value.

The European Dimension of Financial Investigations

As soon as crime-enterprises grow in size, their organizations are bound to change structurally as they have to make use of legitimate world facilities to manage the flow of their goods, services and moneys. The crime-entrepreneur has to develop or reorganize his trading techniques in such a way that his transactions can be blended into the legitimate commercial circuits which are being (ab)used. Here the regional (European) or even global dimensions come to the stage.

Implications for Tactical Investigations

The most important implication for tactical financial investigations concerns the obtaining and processing of information from law enforcement agencies in other jurisdictions. When the participants of the crime-enterprises are residing and operating in more than one jurisdiction and are targets of the CID's in those jurisdictions, if the investigation and prosecution of these "national" targets are not co-ordinated, the investigative agencies tend to adopt a protective attitude towards "their" information, fearing violations of confidentiality as well as the risk that others will "steal the credit" for what they consider "their case". This risk can be enhanced where proceeds of crime are distributed directly to the producers of the case. In that case information protection goes frequently beyond investigative co-operation. What should be the proper European investigative dimension? Operationally one could think of two possibilities in addition to the normal legal aid procedures.
- Integrated multi-national investigation projects
  The idea to form integrated common projects between various national crime squads is not a utopian one: in the field of drug crimes such projects are quite feasible, though are less common than might be expected. Given that the legal requirements are met, there is no reason why financial investigations (and not only drug related ones) should not be carried out in the framework of common multinational projects. When the legal conditions are met, the exchange of financial information, can be covered by the existing treaties on mutual legal cooperation. More important is the material cooperation: formulating common investigative targets, drawing up a timetable, setting up a common crime-analysis task group to integrate the national data, agreeing upon a focal point of co-ordination. While technical difficulties are surmountable, real differences arise in social-cultural police backgrounds.

- European information network of suspicious transaction

The second possibility concerns the European harmonization of the information management. While common investigation projects -which have to be developed gradually- are a first step, this is still a very piecemeal approach which does not cover pro-active preparatory investigations, usually starting with the first indications of suspicious transactions and the analysis of financial information. The development of integrated projects requires a fine tuning of financial information about monetary transactions from various jurisdictions as only its composite pattern may present a plausible legal cause for common investigatory actions in the foreign jurisdictions involved. This implies that the flow of information will have to be improved between the national financial investigation centers, like the British NCIS, the Dutch CRI, the German BKA or the Belgium DEFO). A first step forward may be the harmonization of the information by agreeing on a common list of variables which can be fed into a computerized information exchange system creating a "collective memory".

Implications for strategic financial investigation

The above mentioned collective memory is not only of importance for tactical cross-border investigations. No organizational strategic patterns of behavior can be developed without such organizational memory. What will this "collective memory" contain? Without limiting it unduly, we consider the following to be relevant.

In the first place the abstracted experience from previous investigations: the "lessons from the past". A list of distinctive features of these patterns may later be of help in recognizing similar constructions from scattered observations.

Secondly, data about various crime-markets, the money flows they generate and the economic areas of impact.

Thirdly, analysis of types of crime-groups or networks, their methods of doing crime-business and their social and economic habits and relationships.

Fourthly, the habits and conventions within the legitimate branches of trade and industry in the various jurisdictions in order to have some standards for comparing deviant ways of doing business.

Such storage is not a static hoarding place or some kind of "cupboard" of sleeping data, but functions by developing interactively a growing knowledge base which can strategically be used to direct search processes, to compare or predict international shifts in the various crime-markets and its finances, while its information and analysis can be fed back into ongoing investigations.

Cross-border strategic financial (and economic) investigation, with its potential impact on tactical investigations, requires much shared or mutually accessible information. Given the present electronic communication systems the bottlenecks are not of a technical nature. Strategic financial investigation requires an investment in human intellectual capital first. In addition the products of national investigations and analysis must likewise be accessible electronically to facilitate comparative analysis. It goes without saying, that such devices should not infringe on the national rules concerning the data protection and the protection of privacy. Indeed, discontinuities in data protection and human rights/privacy rights provisions in different European countries -even after the EU Directive on Data Protection is fully implemented by 1999- are likely to continue to give rise to difficulties for practitioners. From this dilemma there is no obvious escape.

Such strategic financial information storage may be a decentralized one. However, it could be argued that such a structure is too loose to represent a "collective memory" at all. Without concentration of this information in a common institution the concept would peter out and become diluted. This would be an argument for allocating such tasks to a European institution like Europol. The High Level Group created by the European Council at Dublin, December 1996, has proposed this in its document in April 1997, which expressed the desire "to set up a system for exchanging information concerning suspected Money-laundering at the European level" and adds that "the European Convention should be supplemented with a provision permitting Europol to be instrumental therein". We would like to add that this should not be interpreted as a switchboard function only and that Europol will also get the facilities to analyze the information which it exchanges in order to provide a more strategic financial service.

In this chapter we have provided in some respects a grand scheme, but in our view a practical one. Whether societies individually or collectively wish to put sufficient financial and organizational resources into it to "make it happen" is an open question: but this sort of mechanism will be required if rhetorical "law and order" dreams are to be made into anything approaching a substantive reality.

Notes

1   This paper is the English revision of "Financieel rechercheren", published by the first author in "Het Tijdschrift voor de politie", April/Mei 1996.

2   The police in Haarlem experimented with a method which implied that a criminal informant was allowed to import huge amounts of hashish on behalf of some wholesalers in order to come near the top echelons of the organized hash-networks. The scheme failed and discredited the police, while the market was swamped with more hashish than a whole population of ardent smokers could consume. The remainder was exported.

3   The need to provide an established database for contacts and accumulated methodologies is one of the rationales for the establishment of the National Crime Faculty at Bramshill Police College.

4   Cross country evaluation of laws and systems in FATF members dealing with asset confiscation and provisional measures. Paper by the Secretariat, December, 1996.

5   One may call this the irony of the fight against the (drug) market: the demand for the basic illegal commodity does not change while the law enforcement efforts are creating a secondary market. In the end more crime has to be fought then before, which has at any rate the benefit of a guaranteed perpetual law enforcement employment scheme (Van Duyne en Kouwenberg, 1994).

6   This does not exclude incidental Money-laundering "at home". The author has come across the sales of collectors articles for fancy prices, because the collector wanted the item "at any price". This occurred with a painting and exclusive cars, presumably bought by strawmen of the crime-entrepreneur. The strawmen was of course unknown and paid cash. The police also mentioned pubs with a high turnover without clients. However, we have seen relatively few substantiated cases.

7   Unfortunately the police all too often publicized its partial triumphs when intercepting contraband or suspicious money couriers. The actors in the cross-border trading networks collect these press messages which they send to their partners abroad in order to explain why certain transactions have failed. If the police would remain silent the interceptions would create much more havoc.

8   Dutch criminal (sub)contractors hardly operate on the Dutch market anymore, but on the German market, where they are less harassed by the tax and labor authorities. This cross-border labor fraud can also be observed in Belgium. The legitimate construction firms benefit (knowingly) from these frauds: the black labor is cheap, skilled, reliable and does not strike.

9   In the Netherlands the assistance of private accountants in organized crime investigations is still a controversy as a part of their clients may (or are) the targets of the police (Pheiffers c.s., 1997).

References

Aronowitz, A.A., D.C.G. Laagland and G. Paulides. (1996), *Value-added tax fraud in the European Union*. Amsterdam, Kluwer.

Boeschoten, W.C. (1992), *Currency use and payment patterns*. Dordrecht, Kluwer Academic Publishers, 1992

Bruinsma, G. and F. Bovenkerk. (1996), "Deelonderzoek II, Branches" In: *Inzake Opsporing, Parlementaire Enquêtecommissie Opsporingsmethoden*. 's-Gravehange, SDU, 1996.

Bovenkerk, F. and A. Lempkens. (1996), "De branches horeca en gokautomaten. Deelonderzoek II, Branches." In: *Inzake Opsporing, Parlementaire Enquêtecommissie Opsporingsmethoden*, 's-Gravenhage, SDU.

Duyne, P.C. van. (1995), *Het spook en de dreigingvan de georganiseerde misdaad*. 's-Gravenhage, SDU-uitgeverij.

Duyne, P.C. van. "The phantom and threat of organized crime." *Crime, Law and Social Change*, 1996, nr. 24, p. 341-377

Duyne, P.C. van, "Organized crime, corruption and power," *Crime, Law and Social Change*, 1997, forthcoming

Duyne, P.C. van, R. Kouwenberg en G. Romeijn. (1990) *Misdaadondernemingen, ondernemende misdadigers in Nederland*, Arnhem, Gouda-Quint.

Duyne, P.C. and R. Block. "Cross-atlantic organized crime. Racketeering in fuels." *Crime, Law and Social Change*, 1995, nr. 22, 127-147.

Enquêtecommissie Opsporingsmethoden.(1996), *Inzake opsporing* 's-Gravenhage, SDU.

Fisse B., D. Fraser en G. Coss. (1992), *The money trail*, Sydney, The Law Book Company.

Gilmore, W. (1995), *Dirty money*. Amsterdam, Council of Europe Press.

Gold, M and M. Levi. (1994), *Money-laundering in the UK.: an appraisal of suspicion-based reporting*. London, The Police Foundation.

Handelman, S. (1994), *Comrande criminal. The theft of the second Russian revolution* London.

Michael, Joseph. (1994), "amesische Zigaretten-Mafia." *Kriminalistik*, 1994, nr. 3, p. 205-208

Pearson, J. (1973), *The profession of violence. The rise and fall of the Kray twins*. London, Weidenfeld.

Pheijffer, M., J.G. Kuijl, A.Th.H. van Dijk and G.J.C.M. Bakker. (1997), *Financieel rechercheren. Theorie en praktijk*, Deventer, Kluwer.

Pfeijffer, M. (1997),*Forensiche accountant: een veeleisend beroep*. Deventer, Kluwer

Walter, I. (1989), *Secret money. The shadowy world of tax evasion, capital flight and fraud*. London, Unwin Paperbacks.

14 Mafia-Type Organizations: The Restoration of Rights as a Preventive Policy

MARIA LUISA CESONI[1]

Introduction

Like "globalization", the words "mafia" and "organized crime" (or "criminal organization") have become particularly fashionable in the 1990s. Whether or not these definitions, which call for political response, are justifiable seems to me to be a fundamental question for both economics and criminal law.

Though the term "organized crime" is applied to a striking variety of organizations and is very diversely defined, and although judicial investigation has revealed the peculiarities of the organizations themselves (for example, the Neapolitan Camorra), there is a perceptible tendency to offer an all-embracing definition of organized crime, making it into a somewhat vague concept which can be used to cover a multitude of sins.

It is high time to look critically at this phenomenon, all the more so because numerous academic studies unquestioningly accept the stereotypes offered by politicians and the media, at the risk of supporting the development of policies whose dangers they may not properly appreciate.

The interaction between the social and legal definition of organized crime on the one hand, and the criminal policies on the other, actually tends to reinforce and rationalize repressive policies which are problematic in that they may involve the violation of fundamental rights and liberties, while doing little to curb the activities against which they are directed.

To be really effective, a preventive policy must take account not only of the diverse forms assumed by organized crime, but also of the environments which fostered their development. In particular, a proper understanding of the political and economic (as well as socio-cultural) conditions which favored the development of mafia-type organizations ought to shift the focus on to preventive policies based on a restoration of the socio-economic and political rights of people living in the affected regions. This approach would also reduce the need for emergency legislation, and so would doubly reinforce respect for human rights.

Problems of Definition

The Ministerial Conference on transnational crime, organized by the UN, which took place in 1994 produced a Political Declaration and the Naples World Action Plan against transnational organized crime; both were approved by the UN General Assembly. According to the Plan, the international community should agree on a common definition of the concept of organized crime in order to harmonize measures taken at the national level and make international co-operation more effective (art. 11). To underpin this definition the Conference, basically following the American approach, identified "organized crime" essentially on the basis of the criminal activities it covers.[2] These activities are very diverse: from international car theft to the black market in nuclear materials; from the organization of illegal immigration to crimes against the environment, software piracy to illicit gambling, white slave trafficking to money laundering to corruption. These different activities involve different social actors, are managed in different ways, and may be variously combined - among themselves and/or with other activities that are perfectly legal.

Thus the attempt to find a unitary definition of the term "organized crime" immediately comes up against the heterogeneity of the phenomena to which it can be applied. This applies as much to academic definitions as to legislation and fieldwork.

Academic Definitions

Three examples of the academic approach will suffice to show that the American definition of organized crime do not (all) coincide with definitions of the Mafia and other, similar Italian organizations, not with those of the "new mafia" in Russia.

The traditional literature in North America has been based mainly on the Mafia as it exists in the USA. This is a centralized, family-based organization which was thought to constitute a secret society, or at least to be totally separate from society at large (Smith, 1975). It was believed to control illegal markets (Schelling, 1967). More detailed research showed that this Mafia control was in fact only partial (Anderson, 1979), and towards the end of the 1970s some scholars dropped the term "organized crime" and "in their efforts to construct a more responsible history" (Block, 1991, p. 12), began to speak instead of "illegal enterprises". In particular, the economist Peter Reuter (1983) challenged the "monopoly" theory and showed, through a study of three illegal markets, that they were neither monopolized nor controlled by the Mafia. Reuter believed that the groups which constituted "organized crime" were heterogeneous and ever-changing. This opinion was to be confirmed by various empirical studies (cf. Albanese, 1989).

However, J.P. Brodeur (1996, pp. 2, 5) remarks that even today "we have never been further from a precise understanding of what is meant by 'organized crime'". He acknowledges that most of the North American definitions are similar, but this (he thinks) is because they are based on the model of a mafia-type crime syndicate, i.e. associations which are "unitary, with a powerful internal structure and completely cut off from the rest of society and its institutions, to which they are connected only by transaction (supply of illegal services), predation (violence) and corruption".

The Italian literature offers more differentiated definitions based on the model of national "mafias". The problem of definition is most often tackled with regard to the Sicilian Mafia and is often based on an examination of its socio-economic role.[3]

For example, Nando Dalla Chiesa (1976) identified the Mafia with the dominant social class in Sicily and so defined it as a *"mafiosa bourgeoisie"* (or vice versa). This definition of Mafia as a kind of criminality - particularly economic criminality - indulged in by the powerful has been accepted by some authors (Borré and Pepino, 1983; Santo and La Fiura, 1990).

Pino Arlacchi introduced into Italian studies the model of the mafia as a business undertaking (i.e. what best characterizes a mafia-type organization is business-style management of illegal activities: *mafiosi* as Schumpeter-style entrepreneurs), and distinguished between "organized crime" - Mafia family business - and "gangs" - meaning a galaxy of smaller scale criminal groups, chiefly gangs of young criminals, or more firmly established groups of urban gangsters (Arlacchi, 1983 and 1991).

Diego Gambetta (1992) argues that the Mafia is an undertaking whose chief objective is simply the production and sale of private protection. CENSIS (1991), however, tends to group all illegal (profit-making) activities carried on in Italy under the label of a single "Crime Company", extending the definition of "mafia" to an undertaking with a variety of different activities.

As for the now-(in)famous "Russian mafias", it is difficult to tell where their observers are situating the boundary between organized criminal groups, various disparate types of illegal economy, and political and administrative corruption (cf. Fituni, 1996). Indeed, Yuri Voronin[4] argues that the Russian mafia is usurping the principal activities of state, which it has infiltrated so thoroughly that it is impossible to say where one ends and the other begins. This recalls some authors' definition of the Italian Mafia as a state within a state (cf. Padovani, 1987).

Finally, it also seems necessary to take account of the comment by the "Observatoire Géopolitique des Drogues" in Paris that "the generic term 'mafia' is used as a convenient label for a collection of different things. However, it has the merit of indicating the fundamental nature of the phenomenon, in spite of its numerous variants: each is a manifestation of organized crime, and not of isolated actions or independent perpetrators" (OGD, 1996 p. 67).

The application of the concept of organized crime in legislation and the courts is, however, more complex.

Legal Definitions

A few examples will show that American legal definitions of organized crime only partially overlap with European ones; and the latter often differ among themselves.

In the United States, the law of the State of Washington defines the direction of organized crime as the act of organizing, directing or financing at least three persons with the intent to engage in a pattern of criminal profiteering activity; or inciting third parties to engage in violence or intimidation with the same intent (Criminal Profiteering Act, 1985).

Federal legislation (Racketeer Influenced and Corrupt Organizations Law, title IX, Organized Crime Control Act of 1970) focuses on the notion of a (criminal) undertaking and on the acquisition of control over a legal business activity, or of real property, by means of organized criminal acts.

In Europe, the most detailed example seems to be the Italian penal code, which has two articles running side by side, one covering "association in order to commit crimes", i.e. "three or more persons associating in order to commit crimes" (art. 416 CP) and the other "mafia-type organizations", for which a much more complex definition is offered (art. 416*bis* CP): "An association is a mafia-type association when its members make use of intimidation derived from their association, and the ensuing subjection and 'gagging' in order to commit crimes or to manage either directly or indirectly or otherwise control, business activities, concessions, authorizations, public markets or public services, or to obtain unfair profits or advantages for themselves or others." This initial definition (1982) was supplemented in 1992 by adding the aim of "preventing or impeding the free exercise of voting rights or procuring votes for oneself or for other persons during elections".

Thus it is untrue (except in a purely formal sense) to say, as Martens (1991) does, that only American law has adopted the concept of "criminal undertaking", since the Italian definition also envisages business activity by an undertaking, and case law has shown that this law can apply to "legal" undertakings (Cesoni, 1995a). The Italian Supreme Court, while differentiating between "gangs" and mafia-type associations, confirms that these associations may be aiming only to control business activity, without actually committing any crime (Minna, 1995).

Paradoxically, the Swiss definition of a criminal organization, introduced in 1994 in the penal code ("an organization which keeps its structure and personnel a secret and whose aims are to commit criminal acts of violence or procure financial advantage by criminal means", art.260*ter* PC), reads like a partial reproduction of an old-fashioned, sociological definition of the Italian Mafia as a secret organization, rather than drawing on recent Italian legislation, which (like French law) does not include the notion of secrecy.

The French penal code defines an association of criminals as "any group or understanding created with a view to planning one or more crimes or offences, in a way which includes certain material acts"(art 450-1PC).

Empirical Definitions

When we pass from theoretical and legal definitions and look at knowledge gained in the field, by the police, by researchers and some journalists, the diversity of the phenomenon is immediately obvious.

Criminal organizations within a single country "Criminal organizations" differ even within countries. For example, what in Italy is called "mafia" is a compendium of groups which differ both among and within themselves (the Mafia proper in Sicily, the Camorra in Naples, the "Ndrangheta" in Calabria, the "Sacra Corona Unita" in Apulia). Besides these "mafias" there are all sorts of more or less autonomous and organized groups devoted to illegal activities (cf. Smuraglia, 1985; Zamagni, 1993; Arlacchi, 1991).

In North America, too, it seems hard to find a common denominator between the Chinese Triads (Posner, 1990), Canadian roadsters, gangs of youths, the new Vietnamese gangs and convict gangs (Brodeur, 1996).

And in sub-Saharan Africa, where organized crime is a recent phenomenon, it is equally hard to find a common denominator between the Nigerian organizations which control the drugs trade in a number of countries (OGD, 1996); the Chinese Triads in South Africa[5]; military or paramilitary organizations engaged in hijacking humanitarian aid; illicit traders in diamonds or natural resources; mercantile networks importing counterfeit money on a colossal scale - and even smuggling by persons in government (Bayart, Ellis, Hibou, 1997).

Globalization and Internationalization All markets are tending towards globalization, and illicit markets are no exception. However, this "globalization" or "internationalization" of organized crime covers a number of different configurations.

A) An organization based in a single country engages in international activities. The classic example is the export of cocaine by the Colombian mafia, or the processing and re-exporting of heroin by the Italian Mafia.

B) An organization based in one country spreads beyond that country's frontiers. This happened with the Chinese Triads and the Italian mafia-type organization. The internationalization of the latter, however, seems to affect only some foreign activities (sometimes legal ones), which do not seem to be monopolized by the organizations concerned (this seems to apply to Camorra members in the south of France and in certain African countries).[6]

C) Criminal organizations interact with one another and extend their networks in order to manage and expand the market in an illegal product. For example, it appears that agreements were made in the late 1980s between mafia-type organizations in Latin America and Italy - most notably between the Sicilian Mafia and the Cali Cartel of Colombia - to manage the export and import of cocaine to Europe (cf. Ministero dell'Interno, 1989; United Nations, 1995 p.9). One of the most recent and complete accounts of the international drugs trade (OGD, 1996) describes a complex and diverse situation. There is a plethora of unconnected channels which are used by different social actors in different ways: thus some ethnic "mafias" (or example, the Chinese Triads), which are represented in a number of countries, control one supply line, while different criminal organizations in various countries cooperate to maintain a supply system, and others merely manage one small area of the trade.

D) Criminal organizations are interacting more and more, on various different markets and in diverse countries, as required by their activities. This may be the consequence of improved communications and freer circulation of people, goods and capital, which have facilitated interchange not only between dealers on illegal markets, but also with any (political or business) grouping which pursues both legal and illegal objectives - or pursues legal objectives by illegal means.

The complexity and diversity of these phenomena cannot be encapsulated by any over-simplified and unambiguous definition. One of the oldest "criminal organizations" in Europe, the Neapolitan Camorra, shows that even the definition of an apparently straightforward phenomenon may not be unproblematic. If we examine three of the principal Camorra clans between 1970 and 1990, on the basis of the judicial procedures and the parliamentary reports (see Cesoni, 1995a), we shall find that they differ among themselves in many ways: there is not just one "Camora", but a multiplicity of Camorrist organizations, as Isaia Sales correctly remarked (1988).

Organized Crime as a Factor of Rationalization

At this moment in time, the strategies for combating organized crime are moving form the national to the supernational level. Indeed, the subject of organized crime - sometimes replaced by, or included in, that of "serious crimes" - is now replacing drugs in international circles. There are numerous analogies between them.

An Undifferentiated Concept

Since the 1960s, political discourse, (and usually) political action on drugs have very largely failed to differentiate between the various products and types of consumer. It took the AIDS epidemic, and the arrival of the new synthetic drugs, to focus attention on the complexity of the "drug phenomenon".

Equally vague, as it oscillates among different definitions, is the concept of organized crime, caricatured in the media as an "octopus," a notion which has even found its way into the international vocabulary.[7]

The definition of organized crime now emerging in United Nations circles refers to a plethora of different social actors and different activities, and so widens the application of existing national laws by creating an elastic regulation open to a wide variety of interpretations and able to include a constant influx of new activities. This progressive broadening of the definition of organized crime has already been put into effect in some countries, such as Italy. The result can be a change of objectives, from the repression of illegal activities to the repression of various categories of perpetrators; guilt, instead of attaching to a person's acts, attaches to his position in life. That is a dangerous attitude in a democracy.

Moreover, this broadening of the interpretation violates the principle of legality, because it criminalizes types of behavior which are not explicitly and precisely determined in the law. Thus Italian courts have been know to prosecute, for involvement in a mafia-type organization, corrupt politicians or entrepreneurs whose business methods may be unorthodox.

A New Public Enemy

The vagueness of the emerging UN role, owing to its promotion as a weapon against a world-wide peril, could supply an excuse for continually advocating exceptional legislative measures capable of eroding fundamental rights and liberties, as has been done in attempts to counter other dangers perceived as global, such as drugs and terrorism.

The drug trade provoked declarations of war.[8] It has now been replaced, in political discourse, by a new collective peril, organized crime, the substitution being facilitated by the fact that organized crime includes drug trafficking. Organized crime is perceived as undermining the foundations of development and democracy.[9] The fact that these dangers are thought to be universal encourages the notion that the end justifies the means.

The need to fight the drugs trade was one of the reasons why the 1988 Vienna Convention urged the universal criminalization of consumers - who hitherto had been described as sufferers, rather than criminals, in international treaties. The Convention also sanctioned extraordinary police practices such as surveillance of deliveries, which had previously been considered excessive.

In countries such as Italy, the struggle against organized crime has already justified the admission of evidence from *pentiti* (co-defendants or defendants in a connected trial) in a way which has not always respected the rights of the defendant;[10] and regulations have been introduced which reverse the burden of proof with regard to confiscations. The same reversal occurs in the laws covering money laundering, which have helped to encourage the merging of legislation on drug trafficking and on organized crime.

A Factor in Foreign Policy

American declarations of war against the drugs trade have been considerably useful for the foreign policy of the United States. Among other things, and thanks in particular to the Cartagena conference in 1990, they helped the US renew its grip on the Latin American countries, which had loosened towards the end of the 1980s owing to institutional changes and increasing economic convergence in that continent.

The role of organized crime in international relations is not yet clear. Could it - for example - constitute an excuse for claiming the right to monitor the domestic policies of Eastern European states? Certainly organized crime appears to have replaced drugs as a factor in relations between EC countries - a useful pretext for demanding the harmonization of judicial procedures inside the community.

An Inducement to International Co-operation

The drugs trade, being an international activity *par excellence* - because the illegal substances consumed in the West are mostly produced elsewhere - has already brought about an increase in, and rationalization of, international police co-operation[11] which developed in the absence of effective controls. Judicial mutual assistance developed somewhat earlier: article 36 of the 1961 Single Convention established a universal right of prosecution for serious drugs-related offences.[12]

How does this affect organized crime? We have seen that the Naples World Action Plan against transnational crime acknowledged the need for a common definition, one aim of which was to rationalize international co-operation on criminal matters. To this end, the Naples Conference proposed an international convention on organized crime.

An Influence on National Legislation

From the beginning of the present century, legislation on narcotics has emerged from an interaction between international conventions and national legal systems: the former have decisively influenced the development of the latter. Subsequently there has been an increasing tendency for national criminal law, both substantive and formal, to be shaped in an international context: in Europe, this applies to laws on money laundering, and to legislation now being developed to assist the criminal prosecution of those who corrupt foreign officials. The same thing would happen, in the wider context of the United Nations, if there were to be a convention on organized crime. There is therefore a growing tendency for international law to influence national criminal law, and to promote harmonization - or even homogenization - in this field.

This poses the problem of democratic control over the legislative process, because national parliaments are much less involved in the drafting and adoption of international conventions than in those of national legislation.

Thus it can be seen that definition and action are closely connected. Before an international convention can be developed, there must be a consensus on the definition of organized crime. In the meantime, although the concept remains ambiguous, it is nonetheless operational, and is sustaining a political approach founded upon repression.

Prevention Strategies

Two conclusions can be drawn from the Italian example. Firstly, attempts to create an unambiguous definition of organized crime fails to embrace the complexity of the phenomenon and the way it interacts with its environment. Secondly, a tendency to respond purely in terms of criminal *repression* will hamper attempts at *prevention*.

Repressive responses arise from the view - held by both politicians and by numerous academics - that organized crime is responsible for cracks in the democratic fabric, failures of economic policy and violations of human rights. This "tunnel vision" discourages proper examination of the conditions which enable groups involved in organized crime to consolidate their power, often on the interface between the legal and the illegal. In fact, such groups can have a real negative effect on their environment only once they are firmly established and have consolidated their power - and even then the effect, in economic terms at least, may not be wholly negative, or else why are such groups often accepted as part of the social fabric?

Therefore, if we wish to curb the development and/or reinforcement of such groups, we must do something about the external conditions which favor them.

The Restoration of Rights and the Assumption of Political Accountability

In the Italian Mezzogiorno, and in other similar environments, the first step is to restore the socio-economic and political rights of people living in conditions which foster the development of mafia-type organizations. That would reduce the pressure to engage in illegal activities - and the opportunity of doing so as well.

The first priority is the education of children and young people. An effective educational policy can be "preventive" in many ways: it reduces the sub-cultural factors which encourage cultures marked by prevarication and violence; it offers alternatives to children who are at risk of an early initiation into juvenile crime; it gives young adults a passport to the (legal) world of work. The other imperative is to encourage production and job creation: otherwise the society will fall apart, leaving individuals to fend for themselves in informal or criminal markets - or leaving them dependent on a welfare system riddled with clientelism.

Effective economic policies and public expenditure are indispensable in order to create viable industries, and therefore jobs, in depressed areas. But these policies must be such as to discourage corruption. They must be plainly visible - in fact, transparent - and must be subject to effective scrutiny on behalf of the community concerned. It is essential to adapt legislation on public markets and on local government finance, and there must be control over political responsibility. Financial dealings must also be controlled, not only to prevent money laundering but also - and particularly - to ensure the transparency of financial organizations which manage public funds. The fewer opportunities there are for corruption in politics and administration, the harder it is for mafia-type organizations to forge links with corrupt officials - which will curb both their economic and political power.

It is also essential to foster a culture of public service, though this must be on a voluntary basis and is therefore harder to develop. Such a culture will ensure that public money is managed for the public good, rather than for the benefit of the bosses and their clients, and will also create public pressure for the political accountability of politicians acting illegally in local and national government. Political sanctions on such conduct prevent its propagation, contrasting with a situation in which people will vote for candidates who are under investigation, or have been found guilty.

Enhanced Protection of Liberties and Rights

If we can diminish the factors which favor the development of mafia-type organizations, we will reduce the reasons (or pretexts) for demanding increased repression at the expense of human rights and fundamental liberties.

Furthermore, it seems logical that if socio-economic rights are respected and the accountability of politicians and administrators affirmed, it should be possible to develop criminal legislation which respects the rights of the citizen as part of a general process prevention.

A self-limiting criminal law, operating alongside a redistribution of educational and job opportunities and a (re)assertion of the ethics of public service, would contribute to reinforcing a positive self-identity among members of the community.

That may be a utopian view. Meanwhile, if we want to create a culture of legality we must at least begin by confining the conception and implementation of law - particularly criminal law - within boundaries determined by fundamental principles, national constitutions, and international conventions on human rights.

Conclusion

It is misguided to restrict the struggle against "organized crime" to repressive responses developed and rationalized by the introduction of new, substantive legal definitions formulated or sustained by academic theorists, while failing to tackle the structural conditions which allow that phenomenon to flourish. Such an approach threatens human rights without offering any substantial and/or durable results.

But that is not the worst of it.

To lump together different offences under a single definition of "organized", and accuse the latter of destabilizing democracy, causing corruption and inhibiting economic development, is tantamount to evading political responsibility for those same problems. For, if certain corrupt politicians are involved in organized crime, this makes "ordinary" (and more widespread) corruption appear less serious. Moreover, if organized crime is responsible for economic problems, this removes the need to develop new economic policies: repression alone will do the trick.

But in a world of omnipresent unemployment (or precarious employment), political disaffection, increased migration and (last but not least) growing demand for illegal goods and services, it seems inevitable that there will also be an increase in the "criminal workforce" and in white collar crimes.

Therefore we need to safeguard not only those rights which are protected by the European Convention on Human Rights, but also all the social, political and economic rights of the ordinary citizen. Only by a redistribution of opportunities and of wealth, and a shift towards a kind of democracy which holds political figures responsible for their actions, will it be possible to reduce the scope for economic offences, and consequently the violence which can accompany them.

Notes

1   Translated by Mrs. Rosemary Morris
2   In the US, the Racketeer Influenced and Corrupt Organizations Law is applied to a list of criminal activities.
3   For an examination of economic approaches to, and definitions of, mafia-type organizations see Cesoni, 1995b.
4   Personal communication at the conference on "Crime and Social Order in Europe," Manchester, 7-10 September 1996. (Yuri Voronin is director of a research project on organized crime at the Urals State Law Academy, Russia.)
5   B.J.M. Wagener gave a paper about his research on this subject at the conference on "Crime and Justice in the Nineties," Pretoria, 3-5 July 1996.
6   The relationship between Sicilian and American Mafias goes back much further.
7   "Octopus" is the nickname of the joint project of the Council of Europe and the European Commission on Corruption and organized crime in States in transition (PHARE program).
8   Especially since 1989, not only by the United States (witness the pronouncements of President Bush) but also, for example, by the former French minister Pierre Joxe.
9   See e.g. Cooney, 1992 and United Nations, 1995.
10   As shown by a recent modification to art. 513 of the Penal Code, which, until it was revised allowed the courts to admit, at a session of the actual trial, evidence given by *pentiti* during the pre-trial investigation - a contravention of the principle that both parties must be heard.
11   As an example, the first European police liaison officers were appointed to combat drugs trade (cf. Bigo, 1996).
12   The aforesaid serious offences, whether committed by nationals or foreigners, will be prosecuted by the Party on whose territory the offence was

committed, or by the Party on whose territory the offender is found, if the laws of the Party to whom the request is addressed do not permit extradition, and if the offender has not already been prosecuted and sentenced (art. 36.2.a.iv).

References

Albanese, J. (1989), *Organized Crime in America,* Cincinnati: Anderson.

Anderson, A. (1979), *The Business of Organized Crime,* Stanford (Calif.): Hoover Institute Press.

Arlacchi, Pino. (1983), *La mafia imprenditrice,* Bologna: Il Mulino.

Arlacchi, Pino. (1991), "Organized crime and criminal gangs." In *Illicit drugs and organized crime: issues for a unified Europe,* edited by S. Flood, Chicago: Office of International Criminal Justice, University of Illinois.

Bayart, Jean-François; Ellis, Stephen and Hibou, Béatrice. (1997), *La criminalisation de l'Etat en Afrique,* Bruxelles: Complexe/Paris: CERI.

Bigo, Didier. (1996), *Polices en réseau l'expérience européene,* Paris: Presses de la Foundation nationale des sciences politiques.

Block, Alan. (1991), *Perspectives on organizing crime. Essays in opposition.* Dordrecht, Boston, London: Kluwer Academic Publ.

Borré, Giuseppe; Pepino, Livio. (1983), *Mafia 'ndrangheta e camorra. Analisi politica e intervento giudiziario.* Milano: F. Angeli.

Brodeur, Jean-Paul. (1996), "Le crime organisé hors de lui-même: tendances récentes de la recherche," Montréal: *Les cahiers de l'école de criminologie* (forthcoming in *Annales internationales de criminologie*).

CENSIS. (1991), *Contro e dentro. Criminalitá, istituzioni, società,* Milan: Franco Angeli.

Cesoni, Maria Luisa. (1995a), *Mezzogiorno et criminalités: la consolidation économique des organisations camorristes.* Doctoral thesis, Paris: Ecole des Hautes études en sciences sociales.

Cesoni, Maria Luisa. (1995b), "L'économie mafieuse en Italie: à la recherche d'un paradigme. . ." *Déviance et société* n. 19, pp. 51-83.

Commissione parlamentare antimafia. (1990), *Mafia e politica in Italia,* Rome: Ed. Associate.

Commissione parlamentare antimafia. (1993), *Mafia e politica,* Rome-Bari: Laterza.

Cooney, Patrick. (1992), *Rapport de la commission d'enquête sur la diffusion dans las pays de la Communauté de la criminalité organisée liée au trafic de drogue,* Strasbourg: Communautés Européennes-Parlement européen.

Dalla Chiesa, Nando. (1976), "Il potere mafioso. Economia e ideologia'" Milan: Mazzotta.

Fituni, Leonid. (1996), "I padrini della nazione. Il ruolo delle mafie nella crisi russa."In *Mafie e antimafie Rapporto '96,* edited by L. Violante. Roma-Bari: Laterza.

Gambetta, Diego. (1992), *La mafia siciliana. Un'industria della protezione privata.* Turin: Einaudi.

Lamberti, Amato. *La camorra. Evoluzione e struttura della criminalitá organizzata in Campania,* Fuorni-Salerno: Boccia.

Martens, Fredrick. (1991), "Transnational enterprise crime: A comparative perspective." In *Illicit drugs and organized crime: issues for a unified Europe,* edited by S. Flood, Chicago: Office of International Criminal Justice, University of Illinois.

Ministero del'Interno, Servizio centrale antidroga. (1989), *Attività Antidroga delle forze di polizia nel 1989,* Roma.

Minna, Rosario. (1995), *La mafia in cassazione,* Florence: La Nuova Italia.

Nations Unies. (1995), La Conférence ministérielle mondiale sur la criminalité transnationale organisée, *Prévention du crime and justice pénale, bulletin d'information,* n.. 26/27.

OGD - Observatoire géopolitique des drogues. (1996), *Atlas mondial des drogues.* Paris: PUF.

Padovani, Marcelle. (1987), *Les dernières années de la mafia,* Paris: Gallimard.

Posner, Gerald. (1990), *Triades. La mafia chinoise,* Paris: Stock.

Reuter, Peter. (1983), *Disorganized crime. The economics of the visible hand,* Cambridge (Mass.), London: MIT Press.

Rey, G.M. and Savona, Ernesto U. (1993), "The mafia: an international enterprise?" In *Mafia issues: Analyses and proposals for combating the mafia today,* edited by E.U. Savona, Milan: ISPAC.

Sales, Isaia. (1988), *La camorra le camorre,* Rome: Editori Riuniti.

Sales, Isaia. (1994), "Ciro Cirillo," In *Cirillo, Ligato, Lima. Tre storie di mafia e politica,* edited by N. Tranfaglia, Rome-Bari: Laterza.

Santino, Umberto and La Fiura, Giuseppe. (1990), *L'impresa mafiosa. Dall'Italia agli Stati Uniti,* Milano: Franco Angeli.

Schelling, Thomas. (1967), "Economic analysis of organized crime." In *Task force report: Organized crime.* Washington D.C.: U.S Government Printing office.

Sim, J.; Ruggiero, V. and Ryan, M. (1995), "Punishment in Europe: perceptions and commonalities." In *Western European Penal Systems: A critical anatomy,* edited by V. Ruggiero, M. Ryan and J. Smith, London, Thousand Oaks, New Delhi: Sage.

Smith, Dwight. (1975), *The mafia mystique,* New York: Basic Books.

Smuraglia, Carlo, ed. (1985), *La criminalitá organizzata in Lombardia. Il fenomeno-rimedi,* Milan: Giuffré.

Wolleb, E. and Wolleb, G. (1990), *Divari regionale e dualismo economico.* Bologna: Il Mulino.

Zamagni, Stefano, ed. (1993), *Mercati illegali e mafie. L'economia del crimine organizzato.* Bologna: Il Mulino.

15 Repeal Drug Prohibition and End the Financing of International Crime

ARTHUR BERNEY

It is my view that the harms associated with illicit drug trafficking, perhaps the most widespread form of transnational crime, can be reduced and even eliminated by decriminalizing all forms of the drug trade.

I draw courage to present this position to the Conference on Global Organized Crime and International Security from the "Rationale for the Workshop" offered by the chairperson, Professor Emilio Viano:

> Transnational crime is presently the most serious security threat to democratic institutions, the rule of law, community welfare, and basic values and norms. . . The menace represented by emerging forms of transnational crime. . . goes to heart of what is security, democracy and development.

At the outset then I will try to briefly give some specificity to the referenced threats to "democratic institutions, the rule of law, community welfare", drawn from my own study of illicit drug enforcement efforts in the United States. I am not a social scientist or criminologist. My interest in organized crime, and in particular drug trafficking, arose as an aspect of my studies on discrimination against minorities in the Unites States. One cannot be a student of American law without acknowledging the terrible history of racism in the United States. Even given this, I was not fully prepared for the charge that the "war on drugs could more aptly be called a war on minority populations",[1] This charge was backed up by statistics in the Unites States that beg any explanation other than racial and ethnic discrimination.[2] Throughout the conference we heard accounts that in a like manner other societies laid the blame for drug trafficking on the heads of foreign ethnic gangs and outsiders. This echoes the xenophobic nature of the perception of the drug problem in almost all countries. With the possible exception of the babies born addicted, everyone else involved in this "dirty business" of illicit drugs is made the object of contempt and vilification. If this were not, in itself bad enough, this stereotyping merges and seems indistinguishable, in the general "public's mind",[3] from the more ancient and invidious forms of stereotyping to wit: race, alienage and class.

As I began to study the "war against drugs" I also perceived the threat that the extreme means of fighting this war posed to civil liberties. In 1989 Milton Friedman, no social radical, wrote an open letter to William Bennett, the then "drug czar", in which he said:

> Every friend of freedom. . . must be revolted . . . by the prospect of turning the United States into an armed camp, by the vision of jails filled with casual drug users and of an army of enforcers empowered to invade the liberty of citizens on slight evidence, a country in which unidentified planes may be shoy down 'on suspicion'[4] . . . is not the kind of United States that either you or I want to hand on to future generations.[5]

Another commentator, noted that "[t]hroughout the history of the United States, the government has used exigencies of war as an excuse to constrict the constitutional liberties of American citizens". Applying this insight to the drug prohibition program, he observed that driven by the "war propaganda" in the "metaphorical war" against drugs, the American people have been willing to "countenance all manner of civil liberties abuses".[6] To prove the point, he cited opinion polls that found that 52% of Americans said "police should be able to search homes of suspected drug dealers without a warrant",[7] and quoted former New York City Mayor Koch's proposal "to strip-search everyone entering the United States from Latin America or Asia".[8]

This kind of talk is unnerving, but perhaps it is "just talk". Would that this is so. Unhappily, the evidence supports the charge that government anti-drug policies - at home and abroad[9] - grievously abridge civil liberties and human rights.[10] Beyond the summary of patent offenses of civil liberty lies an entire field of indirect, subtle and systematic injuries to democratic processes and protected rights. Among these are: the numerous instances of unequal application of the law, disparate sentencing under inflexible penalty guidelines,[11] growing police brutality[12] and corruption,[13] overcrowding in and appalling conditions of jails,[14] and the overwhelming of the judicial criminal system.[15]

The cumulative effect of these ravages upon the delicate reticulation of civil liberties, painstakingly stitched over the centuries into the fabric of a free society,[16] may be nothing short of devastating. The prediction of a coming "new conservatism, employing repressive, police-state tactics"[17] removed from the following proposals offered by some of our leasers and opinion makers: establishing large internment camps for drug offenders; using federal troops to break the back of [Washington, D.C.'s] lucrative drug racket; using troops along U.S. borders for interdiction and for defoliating source countries.[18] Some of these ideas can be dismissed as wild, but the proposed use of military force in particular, because it already has been tried to some degree, cannot be ignored in any final assessment of the threat to civil liberties posed by prohibition policy. Of course, if the military poses a threat to civilian control and republican governance in the U.S. that threat is remote as compared to that posed by heightened military intervention in Latin American. In pursuit of its drug policies the United States has made common cause with the military in various countries in the Andean and Caribbean regions and has even deployed forces in largely futile efforts to interdict the drug trade,[19] thereby placing civilian and democratic governments at immediate risk.[20]

Ultimately the most fundamental civil liberties threat that the prohibition of drug use involves entails a form of statism that strikes at the values associated with individual autonomy.[21] In the interest of time I will not make this argument here but will merely refer you to an extraordinary recent decision of the Supreme Court of Colombia.[22] I cannot let pass the hypocritical nature of the application of a moral and criminal code that selectively proscribes only some forms of drug use. Consider the case of a hypothetical drug which has an addiction risk similar to opiates, and which has an acute toxicity syndrome including: "nausea, tremor, tachycardia and in high doses, hypertension, bradycardia, diarrhea, muscle twitch and respiratory paralysis." In addition this drug's chronic toxicity syndrome includes: "coronary, cerebral and peripheral vascular disease, gangrene, gastric acidity, peptic ulcer, withdrawal irritability, impaired attention and concentration, retarded fetal growth, and spontaneous abortion." Finally, you might recognize this drug if I told you that it is delivered ordinarily by introduction to the lungs, which delivery system contributes to the incidence of lung diseases, including pneumonia, emphysema and cardiogenic lesions, of users and persons incidentally exposed to such use.[23] If in the face of these proven factors, the government acts to ban the growth of the plant from which the drug is derived, as well as the manufacture, distribution and sale of the product, would the police and national security forces recommend, in view of projected costs and likely success of maintaining the ban, the adoption of such a ban? Of course, the hypothetical drug referred to is nicotine and the product, tobacco. The idea that we adopt a prohibition policy toward tobacco would be considered foolhardy, if not absurd. The experience of alcohol prohibition early in this century, probably would be sufficient to head off any such approach concerning tobacco use. If this is the case with respect to tobacco, why does the same logic not apply to the prohibition of so-called illicit narcotics? The associated health risks of alcohol and cigarettes is, if anything, greater than the risks of cocaine and opium use.[24] Similarly, although abuse of prescription drugs such as amphetamines and barbiturates does not cause tissue damage equal to cigarettes and alcohol, the health risks they create are no less severe than those created by illicit drugs. Again we have to ask: why are these drugs prescribed and illicit drugs proscribed?[25]

The answer to this key question, in my view, is primarily a matter of economics. In contrast to cocaine, which is produced solely in South America, and opiates mainly in Asia, the production of alcohol, cigarettes and prescription drugs is largely supported and controlled by resources and industries within the United States and other developed economies. These three major industries play a significant role in the western economies, providing substantial revenue and jobs as well as generating billions of tax dollars. Let us compare, however, the economic data respecting the illicit drug trade. Based on 1992 figures, total global imports were $3,849.4 billion. Trade in oil, mineral fuels and lubricants amounted to 9.5% of this total. Food, animals, beverages and tobacco, combined, equaled another 9%. Conservative estimates of the illicit drug trade was between $400 and $500 billion, or 10-13%! Such comparative figures are hard to give credence to. Who, for example, would believe that illicit drug trade would exceed chemicals and pharmaceuticals by $100 billion or motor vehicle sales by 100%? Paradoxically, these figures can be explained by realizing that more than 90% of the gross profit in the illicit drug trade is generated at the distribution stage and that this out-sized distribution "value" is the direct result of the risks imposed by the effort to prohibit the trade. In other words, most of the profits of the illicit drug trade can be traced to government police efforts.[26]

According to this analysis it would appear that there are three major groups which benefit directly from the existing drug regime: 1) The organized crime elements which derive most of the income for all of their criminal enterprises form the profits in the production, distribution and sale of illicit drugs.[27] 2) The licit drug businesses (the tobacco, alcohol and the pharmaceutical companies) that are substantially protected from open competition, maintaining a corner on the demand for psychotropic substances in the open "white" market.[28] 3) The law enforcement agencies and personnel that are essentially in a symbiotic relationship with the drug traffickers, deriving a great part of their budgets and income from the world wide (losing) war against illicit drug use.[29]

When the prohibition (of alcohol) era finally ended in the United States organized crime lost one of its major sources of income almost over night. Today alcoholic beverage companies, some of which trace their roots to the illicit (bootleg) businesses of the prohibition era, are among the largest and most successful commercial enterprises in the global economy. Hundreds of thousands of people derive their livelihood directly and derivatively from this vast enterprise and billions of dollars in tax revenues are generated in the form if income, sales and excise taxes from this activity. There is no reason to doubt that if other prohibition regimes (against prostitution, gambling and narcotics) were curtailed all of these "vices" would become, like alcoholic consumption, a normal activity subject to the constraints of reasonable regulation and limits.

The obvious conclusion does not need to be belabored. Illicit drug trade has not been reduced by the prohibition effort, indeed, as suggested, the high profits in the trade are largely traceable to the prohibition effort. In addition, harking back to my opening points "'the most serious security threat to democratic institutions, the rule of law, community welfare, and basic values and norms'" is not drug trafficking itself but the futile law enforcement effort to stop it. Therefore, I believe the only sensible thing to do is to call an end to the prohibition approach.[30] Diminishing the economic power of drug traffickers, some of whom are without doubt ruthless sociopaths, is surely a worthwhile end in itself. However, beyond that direct benefit, the list of salutary effects this action might well lead to are quite impressive:

- It would bring the international trade in the commodities (heroin, cocaine, cannabis and synthetic drugs) into the normal course of trade - contributing to tax revenues and GNP.
- It would serve to marginalize, reduce or eliminate criminal cartels and organization, diminishing their capability to underwrite other criminal activity. This in turn will reduce the corruptive power of criminal organizations.

- It would reduce the violence and social displacement directly connected to the present drug trafficking system, and indirectly reduce property crime (a major source of money needed to maintain drug habits).

- It would substantially cut the costs of the criminal enforcement and justice system, thus freeing enforcement resources for protecting the welfare of the community against "victim" crime.

- It would release public funds for educational and health care programs that have proven to be the most effective way to reduce drug dependency and addiction.[31] Just eliminating the activity of pushers and perverse role models will probably reduce use, especially among the young.

- It will reorient the thinking about addictive and self-harmful behavior, probably in the direction of focusing on addictive behavior as mental and physiological matter that is best addressed by scientists. One immediate health consequence may be the reduction of diseases communicated by contaminated needles and prostitution.[32]

- It will make it possible to promote a policy of shifting the deleterious cost of drug use and abuse to those who profit from it. (In the U.S. there already is a move afoot to reach a "settlement" with the tobacco industry. There is no reason why the social, health and economic costs of enterprises that thrive on and induce the consumption of harmful substances ought not, to bear - perennially - the costs they impose on society.)

Even as I would like to close on what I consider the hopeful note that the international community is drawing closer to the abandonment of the policy of prohibition, there are few signs that this will occur in the foreseeable future. Nevertheless, there are steps that are attainable and which may prepare the ground for a turn away from the present policy. A first such step would be to convince the law enforcement community to de-emphasize the programs aimed at curtailing production and interdicting the movement of drugs, and to stop arresting, prosecuting and incarcerating users, and instead to gradually shift all of its modern technological capability toward the effort to forestall the movement of profits, through money laundering.[33] Related to this latter emphasis on "following the money", anyone found complicit in the transfer of money, including the international banks, should be required to underwrite a proportional share of the health care and rehabilitation costs related to drug use. Finally, the recent proposals to call on the licit drug companies (tobacco, alcohol, and pharmaceutical companies) to bear the cost of the harms that their products cause, should be adopted at the international level. If that final step is achieved it will be more likely that the nations of the world will come to see that the same technique could and should be applied to the devastation caused by the worldwide illicit drug consumption.

Notes

1   Powell, J. and Hershenov, E. (1991) "Hostage to the Drug War: The National Purse, the Constitution and the Black Community," UC Davis Law Review, n. 24, pp. 557, 559.

2   Before the age of twenty-five, a black man is today more likely to die in streets than a United States soldier was to perish in Vietnam. . . [emphasis deleted]. Fully eight to ninety percent of drug arrests nationwide involve African American males . . . despite the fact . . . that blacks make up only 12% of the nation's drug users. Fully eighty-two percent of a population of 55,000 inmates in New York's state prisons are black or Latino . . . [M]inorities now comprise ninety-five percent of New York City's jail population . . . "In Florida, state researchers predict that . . . nearly half of black men in 18-34 age group will be locked up or under court supervision." Although substance abuse was equally prevalent among white and black women, a black woman who uses drugs or alcohol during pregnancy is almost ten times more likely to be reported to the state authorities than a white woman. *Ibid* pp. 608-612.

3   If, as apparently the case, most consumers of cocaine in the United States are white, why are journalists not questioning or explaining the odd fact that most of the "drug busts," police raids and arrests take place in the minority neighborhoods of U.S. cities.

4   The reference is to the vote by the Senate, reversed the following day, in favor of a proposal to "shoot down unidentified airplanes entering the United States". See 1989 Washington Times, 6 October at A2, col. 1.

5   Friedman, Milton. (1989), "An Open Letter to Bill Bennett", Wall Street Journal, 7 September sec. 1 p. 14 col. 3.

6   Boaz, David. (1991), "A Drug-Free America - Or a Free America", UC Davis Law Review, n. 24, pp. 617-626.

7   Boaz. p. 626, referring to Morin, M. (1989), "Poll Say Bush Plan Is Not Stringent Enough", Washington Post, 8 September, p. A18, col. 1.

8   Boaz. p. 627, referring to United Press International release 7 July 1984.

9   Professor Peter Smith, director of the Center for Iberian and Latin American Studies at the University of California, describes the effect of the "U.S. - sponsored drug wars" in this fashion: "The wars have altered society and politics in important and far-reaching ways. First, they have subjected the countries and peoples of Latin America to staggering levels of violence and intimidation. The human toll of anti-drug campaigns has been extremely high - not only in Colombia but also in Peru and Mexico" (Smith, 1992 and Americas Watch Committee, 1990). In 1995 "nearly 1,000 Columbia law enforcement and military personnel were killed or wounded fighting drug traffickers" (Kitfield, 1996).

10   Berney, Arthur. (1995), "Cocaine Prohibition: Drug Induced Madness in the Western Hemisphere", Boston College Third World Law Journal, n. 15 pp. 19, 37-43.

11   The Comprehensive Drug Abuse Prevention and Control Act, as amended in 1986, provides that the possession of one hundred times the amount of powdered cocaine carries the same penalty as the possession of crack cocaine. Anti-Drug Abuse Act of 1986, Pub L 99-570 Stat. 3207, Title I section 1005, codified at 21 U.S.C. section 801 (1988 and Supp. V. 1993) See 21 U.S.C. section 841 (b) (1988 and Supp. V. 1993) African American males tend to use crack cocaine more often, while powdered cocaine is mainly used by whites. See the National Household Survey on Drug Abuse 1992 pages 32-39.

12   See Letwin, Michael. (1990), "Report from the Front Line: The Bennett Plan, Street Level Drug Enforcement in New York City", Hofstra Law Review n. 18 pp. 795, 819-821.

13   See Special Committee on Criminal Justice in a Free Society, American Bar Association, 1988 at 47 stating, "bribery, even complicity in [drug] trafficking by law enforcement officials or lawyers and judges is inevitable". See also Ostrowski, James. (1990), "The Moral and Practical Case for Legalization". Hofstra Law Review, n. 18, pp. 607, 663-664. This analysis states: "Drug corruption charges have been leveled against FBI agents, policemen, prison guards, U.S. Custom inspectors, even prosecutors." Ostrowski, p. 663, citing a long list of newspaper reports, at n. 264.

14   "In 1993, 59.5% of federal prisoners were committed for drug offences". U.S. Department of Justice, Bureau of Justice Statistics, Sourcebook. (1993), p. 633. See Schuler, J. and McBride, A. (1990), "Notes from the Front: A Dissident Law-Enforcement Perspective on Drug Prohibition", Hofstra Law Review, n. 18, pp. 183, 917.

15   See Bishop, Katherine. (1990), "Mandatory Sentences in Drug Cases: Is the Law Defeating its Purpose?" New York Times, 8 June, p. B16 (discussing judges' concern that surge in drug cases is overwhelming the federal courts).

16   See, e.g. Olmstead v. United States 277 US 438, 485 (1928) (J. Brandeis in a now classic dissent describing the importance of the protection of civil liberties to a free society).

17   DeParle, Jason. (1994), "The Most Dangerous Conservative", The New York Times Magazine, 9 October pp. 48, 50 (a profile of Charles Murray, co-author of *The Bell Curve*, The Free Press, 1994).

18   See Schuler and McBride, supra note 14, p. 896.

19   Gugliotta, Guy. (1992), "The Colombian Cartels and How to Stop Them", in *Drug Policy in the Americas*, ed. Peter Smith, pp. 120-122. and Bagely, Bruce. (1992), "Myths of Militarization: Enlisting Armed Forces in the War on Drugs", in *Drug Policy in the Americas*, p. 140-141.

20   Walker, William. (1992), "International Collaboration in Historical Perspective", in *Drug Policy in the Americas*, pp. 272-273 (describing the continous U.S. efforts to intercept drug production in Mexico).

21   If for example, a person has the right to refuse medical intervention, does that same person not have the right to consume substances of his choice? C.f. Washington v. Harper, 110 S.Ct. 1028 (1990) wherein the U.S. Supreme Court recognized a prisoner's "significant liberty interest in avoiding the unwanted administration of anti-psychotic drugs".

22   See In re *A. Sochandamandou*, (File N. C-221/94, Constitutional Court of Justice, Republic of Colombia) May 5, 1994. The Court declared that those provisions of Colombian law that punished persons for possession of addictive drugs in amounts described in the law as "doses for personal use" (which in the case of cocaine was set at one gram or less), or in the case of addiction required commitment to a psychiatric clinic were unconstitutional. The court rested its decision on constitutional norms that "respected human dignity", recognized the "priority of the inalienable rights of an individual, such as autonomy as an immediate expression of freedom".

23   See Goldstein, Avram and Kant, Harald. (1990), "Drug Policy: Striking the Right Balance", Science, 28 September, p. 1514.

24   The addictive qualities of the three different drugs are comparable; moreover, the adverse effects of most psychotropic drugs are related to the central nervous system whereas alcohol and cigarettes cause substantial damage to the heart, liver and lungs. Goodin, Robert E. (1989), *No Smoking* pp. 26-27; Arif, A. and Westermeyer, J. (1988), *Manual of Drug and Alcohol Abuse*, pp. 137, 224 and 217.

25   The health costs imposed on society by the use and abuse of alcohol, prescribed psychotropic drugs, and cigarette are enormous. In the United States a 1984 report put the direct medical cost from smoking related diseases at $11 billion and losses due to reduced productivity at $36 billion! Whelan, E. (1984), *A Smoking Gun: How the Cigarette Industry Gets Away with*

Murder. Comparisons between illicit drugs and to all forms of licit drugs, both in terms of direct health costs and derivative costs are problematic because predictions of how much drug use would increase if all drug use was decriminalized vary substantially. However, it is instructive that even now "the drug most associated with crime and violence is alcohol". This suggests that the nature of a substance and its impact on behavior is more relevant to the harm and costs it imposes than whether or not it is prohibited.

26   The economic extrapolations are based on figures reported in the United Nations International Drug Control Programme (UNDCP), Economic and Social Consequences of Drug Abuse and Illicit Trafficking: An Interim Report, E/CN.7/1995/3 (9 November 1994) 7-8, 11. [Herafter UNDCP Report].

27   The enormous influence that drug organizations have in many countries and the pernicious activities they finance, including terrorism, demonstrate how critical the drug money is to all criminal activity. UNDCP Report at 38 paragraph 107-109.

28   The abuse of synthetic drugs (hallucinogens, amphetamines and sedatives diverted from illicit trade) is already higher than that of heroin and cocaine combined UNDCP Report at 15 paragraph 35.

29   A five-year study at the University of California reported that the annual expenditure in the United States was $11 billion plus for police activity, the criminal justice system and the correction systems in connection with the ban on illicit drugs. Vallance, T. (1993), *Prohibitions Second Failure*, Praeger, pp. A more recent estimate put the total antidrug budget at roughly $15 billion for 1997. Kitfield, J. (1996), "Four Star Czar", CIS Congressional Compass p. 4, The National Journal, 13 April. Another measure of the expenditure efforts going to the drug control can be extrapolated from federal budgetary figures for fiscal 1997 in the U.S. Of $6,339,000 budgeted to the Office of the President, fully 48% was assigned to the Office of the National Drug Control Policy and Federal Drug Control Programs. In a billion dollar state department appropriation request more than one-fifth of this figure was for "international narcotics control". Although there are surely no other nations that spend at the level of the U.S. in an attempt to reduce illegal drug activity, the costs internationally are some multiple of that of the U.S., particularly if, as reported at the Oñate conference, included in the income of law enforcement bodies we count the bribes and other forms of official corruption in many nations.

30   Probably the only people in the world more opposed to and frightened by this idea than the "drug war crusaders" are the drug traffickers themselves.

31   Dr. Herbert D. Kleber, Medical Director for Addiction and Substance Abuse at Columbia University, stated that data indicated that $1.00 spent on

addiction treatment saves about $5.00 elsewhere in the health care system. Kitfield note 26 supra at 10. In 1991 the economic cost of drug abuse in the U.S. was estimated to be $76 billion. UNDCP Report at 34 paragraph 88.

32   See UNDCP Report at 34, paragraph 88.

33   It has been estimated that $350 billion of the total $500 billion of the illicit drug trade is available for laundering every year. UNDCP Report at 27, paragraph 71. As importantly, by focusing almost all the enforcement efforts on the flow of money to the crime organizations, we would reduce a great deal of the terror and violence associated with the current system. Weapons are not useful tools against inhibitions of electronic money transfers.

16 The Criminal Justice System Facing the Challenges of Organized Crime

EMILIO C. VIANO

This chapter offers an overview of the major federal laws enacted recently in the United States to combat organized crime. Surprising as it might seem, there are still countries that do not have any meaningful legislation that defines or addresses the problem of organized crime. While the transnational nature of today's syndicate makes it imperative that international conventions and treaties be developed, ratified and applied, the first step is still each country's development of the appropriate legal tools for the fight against organized crime. The United States has been at the forefront in developing related legal approaches, models and techniques that have greatly influenced other countries and provided appropriate models. This chapter intends to offer an overview and analysis of the U.S. legislation as an example of concerted and aggressive approach to combating organized crime.

Federal Organized Crime Control Provisions

The federal organized crime control laws are designed to attack varying elements of organized criminal activity. Largely building upon Congress' interstate commerce powers, several of the statutes regulate abuses or misuses of commercial avenues. For example the Hobbes Act, 18 U.S.C.S. section 1951, criminalizes any activity in which an individual uses robbery, extortion, conspiracy, or threats to obstruct, delay, or interfere with interstate commerce. A person convicted under this act is subject to either a $10,000 fine, up to twenty years imprisonment, or both.

The Travel Act, 18 U.S.C.S. section 1952, makes it a crime to travel interstate or use interstate facilities, including the mail, with the intent to aid or conduct racketeering activities. These offenses include the distribution of proceeds from unlawful activity, committing a crime, violence, or furthering unlawful activity, or otherwise promoting, managing, facilitating, etc., any unlawful activity. Punishment for violation of this act is a $10,000 fine, imprisonment of up to five years, or both. Eighteen U.S.C.S. sections 1953 and 1955 relate to illegal gambling activities. Section 1953 makes it a crime to transport interstate any paraphernalia used, or designed for use, in bookmaking, sports wagering pools, or numbers games. Section 1955 defines "illegal gambling business" and prohibits engaging in any of the specified activities. Such activities are considered illegal if they involve five or more persons and either remain in substantially continuous operation for over thirty days or gross $2,000 in one day. Violations of section 1955 are punishable by a $10,000 fine and/or five years imprisonment, while section 1955 carries a $20,000 fine and/or five years jail time. Finally, section 1954 and section 1958 relate to other criminal conduct associated with organized crime-influencing operations of an employee benefit plan and commissioning or conducting murder for hire. Under section 1954, a person who offers or receives any money, loan gift, kickback, or other item of value in exchange for influence regarding decisions or other duties concerning benefit plans is subject to a $10,000 fine and/or three years imprisonment. Similarly, any person who travels or uses, or causes another (including the intended victim) to travel or use, interstate facilities with the intent to commit a murder has committed a crime. The penalty for this crime varies depending upon the resulting injury: $10,000 and/or ten years imprisonment if no personal injury results; $20,000 and/or twenty years if personal injury results; and $50,0000 and/or life imprisonment if death occurs.

In addition to the above statutes, provisions of the Drug Prevention Act related to continuing criminal enterprises are also intended to punish those engaged in organized crime. This section defines "continuing criminal enterprise" as any violation of the act which is a felony and which is part of a continuing series of violations taken in concert with five or more persons and from which such a person obtains substantial income.

The Racketeering Influence and Corrupt Organization Act   (RICO)

A number of federal and state laws exist to prevent activities associated with criminal operations. An important piece of federal legislation is the Racketeering Influence and Corrupt Organization Act (RICO).[1] The majority of RICO-type acts are patterned after the federal laws which seek to control abuses or misuses of commercial avenues. These federal laws are generally based on Congress' power to regulate interstate commerce under the United States Constitution.[2] The law places special emphasis on gambling and drug trafficking because these are two activities typically associated with organized crime.

The origins of the RICO Act can be traced to two bills proposed in 1967 by Senator Roman Hruska of Nebraska. These bills sought to stop organized crime's infiltration of legitimate businesses by amending the Antitrust laws and borrowing antitrust remedies. In 1971, as part of the Organized Crime Control Act, the Congress enacted RICO, which strengthened prosecutorial tools available to law enforcement personnel. Changes in the Federal Witness Protection Program, wiretap surveillance regulations, and the Continuing Criminal Enterprise (CCE) statutes[3] resulted in increased numbers of prosecutions and longer sentences. RICO and CCE rely on a legal concept that makes participation in the affairs of a criminal enterprise a crime in itself, with punishment more severe than for the underlying behavior. For example RICO requires for conviction that the defendant commit certain predicate acts that constitute racketeering activity. The predicates are 37 federal and 8 state felonies. They include gambling, prostitution, drug offenses, fraud extortion, bribery, labor law violations, even cigarette bootlegging-offenses commonly found in organized crime activities.

RICO is a liberally constructed piece of legislation similar to conspiracy law but using the new tactic of enterprise forfeiture to battle organized crime.[4] There is no problem of overlap between these "new" varieties of crime and traditional crimes. In fact, the percentage of RICO cases that involve traditional racketeering has been shrinking drastically. RICO does three things. It creates new crimes, posits new criminal penalties, and establishes grounds for new civil suits. RICO's far and most controversial objective is to make it unlawful for individuals to function as members of organized criminal groups. Under RICO, participation in an organized criminal group is a violation in itself. The statute defines "enterprise" to include any individual, partnership, corporation, association, or other legal entity, or any group of individuals who, though not a legal entity, are associated in fact.

Faced with such severe penalties for their very association in a criminal enterprise, defendants charged with RICO and CCE violations are increasingly turning to the federal protection program. The code of silence in the criminal brotherhood, epitomized in the Mafia's omertà, has apparently been broken. Every leader of the five organized crime families operating in the New York metropolitan area are in prison, including the "Teflon don", Gotti. Almost all of them are there because trusted members of their "family", under threat of spending most of their remaining lives in prison, have turned state's evidence and testified against their leaders (Ryan, 1995, pp. 24-25).

While law enforcement officials trumpet and take pride in victories won under RICO, prosecutions of the rich and powerful have produced loud claims of overreaching, bringing in the advent of civil RICO suits, often founded on ordinary business disputes. RICO critics argue that Congress' sole intent was to end Mafia infiltration of legitimate businesses. These critics maintain that Congress did not want RICO to be used against people having no Mafia ties. Some critics further contend that even Mafia figures were not to be prosecuted for activities other than the infiltration of legitimate businesses (Alito, 1989, p. 3).

Besides arming the prosecutors with new criminal charges, RICO introduced several important procedural changes. RICO at the trial judge's discretion permitted all members of the enterprise to be charged and tried together, thereby allowing the jury to view each defendant and each crime in a broader context. Defense attorneys have been very critical of this kind of system. They argue that it permits a spill-over of evidence from one defendant to the other and from one charge to another. Although the Double Jeopardy clause of the U.S. Constitution prohibits a defendant from being tried and convicted more than once for the same offense, RICO permits a crime to be charged as a RICO predicate even if the defendant was previously convicted and served a sentence for the predicate offense. This is a distinct difference between the way old traditional crimes were charged and tried, and the way new crimes are being handled today by using RICO. While evidence rules generally restrict proof of a person's character and association, RICO permits proof of membership in any criminal group charged as the enterprise.

Violations of RICO carry heavy criminal penalties. In addition RICO contains broad, innovative, and highly effective forfeiture[5] provisions. Before RICO, forfeiture was not generally viewed as an important weapon or deterrent against crime. As a result RICO revived the concept of criminal forfeiture, which had laid dormant since colonial days. Under this procedure, criminal forfeiture may result in a judgement ordering the defendant to pay a sum of money even if the cash or property subject to forfeiture has been hidden, squandered, transferred or converted into some other form of wealth (Alito, pp. 8-90).

There is also what might be called the moral relativity defense of RICO, which equates the activity of organized criminals with the activities of legitimate business and is unable to or unwilling to differentiate between the two. Under this view, the rigorous penalties of RICO are just as applicable against an investment banker or accountant as against the head of a Mafia family that runs drugs and commits murder. Until 1988 the RICO Act permitted the Department of Justice to prosecute attorneys and seize fees from tainted sources. Defense attorneys argued that this created a situation in which a defendant cannot retain an attorney because of the government's threat of criminal and civil sanctions against any attorney who takes the case. This in turn forces the defendant to depend on a public defender, who is not always able to defend his client adequately against the often complex nature of RICO.

As a result of this controversies, in 1988, President Ronald Reagan, signed an anti-drug abuse bill that contained an amendment to 18 U.S.C. section 1957. The amendment excluded defense attorneys fees from the criminal money laundering provisions.[6] Thus, while criminal defense fees could still be subject to forfeiture, attorneys who accept tainted fees are exempt from criminal prosecution. Under RICO, the U.S. has been able to extend its laws extra-territorially, especially when it is a prosecution for money laundering and drugs trafficking. This of course presupposes the cooperation of the nations in which these money laundering and drug activities are taking place and which have a direct effect in the U.S.

All state statutes related to interstate activities are preempted by the federal RICO statute; however, they still apply to intrastate offenses. The majority of state RICO-related acts are patterned after the federal laws. The state statutes are generally similar. Each begins with a detailed listing and definition of "crime related" or "racketeering" activity. Next, each establishes criminal liability for a racketeering offense and defines the penalty, which includes jail time, a fine or both. An alternative to a fine is also defined in both measures by the amount of pecuniary loss caused by the defendant. Statutes also define civil penalties including forfeiture of property, seizure of property, injunctions or suspension or revocation of one's license. Many statutes clearly state that the civil remedies are not mutually exclusive, nor are they a substitute to criminal sanctions.

Money Laundering

The primary motivation of those engaged in international organized crime is financial gain. Money laundering was made illegal by the Anti-Drug Abuse Act of 1986, which clearly sought to expand the scope and intensity of money-laundering enforcement. In a practical sense, money laundering involves the day-to-day, dollar-to-dollar flow of cash generated from drug sales.

Launderers generally have two purposes in mind when they set in motion the cumbersome laundering process. First, they wish to hide the source of their drug-generated cash. Second, they want to transfer this money in a manner which is difficult to trace and ultimately beyond the reach of law enforcement. Usually, but not in all cases, this means that the money leaves the country, where its trail is further obscured and where it is often not subject to restraint or seizure.[7] Money laundering is a criminal attack on the integrity and safety of the international economic order.

The laws that most assist launderers of the proceeds of crime are those ensuring bank secrecy, a practice which allows and/or mandates financial institutions to keep information received about their customers in the course of business, secret and confidential. Bank secrecy can create insurmountable difficulties in the detection and investigation of laundering cases. This is because records of financial transactions are needed to uncover physical transactions and often are the only proof that such transactions took place.

Additionally, financial gains from crime are generally returned to those planning and directing the commission of the crime. Financial transactions are also useful in the investigation of highly profitable crimes because they reveal the identities of those involved in them. It must be recognized, of course, that individuals have a legitimate interest in protecting the privacy of their financial affairs. This interest clashes with the government's interest when the latter requires the disclosure of financial information to assist its investigations.

Laws pertaining to money laundering illustrate the tension which can exist between individual rights and the needs of law enforcement. Although in the United States individuals expect and are entitled to privacy in matters pertaining to banking and financial activities, records of financial transactions can help law enforcement personnel find the perpetrators of certain crimes.

Three important laws address this problem in slightly different ways. These laws are: (1) The Bank Secrecy Act of 1970; (2) The Right to Financial Privacy Act of 1978; and (3) The Money Laundering Control Act of 1986. One should note that the Money Laundering Control Act creates two new money laundering crimes: "money laundering" and "monetary transactions". The first crime involves the use or transport of money which one is aware represents the proceeds of some unlawful activity with the intent to either promote such activity, conceal its nature, or avoid a legally required transaction-reporting requirement.[8] The Monetary Transaction Crime is broad and defined as use of criminally-derived property in monetary transactions such as deposits, withdrawals, transfers, and so forth.[9] Persons convicted of a money laundering crime are subject to both fines and imprisonment; however, monetary transaction violators receive only criminal fines and civil penalties. Both these crimes, and the text of the Money Laundering Control Act as a whole, represent the current legislative trend in favor of greater limits on individual privacy rights in exchange for better law enforcement procedures.

The Money Laundering Crime

The focus of the law, however, is not so much on the actions but rather on the specific intent or knowledge of the underlying activity on the part of the accused. The defendant must know that the financial transaction or transportation is meant either (1) to conceal or disguise the nature, location, source, ownership, or control of the proceeds of some kind of crime, which is a felony under federal or state law, or (2) to avoid a transaction-reporting requirement under federal or state law. Thus, negligent involvement in a money laundering scheme cannot be punished under this law. Engaging in a legitimate and ordinary business exchange, while suspecting that it may be part of a laundering plan or that the money has been obtained through criminal activities, is not forbidden. People can rely on some assurance that they will not be accused and prosecuted simply because the transaction raised suspicion unless they have some specific knowledge of acts and omission that can be described as "willful blindness", the intentional and knowing disregard of the nature of the funds involved

The act imposes some jurisdictional limitations on police and prosecutorial activities. U.S. extra-territorial enforcement efforts have been controversial. The act is applicable to transactions involving more than $10,000 when the interest of the U.S. is clearly involved, either because the defendant is a U.S. citizen or because the transaction took place wholly or partially in the U.S. (e.g., a wire transfer of funds from a U.S. bank to one in another country or a phone call placed from the U.S. to a financial institution abroad). Thereby, jurisdiction could be problematic and not meet the "reasonableness" standard in court.

The "Monetary Transaction Crime"

The monetary transaction crime prohibits monetary transactions in criminally derived property. The property must in fact have been derived from "specific unlawful activity", and its value must exceed $10,000. The defendant must know that he or she is engaging in a monetary transaction, that the property affected is criminally derived, and that the offense from which it derives was generally a crime. This measure of the act has the potential of being applied quite expansively both in terms of who can be accused of engaging in it or benefitting from it (including the defense attorneys) and also in its jurisdictional reach. The nationality basis of the accused is broader in this case than for the "money laundering crime". Also, the "effects doctrine" can be used to establish territorial jurisdiction. This means that any conduct that meets the definition of the monetary transaction crime and has some effect in the U.S. can be investigated and prosecuted by U.S. authorities.

The principal penalty for both money laundering and money transaction crimes is the forfeiture of the defendant's gross receipts and property derived from such illegal activity. This provision has been critized as threatening a defendant's ability to mount an effective defense and right to counsel. The Right to Financial Privacy Act represents an effort to redress the balance between individual rights and the needs of law enforcement. With several important exceptions, the law requires the U.S. government to first obtain a subpoena, search warrant, or other appropriate authorization, and observe other formalities, before a financial institution must comply with a government request for information about an individual customer's financial records. Corporations are not so protected because it is held that they lack privacy rights. Finally, just as criminal activity may undermine the rule of law, so too the violation of people's rights by the government may lead to disrespect for the law and the defeat of law enforcement measures. Therefore, a careful balance must be reached between fighting increasingly sophisticated criminal activity and protecting the fundamental rights of individuals.

Cooperating Witnesses or Defendants

Witness Protection

A witness who testifies in an organized crime case faces potentially serious undesirable consequences. To protect such witnesses from retribution, the Witness Protection Program was authorized by the Organized Crime Control Act of 1970. The program was entrusted to the U.S. Marshals Service which, initially, was not prepared for these responsibilities. Also, the success of the program had not been anticipated: 6,500 witnesses and 9,000 dependents by the end of 1996. Initial estimates had been much lower. There was also criticism that the program shielded criminals not only from organized crime's revenge but also from debts, lawsuits, payment of child support and alimony, and responsibility for crimes committed while being protected. In response, an amendment to the 1984 Comprehensive Crime Control Act orders the U.S. Justice Department to stop hiding witnesses who are sued for civil damages and to dismiss from the program those who engage in new crimes. Because estranged or divorced spouses had also been unable to locate and visit their children who had accompanied the other spouse-parent into the protected program, often a sudden and unexpected disappearance, Congress also amended the law to provide greater rights for the other parent in those situations; permit monthly visits organized and supervised by the Marshals in a third, "neutral" city; but no input into the child's upbringing.

The Department of Justice manual in Chapter 9-21,[10] sets forth procedures for a person who is a witness to a crime to obtain the status of a "protected witness" under the Witness Security Program. As a protected witness, the person will be protected by the United States Marshals Service and may be relocated and receive a new identity and financial assistance. An applicant to the program must be an essential witness in a specific important case, including organized crime, drug trafficking, a serious federal felony for which the witness may be subject to retaliation by violence if he or she testifies, a state offense similar to these federal offenses, or a civil or administrative proceeding in which testimony may place the witness's safety in jeopardy.

Because of the expense of the program, peoples are considered for entry into the program only if they commit themselves to giving testimony that is credible and significant. Applicants must submit a criminal history and psychological evaluation for themselves and family members who will enter the program with them. In each case, the Justice Department makes a written assessment of the risk the witness may pose to the new community in which he or she may be relocated. Applicants are interviewed by the U.S. Marshals Service to evaluate potential problems. Before a protected witness can be used as an informant, consent of the Justice Department's Office of Enforcement Operations is required. This office will consider the potential benefits, risk, and costs of using the witness as an informant.

Victim - Witness Assistance

In 1981, the Attorney General established a Law Enforcement Coordinating Committee (LECC) in each federal judicial district to promote cooperation between federal, state, and local law enforcement agencies. In 1982, U.S. Attorneys were given the additional function of providing Victim-Witness Assistance (VWA). In each district, there is a LECC/VWA coordinator, responsible for administering both programs. Under the Victim's Rights and Restitution Act of 1990, federal crime victims are entitled to certain services. Each federal judicial district has written procedures, guidelines, and materials for providing victim-witness services. The offices develop and maintain resource materials which identify available public and private programs for providing counseling, treatment, or support services to victims.

Informers and Undercover Agents

Undercover investigations are very sensitive matters in the U.S. because they require government employees to deceive persons who are targets of criminal investigations in order to invite them to engage in criminal conduct that the government can monitor. The guidelines are adopted by the U.S. Attorney General in order to ensure that formal procedures and guidelines are available to law enforcement officers engaging in undercover investigations. The central concern is that government officials should avoid causing a person to engage in an illegal activity in which that person would not otherwise be predisposed to engage in. Approval is given only if certain criteria are met. Moreover, only under limited circumstances may undercover employees participate in "otherwise illegal" activities. Approval for such activity is guaranteed only if the activity is required (i) to obtain information or evidence necessary for paramount prosecutive purposes; (ii) to establish or maintain the "cover" of the operation; or (iii) to prevent the death or danger of serious bodily injury to the undercover operative. Thus, measures exist to help ensure that a given undercover operation is only undertaken in a reasonable manner, when it is likely to reveal illegal activity.

Approval from headquarters is required for operations that involve a substantial expenditure of government funds, involve "sensitive circumstances", such as public corruption, or present risks of harm to innocent persons. Other operations may be approved by the Special Agent in charge of the local FBI office.

U.S. Legislative Initiatives

Measures against the laundering of the proceeds of crime can be divided into three major categories: legislative initiatives, measures of a regulatory nature, and infrastructure-building measures. Prior to the passage of the Money Laundering Control Act of 1986, money-laundering was not a federal crime, although the Department of Justice had used a variety of federal statutes to successfully prosecute money-laundering cases.[11] Legislation enacted in 1988 allows the government to file a suit claiming ownership of all cash funneled through operations intended to disguise their illegal source. The courts have the power to freeze the assets until the case is adjudicated.

An amendment to the Drug Abuse Act of 1988 requires offshore banks to record any U.S. cash transactions in excess of $10,000 and to permit U.S. officials to have access to the records. In addition, offshore banks that fail to comply can be banned from holding accounts in the U.S. banks and be denied access to U.S. dollar clearing and money-transfer systems. Under the Currency and Foreign Transactions Reporting Act (13 U.S.C. Sec. 5311, as amended) the United States can compel other countries to maintain certain financial records similar to those required under the Bank Secrecy Act. If a country fails to negotiate an acceptable record system, its financial institutions can be denied access to the U.S. banking system. There have been problems implementing this legislation, because in some of these countries there are strict limitations on the dissemination of cash reports to third parties.

In 1993 the Supreme Court ruled unanimously that the Eight Amendment's protection against "excessive fines" requires that there be a relationship between the gravity of the offense and the value of the property seized. It should be noted that money-laundering operations are not limited to banks; car dealerships, jewelry shops, and real estate agencies have been involved, too.

In support of the on-going multilateral efforts to bring all nations into conformity with international standards against money laundering, President Clinton has ordered that the U.S. identify the most egregious overseas sanctuaries for illegally obtained proceeds. The U.S. will then enter into active negotiations with those nations to achieve conformity with international standards and end their safe haven status. If they fail to comply within a reasonable time, the President has authorized the Secretary of the Treasury, in consultation with the Secretary of State and the Attorney General, to consider applying unilateral sanctions against those countries and encouraging other states to do the same (*Trends in Organized Crime*, 1956, p. 25). The

President's actions recognize that international criminal enterprises now move vast sums of illicitly derived money through the world's financial systems, buy and sell narcotics, arms, smuggle aliens, nuclear materials, and weapons of mass destruction. Since international criminals know no geographical boundaries, the ultimate purpose of the President's initiative is to protect the welfare, safety, and security of the U.S. and its citizens.

International Forfeiture Cooperation and Sharing of Confiscated Assets[12]

Major drug traffickers and other organized criminals often hide their illicitly generated proceeds outside the country where they commit their crimes. Thus, one country's forfeiture efforts, however effective and comprehensive, may not be enough to take the profit out of transnational crime. For forfeiture laws to work effectively, the U.S. and its international partners must apply and enforce their domestic confiscation measures in increasingly multinational settings. The U.S. Department of Justice has placed the development of international forfeiture cooperation among its top priorities. The paramount objective is to take the profits out of crime. Secondarily, domestic efforts have shown that forfeited wealth, when shared with cooperating law enforcement agencies, serves to enhance interagency cooperation by replenishing the resources needed by all to combat crime. This concept is equally true in the international setting. While law enforcement is always the prime objective, the sharing of forfeited assets among participating nations also creates an incentive for future cooperation and provides the means to carry out such costly efforts.

Bilateral Treaties, Executive Agreements, and Letters Rogatory

Recent bilateral and multinational agreements providing for mutual forfeiture assistance, attest to the emergence of forfeiture as an international law enforcement sanction. Currently, the U.S. has ratified mutual assistance treaties (MLATs) with twenty-two jurisdictions (Anguilla, Argentina, Bahamas, British Virgin Islands, Canada, Cayman Islands, Italy, Jamaica, Mexico, Morocco, Montserrat, Netherlands, Panama, Philippines, Spain, Switzerland, Thailand, Turkey, Turks and Caicos Islands, United Kingdom and Uruguay). Where there is no treaty or executive agreement in place, the State Department will draft a case-specific agreement with the proposed recipient country. In addition, letters rogatory, the more time consuming but traditional means of obtaining assistance from a foreign court, remain available for use in cases where the U.S. and the foreign jurisdiction in question are not parties to a forfeiture related bilateral treaty or agreement.

Bilateral MLATs and executive agreements have helped to regularize international forfeiture cooperation between treaty partners. However, the United Nations Convention Against Illicit Traffic in Narcotic Drugs and Psychotropic Substance, more commonly referred to as the Vienna Convention,[13] is perhaps the single most important development in international forfeiture cooperation to date. Article V of the Vienna Convention details the obligation of the parties to seek the forfeiture of (or, in the term used by the Convention, confiscate) drug trafficking and money laundering proceeds, as well as the instrumentalities used to commit such offenses. It mandates each signatory country to enact laws with domestic and international application.

Civil forfeiture In 1992, Congress enacted 28 U.S.C. section 1355(b)(2), a statute vesting U.S. district courts with extraterritorial jurisdiction over assets located abroad that are subject to civil forfeiture under U.S. laws. Section 1355(b)(2) enhances the U.S. ability to lend international forfeiture assistance. This provision is particularly useful in case where the foreign country in question cannot forfeit the property under its own laws, but may be able to take other steps that assist the U.S. forfeiture efforts (e.g., seize the property, enforce a U.S. forfeiture judgement, or repatriate the assets). In such case, once the assets have been civilly forfeited in the U.S., cases brought under section 1355(b)(2) must be closely coordinated with the authorities of the foreign government where the forfeited assets are located. The final civil forfeiture judgment can be transmitted to the foreign country for enforcement or for repatriation of the assets.

Criminal forfeiture In the U.S., the plea bargain process is an important part of the criminal justice system. Through a plea agreement, a defendant can consent to the forfeiture of his or her property regardless of its location. To that end, a plea bargain may require the defendant to transfer title to foreign-based assets to the U.S. or to liquidate the property and transfer the proceeds to the U.S. In such cases, the U.S. may request assistance from the foreign government in repatriating the property for forfeiture. Where repatriation is not possible, the U.S. may be able to assist the foreign jurisdiction to forfeit the property under its laws by structuring the U.S. plea bargain agreement so that the defendant is required to cooperate with foreign authorities in their own law enforcement efforts. Similarly, where explicit admissions regarding the illicit source of the property will enable the foreign country to obtain a forfeiture order, the plea agreement might also contain an admission by the defendant that the foreign-based property constitutes proceeds of the particular conduct alleged.

Request to the United States from Foreign Countries

Foreign criminals like their U.S. counterparts, often attempt to protect their illegal profits from their own countries' laws by transferring them elsewhere, including to the U.S. In response, Congress enacted legislation [18 U.S.C. section 981(a)(1)(B)], authorizing the seizure and forfeiture of assets within the U.S. borders that represent the proceeds of drug-related crimes committed abroad. One of the more notable features of section 981 is the use of foreign forfeiture orders and foreign convictions to support a civil forfeiture action against drug proceeds found in the U.S. Also, the U.S. does not require foreign governments representatives to obtain official authorization before interviewing willing witnesses in the U.S. In cases where a witness is not willing to submit voluntarily to a deposition or to produce records and other evidence, the U.S. may be able to secure such assistance through compulsory process under U.S.C. section 1782.

Asset Sharing

It is the policy of the U.S., pursuant to statutory authority, to share the proceeds of the successful forfeiture actions with countries that made possible or substantially facilitated the forfeiture of assets under the U.S. laws. Since 1989, the Department of Justice has transferred more than $65 million from the Asset Forfeiture Fund to 21 different countries. The assistance these countries have rendered has ranged from providing bank records, to engaging in undercover operations in conjunction with U.S. law enforcement agencies, to defending litigation by claimants on behalf of the U.S., and to repatriating forfeitable assets. Asset sharing among nations enhances international forfeiture cooperation by creating an incentive for countries to work together, regardless of where the assets are located or which jurisdiction will ultimately enforce the forfeiture order.

The U.S. does not view international asset sharing as the bartering or selling of law enforcement cooperation among nations, because it stands ready to cooperate with the forfeiture efforts of other nations whether or not there is asset sharing. At the same time, it encourages reciprocal sharing among law enforcement partners. The ultimate decision of whether and how much to share is made, subject to review by the Secretary of State representative, the Attorney General or the Secretary of the Treasury. No U.S. representative has the statutory authority to commit to asset sharing in any given case until an international forfeiture sharing agreement has been approved at the highest levels of the Departments of Justice (or Treasury) and State.

While these provisions are broadly drafted to permit asset sharing for all manners of foreign assistance resulting in the seizure or forfeiture of property, this does not mean that the U.S. can share with foreign governments in all U.S. forfeiture cases. As currently drafted, the sharing laws provide that the forfeiture itself must have occurred pursuant to Chapter 46 of Title 18, Subchapter I of Chapter 13 of Title 21, or under any law (other than   section 7301 or 7301 of the Internal Revenue Code of 1986) enforced or administered by the Department of the Treasury. Thus, if the forfeiture took place pursuant to some other statute, the U.S. would not be able to share with a foreign government, even though their assistance facilitated the forfeiture. In view of these controversies, the Department of Justice has proposed the creation of an omnibus international asset sharing statute authorizing the transfer of forfeited property to foreign countries in any case where they had assisted in the U.S. forfeiture case.

How much to transfer in any specific case is governed by the principle that the shared amount should reflect the contribution of the foreign government in relation to the assistance provided by other foreign and domestic law enforcement participants. Generally, of course, the level or amount of sharing will be in direct relationship with the importance and degree of foreign assistance. The U.S. opposes international sharing agreements that fix a specific percentage to be shared in future cases.

Other Types of Illicit Trafficking

Toxic Waste

An activity that conjures images of organized crime, is the private collection of solid waste. Back in 1931, Walter Lippman (1962, p. 61) noted that "racketeering in many of its most important forms tends to develop where an industry is subjected to exceedingly competitive conditions". Companies "faced with the constant threat of cutthroat competition are subject to easy temptation to pay gangsters for protection against competitors" (Abadinsky, 1997, p. 428). The presence of toxic waste in municipal landfills can be traced in part to the intense competition and under-regulation of private garbage haulers. Because often there is no statewide permit program for these haulers, they operate as "free agents" outside the norms that regulate hazardous waste. This break in the regulatory scheme provides numerous opportunities for criminal trafficking in toxic waste. As far back as 1957 the U.S. Senate Select Committee on Improper Activities in the Labor and Management Field, under the leadership of Senator John L. McClellan, carefully documented organized crimes infiltration of the private sanitation industry in New York state. Hauliers associated with organized crime were exposed for their use of "property rights" to monopolize the industry and drive up the price of garbage collection (Block, 1990, p. 177).

During the late 1970s and early 1980s, a great deal was learned about organized crime and toxic waste, especially in the Northeast. Investigations have revealed that the major New York City and New Jersey syndicates are directly involved in the toxic waste disposal business in these regions. This is especially true of the Genovese and Tieri crime syndicate. Also prominent were the members of the Gambino, Bonanno, Lucchese, and DeCavalcante organizations. In order to combat organized crime infiltration into the waste disposal system, New York has created a Trade Waste Commission that can deny a license to any firm with ties to organized crime.

Allowing a significant portion of the social and economic control of a business like hazardous waste disposal to be held by organized crime syndicates is far more devastating for the public well-being than is typically the case for organized crime activity. The long-term consequence of illegal disposal practices have the potential to affect many more unknowing and involuntary "victims" than all organized crime's illegal operations combined (Bunyan, 1987, p. 125).

Drug Trafficking

The Continuing Criminal Enterprise Statute,[14] which differs considerably from RICO, targets specifically illegal drug activity. The statute makes it a crime to conspire to commit a continuing series of felony violations of the 1970 Drug Abuse Prevention and Control Act when such acts are undertaken in concert with five or more other persons. For conviction under this statute, the offender must have been an organizer, manager, or supervisor of the continuing operation and have obtained substantial income or resources from the drug violation.

Migrant Trafficking

Migrant trafficking is one of the fastest growing branches of organized crime in recent years. It is estimated that in 1992/93 alone as many as 500.000 people (illegal labor migrants and asylum seekers without founded claims) from countries like China and India have been smuggled into Western Europe, at fees as high as $250,000. While the majority of them tend to be young males, there is also illegal traffic in women for the sex market and in children for the adoption market. Women are often lured abroad with promises of marriage or jobs as domestic servants or office workers and find themselves ending up as prostitutes (*Trends in Organized Crime*, pp. 77-78). Most Asian organized crime groups, both in the Far East and in the United States, are involved in prostitution. Since May of 1992, several boats holding undocumented Chinese aliens have been intercepted by immigration authorities in American waters. Points of arrival have included Hawaii, North Carolina, and Massachusetts. Undoubtedly many more of those boats are not being intercepted. Triad societies largely control prostitution in Hong Kong; and triad, tong and street gang members are also involved in prostitution operations in the Unites States.[15] Two triad members who testified before the Subcommittee on Investigations (*The New International Criminal and Asian Organized Crime*, 1992) noted their involvement in prostitution in the early days of their criminal careers. In New York, Subcommittee staff learned of a typical massage parlor employing ethnic Korean prostitutes. These women are frequently legal U.S. residents or citizens because of previous arranged marriages to U.S. service men in Korea for which the service men are paid a fee. Once in the United States, the women typically divorce and begin work in a massage parlor as arranged by the prostitution organization that assisted in arranging their bogus marriages. These women become indentured servants until their debts to the organization are satisfied. The Japanese organized crime has also been linked to "sex trade" in the United States, including prostitution and child pornography in Guam (*Ibid*, pp. 36-37).

There are reports that Asian organized groups are becoming more heavily involved in alien smuggling operations. Usually the aliens being smuggled do not pay the entire charge before departure from their countries.

Recently smuggled aliens are being used as drug couriers and being forced into prostitution to pay their debts. When smuggled aliens are apprehended, they cannot generally be detained for extended periods of time. This is a significant problem in trying to stop the influx of illegal aliens being smuggled into the U.S. Key points of entry are typically overwhelmed with illegal entrants for which there is no adequate detention space. Such aliens must then be released on parole, and often do not appear for scheduled hearings. They simply vanish among the general population.

Racketeering: Effects of these Special Crimes on Criminal Law and Policy

The public perception of the intent of RICO and CCE was that the statute would be used to prosecute traditional organized crime families, particular those that had infiltrated legitimate businesses or labor unions, or were involved in international drug smuggling. While Civil RICO lay dormant throughout the 1970s, it has been used quite frequently in the 1980s as plaintiffs discovered that virtually anyone could be charged with racketeering. Needless to say the business community is not pleased and has lobbied Congress repeatedly to reform RICO and stop stigmatizing them unfairly.

Organized crime is conceptually defined by RICO as a pattern of racketeering activity committed by an individual or group either as part of an enterprise or against an enterprise. The original 24 federal felonies considered racketeering activities included murder, intimidation of witnesses, kidnapping, obstructing justice, counterfeiting, theft of interstate shipments, white slavery, embezzlement of pension funds, certain federal and drug offenses, bankruptcy fraud, mail fraud and wire fraud. In 1984, obscenity and pornography were added as a predicate act.[16] An enterprise can be either illegitimate or legitimate, making it possible for a legitimate business to be subject to forfeiture because its owner has committed a crime in the course of its operation.

There have been a number of RICO cases, both criminal and civil, appealed on the basis that the statutes are in conflict with basic constitutional protections afforded all criminal defendants. A number of the First Amendment cases involve the use of RICO in obscenity trials. This allegedly has created a chilling effect on legitimate publishers. In 1989, the Supreme Court, in *Fort Wayne Books, Inc. v. Indiana*, (Melnick, 1989) relied on the prior restraint argument to disallow the padlocking of an adult bookstore without a court verdict that any of the materials therein were obscene.

Conclusion

The United States has been in the forefront of fighting both domestic end international organized crime using criminal law and the justice system as major tools. Nationwide efforts to combat organized crime began in July 1954 when the then Attorney General Robert Kennedy established the Organized Crime and Racketeering Section (OCRS) within the Criminal Division of the U.S. Department of Justice.

In particular, the legislative history of RICO, introduced in 1970, demonstrates that it was intended to provide new weapons of unprecedented scope for an assault upon organized crime and its economic roots. For the past 20 years prosecutors have increasingly turned to the RICO statute, both because of its relatively strong penalties that can reach up to 20 years and because it provides for forfeiture of personal assets acquired from the proceeds of criminal activity. The RICO statutes have been key prosecution tools in the fight against organized crime. As prosecutors become more experienced, they are prosecuting more successfully under RICO. RICO-type statutes now exist also in the majority of American States, but they are not always used to maximum advantage because state prosecutors are unable to mount the complex prosecutions necessary. However, as mentioned earlier in this report, the RICO statute has also been seriously criticized by academicians and lawyers for its various inadequacies and biases against innocent victims and third parties.

There are those who are reluctant to place too much faith in criminal law and its sanctions in order to combat and defeat organized crime. It is true that the government's approach to apprehend and prosecute as many crime bosses (particularly Italian-American) as possible has had little impact on the overall activities and strength of organized crime. For example, neither the police nor the advent of state lotteries have displaced the numbers game as confidently predicted by their proponents and supporters. The key element to effectively addressing any illegal enterprise is to identify its genesis and the root causes of its spreading; in our case, they are "institutionally induced disabilities" and the control and parceling out of societal resources by powerful patrons. Identifying and recognizing the "cultural repertoires" of different ethnic groups should also improve society's ability to effectively address the key patron-client relationship that supports, nurtures and binds the social system of organized crime. Thus, in order to be successful, penal law must be judiciously used as one element of a multi-faceted and multi-disciplinary approach to combatting organized crime.

Notes

1   18 U.S.C. Sections 1951-1968 (RICO Act).
2   Unites States Constitution, Article I, section 8, Clause 3.
3   CCE; 21 USC Section 848.
4   Cecil Greek: Free Inquiry in Creative Sociology, Vol. 19, No. 1, May 1991.
5   This is the loss of ownership as a civil or criminal penalty for illegal use of the property in question, or as a sanction for the commission of a crime.
6   Money Laundering Control Act of 1986.
7   Remarks of Peter G. Djinis, Trial Attorney, Narcotics and Dangerous Drugs Section, U.S. Department of Justice. Proceedings of a seminar held by The Congressional Research Service, June 21, 1990.
8   See 18 U.S.C.S. section 1956 for specifics of the elements of the crimes and their respective punishments.
9   See 18 U.S.C.S. section 1956.
10   U.S. Department of Justice Manual section 9-110.800.
11   Title 18 U.S.C. section 1956 and 1957.
12   Based on unpublished report by the same title prepared by the Asset Forfeiture Office, Criminal Division, U.S. Department of Justice, September 1995.
13   The Vienna Convention, went into effect on November 11, 1990, and has been ratified by over one hundred and fifteen countries.
14   In 1970, Congress also enacted the Continuing Criminal Enterprise (CCE) provision of Title II of the Comprehensive Drug Prevention and Control Act of 1970
15   Triads are secret fraternities that are primarily headquartered in Hong Kong and Taiwan. Criminaly influenced Tongs are business associations located in many U.S. cities which engage in lawful as well as unlawful activities. Street gangs often operate under the sponsorship of Tongs, but many also operate independently.
16   See 18 U.S.C. section 1961 I a Supp. III 1985.

References

Alito, A. Samuel. (1989), *The RICO Racket*. Washington, D.C.: National Legal Center for the Public Interest.

Abadinsky, Howard. (1987), *Organized Crime*, Fifth Edition. Chicago: Nelson-Hall Publishers. 1997.

Albanese, Jay. (1989), *Organized Crime in America*, Second Edition. Cincinnati, Ohio: Anderson Publishing Co.

Bell, Daniel. "The myth of the Cosa Nostra." *The New Leader* 46 (December 1963):12- 15.

Block, Alan. (1991), *The Business of Crime: A Documentary Study of Organized Crime in America*. Boulder, Colorado: Westview Press, Inc.

Block, Alan. (1991), *Perspectives on Organized Crime: Essays in Opposition*. Dordrecht, Netherlands: Kluwer Academic Publishers, 1991.

Bryum, Timothy. (1987), *Organized Crime in America: Concepts and Controversies*. Willow Tree Press, Inc.

Kelly, Robert, Ko-lin Chin, and Schatzberg, Rufus. (1994), *Handbook of Organized Crime in The United States*. Westport, CT: Greenwood Publishing Group, Inc.

Cilluford, J. Frank, and Raine P. Linnea.(1994), *Global organized Crime: The New Empire of Evil*. Published by Center For Strategic and International Studies.

Fox, Stephen. (1989), *Blood and Power: Organized Crime in Twentieth-Century America*. New York, New York: William Morrow and Company, Inc.

Goldfarb, Ronald. (1995), *Perfect Villians, Imperfect Heroes: Robert F. Kennedy's War Against Organized Crime*. New York: Random House, Inc.

International Drug Money Laundering: Issues and Options for Congress. Committee on Foreign Affairs. U.S. House of Representatives. Washington, D.C.: U.S. Government Printing Office, 1990.

Kleinknecht, William. (1996), *The New Ethnic Mobs: The Changing Face of Organized Crime in America*. New York: The Free Press.

MacDonald, B. Scott., and Zagaris, Bruce.(1992), *International Handbook on Drug Control*. Westport, CT.: Greenwood publishing group, Inc.

Monkonen, H. Eric. (1992) *Crime and Justice in American History: Prostitution, Drugs, Gambling and Organized Crime*. Vol. 8 Pt.2. New York: Reed International P.L.C.

Mustain, Gene., and Capeci, Jerry. (1988), *Mob Star: The Story of John Gotti*. New York: Franklin Watts, the Grolier Company.

Organized Crime: Report of the Task Force On Organized Crime. National Adversory Committee on Criminal Justice Standards and Goals. Washington, D.C.: 1976.

Oversight Hearing on Organized Crime Strike Forces. Subcommitte on Criminal Justice of the Committe on the Judiciary House of Representatives, One

206 *Global Organized Crime and International Security*

Hundred and First Congress. Washington, D.C.: U.S. Government Printing Office, 1989.

Pace, F. Denny and Styles C. Jimmie. (1983, 1975), *Organized Crime: Concepts and Control*. Englewood Cliff, N.J.: Prentice-Hall, Inc.

Ryan, Patrick.(1995), *Organized Crime: A Reference Handbook*. Santa Barbara, California: ABC-CLIO, Inc.

Ruggiero,Vincent. (1996), *Organized and Corporate Crime in Europe: Offers that Can't Be Refused*. Brookfield, Vermont: Darmouth Publishing Company, Ltd.

Stolberg, Mary. (1995), *Fighting Organized Crime: Politics, Justice and the Legacy of Thomas E. Dewey*. Boston: Northeastern University Press, 1995.

Trends in Organized Crime. Washington, D.C.: Published by Transaction Periodicals Consumption for the National Strategy Information Center, 1996.

The New International Criminal and Asian Organized Crime: Report prepared by the Permanent Subcommittee on Investigations of the Committee On Governmental Affairs United States Senate. Washington, D.C.,: U.S. Government Printing Press, 1993.

Venturi, Robert., Scott Brown, Dennise., and Izenour, Steven. (1977), *Learning From Las Vegas:The Forgotten Symbolism of Architectural Form*. Cambridge, Massachusetts: The MIT Press, 1977.

Zuller, F.C. Duke. (1996), *Devil's Pact: Inside the World of the Teamsters Union*. Secaucus, N.J.: Carol Publishing Group. 1996.